■ Pictured with David Wheater.

■ Gary Pallister and myself have remained great friends.

■ Celebrating promotion with Tony Mowbray.

Bernie's About 2

Bernie Slaven's Unedited Interviews

TO PETER
MERRY CHRISTMAS
UP THE DURA! 2014/15

Peter
All the very best

Copyright 2009 7 Enterprises Ltd.

All rights reserved.

The moral right of the authors has been asserted.

First published in Great Britain by 7 Enterprises Ltd.

ISBN no 978-0-9560684-1-5

Cover design by Graeme Bandeira

Printed in Singapore by Tien Wah Press.

ALSO AVALIABLE FROM   7 ENTERPRISES

BERNIE'S ABOUT

This book contains interviews with past Boro stars, Charlton, Clough, Gascoigne,Hardwick, Johnstone, Juninho, Mannion,
Merson, Murdoch, Ravanelli, Rioch, Robson, Souness, Stiles and guest celebrity Chris Rea.
All unedited versions, these candid interviews give the reader a true to life insight into these characters.

PRICE £12.00

AVALIABLE AT GOOD BOOK STORES OR
 E MAIL   seven.enterprises@hotmail.co.uk

Bernies About North east   £12

DVD Legends Uncensored

The common idea that success spoils people by making them vain, egotistic, and self - complacent is erroneous; on the contrary, it makes them, for the most part, humble, tolerant, and kind.
Failure makes people cruel and bitter.

BERNIE SLAVEN

ACKNOWLEDGEMENTS

I would like to thank the managers and players for giving up their time, each and every one of them a character.

A big thanks to Graeme Bandeira, for brilliant art work.

Thanks to Evening Gazette, Highland Studios and the players themselves for providing the pictures.

Massive thanks to Bill O'hanlon and Adam Steel for their contribution.

Thanks to Clarissa for making the book possible.

Also thanks to everyone at Studio Print and a big thanks to Real Radio.

DEDICATION

I DEDICATE THIS BOOK TO ALL THE BORO FANS
WHO SUFFERED THE 2008-2009 SEASON.

As Boro fans you've all gone through the hurt, the anguish, and the pain
watching your local club struggle in every department.

You the fans have been truly magnificent, you have turned up in droves and
got behind your team.
 No doubt many of you have had to put in 40-50 hour shifts, to raise the
money to buy a season ticket, after paying hard earned cash and giving
support and loyalty to your team you all deserve better.

Hopefully next season we can bounce back and become a force in the
Premier League once again

Hope you enjoy your read.

INTRODUCTION

The Bernie's About idea came when I worked for Boro TV between 1998 and 2002.

Over those years I met some of the greatest players ever to wear the red shirt of Middlesbrough as well as some of the high profile managers.

The job involved travelling up and down the country accompanied by a camera man. I met players at hotels, in the comfort of their own homes, at training grounds, even on boats.
Over a period off time I interviewed over 200 players, managers and personalities. And thoroughly enjoyed speaking to every one of them.

Some were clever, outspoken, outrageous, opinionated, quiet, eccentric charming, smug, and even arrogant, but everyone was an individual and to their credit none of them asked for a fee. They gave up their free time and answered my questions openly and honestly and made me most welcome.

It was an honour and privilege to interview World Cup winners, European Cup Winners, people who have been successful in their profession.

After great success with my first book in 2008 Bernie's About, I've decided to write part two. Its brought up to date interviewing both past and present players for this publication.
I hope you enjoy these interviews and get an insight into what the players are actually like on and off the field and what makes them tick.

CONTENTS

Interview 1 Malcolm Allison .... 12 - 23

Interview 2 David Armstrong .... 24 - 33

Interview 3 Stuart Boam .... 34 - 44

Interview 4 Marco Branca .... 45 - 55

Interview 5 Stewart Downing .... 56 - 77

Interview 6 Emerson .... 78 - 89

Interview 7 Paul Ince .... 90 - 101

Interview 8 David Mills .... 102 - 111

Interview 9 Tony Mowbray .... 112 - 123

Interview 10 John Neal .... 124 - 131

Interview 11 Gary Pallister .... 132 - 143

Interview 12 Rolando Ugolini .... 144 - 157

Interview 13 Mark Viduka .... 158 - 187

Interview 14 David Wheater .... 188 - 207

'If you don't have any money, you shouldn't be the chairman.'

On what he told Mike McCullagh.

MALCOLM ALLISON

Interview 1 Malcolm Allison

BIG MAL was born on September 5,1927 in Dartford.
In 1951 after spending seven seasons at Charlton Athletic, he joined West Ham, but his career was cut short when he fell ill with a bout of tuberculosis. As a player he was a tall, commanding centre half.
He arrived at Middlesbrough as a manager in 1982, on the understanding that no players would be sold above his head.
I met up with Mal in Yarm 85 restaurant. As ever he was smartly dressed and well groomed.
We had met on several occasions over the years. I always admired his style, charming, charismatic, laced with panache. His other qualities of course were he was opinionated and outspoken, everything I like in an individual, a larger than life character.
To be honest I didn't know what kind of reception I would receive on the day of the interview, as I had taken his role as summariser for Boro's coverage on Century after he swore on air and was dismissed.

BERNIE

You started your professional career as a centre half with Charlton Athletic back in 1944. I was surprised to see you only made two appearances. What was the reason?

MALCOLM

Well, I signed professional when I was 17. When I was 18, I was called up to the Army and I was posted to Chatham, then I was posted abroad after six weeks.
I was in Austria for two years so I was nearly 21 before I came to Charlton. (Laughs).
I'd been there about six months and one day there was a meeting with the trainer and all the players - we had about seven internationals then.

The trainer said this, that and the other, so and so and I'm standing at the back and I said: "Mr trainer, the training's rubbish."

BERNIE

You told him that?

MALCOLM

Yeah, I told him that. Sam Bartram, Don Welsh - captain of England - they all turned round as if to say who's this upstart? Who is he anyway?
The boss pulled me in the next morning and he said: "Malcolm, I'm going to transfer you to West Ham.
"And I'll tell you why because you insulted the trainer yesterday."
I said: "I didn't insult him I just told him the training was rubbish, which it is." (Laughs)
He said: "Oh, oh well you shouldn't say that."
So I said: "Can I shake your hand Mister?"
"What for?" he said.
"Well I've been here since I was 15," I said. "I'm now 21 and if you've spoken to me three times...
I said: "I want to thank you for teaching me the art of communication."
(Laughs)

BERNIE

What was the reason for joining Boro after pledging never to return to league management? Three months after that pledge you were at Ayresome Park.

MALCOLM

Well, they rang me up and my wife wanted to return to England. We had been in Portugal for two years.
He rang me up so I said: "Alright I'll come and meet you." That's Mike McCullagh and his assistant vice chairman.
So I came back to England and met them at Leicester, on the motorway halfway between Middlesbrough and London and had a chat with them.
I said: "Look, I'll come to Middlesbrough on one condition - that you don't sell any players that I don't want to sell."
Because they had Charlie Amer selling players and I know one or two managers before that had been upset about the situation.

I think when Graeme Souness was sold they were really upset.
Anyway, that was agreed so I said: "Okay, I'll take the job." So I took the job.

BERNIE

After signing a two-year contract for Middlesbrough, in your first season you finished 16th in the league. Was that a disappointment for you personally?

MALCOLM

Well, when I came here they were 10 points behind the next team in the league.
They were bottom of the league, 10 points behind, so it was quite a result to get out of it.

BERNIE

How big a talent was Stephen Bell? You handed him a four-year contract at a tender age.

MALCOLM

Great talent, brilliant talent. He had two nice feet and was very quick. He had to be a good player.

BERNIE

What went wrong?

MALCOLM

What went wrong is that he was indisciplined. As a player he was out in the clubs, he was drinking. He had a car crash, he couldn't control the success and he had no chance.
Any young player who thinks that they can go and drink and enjoy himself has no chance of being a top class professional.

BERNIE

When you were being forced to sell your best players to enable you to finance the club's debts you were quoted as saying: "It's better for the club to die than linger." What did you mean?

MALCOLM

They were selling all the best players, they were just killing off the
club.
Amer did it, McCullagh did it and they were just killing the club.
How can a place like Middlesbrough - you see the 30,000 people that come
to the game?
Now the people love their football. How can you sell your best players? I
don't understand it.

BERNIE

These days it's pure business isn't it?

MALCOLM

It has always been business. Mike McCullagh, the chairman, told me he
didn't have the money. If you don't have any money you shouldn't be the
chairman then.

BERNIE

Your last managing job was at GM Vauxhall Conference club Fisher
Athletic. What made you go there?

MALCOLM

I wasn't doing anything and they sent a helicopter up and landed in the
back garden, you know. (Laughs).
I hadn't been in a helicopter before, so I thought I'll go down. (Laughs)

BERNIE

How did it go? Were you there a few years?

MALCOLM

I was there four or five months. They still owe me the money - you could
never get your wages! (Laughs).

BERNIE

Would you say today's coaches are more knowledgeable than the ones of the past?

MALCOLM

Well, I think they've had better teaching the later coaches, but there's always been intelligent people in football.
I mean like Ronnie Cresswell, he played with Joe Mercer and Joe Mercer was only about 10 stone.
He was a terrific tackler, wonderful tackler and I said: "Why were you such a good tackler, Joe?"
He said: " Malcolm, Ronnie Cresswell taught me to tackle in front of the ball.
"Don't tackle the ball, tackle that much in front, just a few inches and then the ball goes and the fellow goes and it goes over the top.
"It doesn't matter how big he is or how strong he is."
And he was a brilliant tackler, so it's people like that who have got these little ideas, little things you know, but coaching wasn't brought into English football until 1950.
Walter Winterbottom was the teacher. A brilliant teacher, not a great football man but a brilliant teacher, to show people how to organise.
So I was there with Jimmy McIlroy and two boys from Burnley.
The best coach in the country and possibly in the world was a man called Alan Brown.

HONOURS

MALCOLM ALEXANDER ALLISON

PLAYING CAREER HISTORY

       Erith and Belvedere
1945-1951 Charlton Athletic
1951-1957 West Ham United

MANAGERIAL CAREER HISTORY

Bath City
1964-1965 Plymouth Aygyle
1965-1972 Manchester City assistant
1972-1973 Manchester City
1973-1976 Crystal Palace
1976-1977 Galatasaray
1978-1979 Plymouth Argyle
1979-1980 Manchester City
1980-1981 Crystal Palace
1981-1982 Sporting Lisbon
1982-1984 Middlesbrough
1985-1986 Kuwait
1986-1988 Vitoria Setubal
1988   SC Farense
1992-1993 Bristol Rovers

MANAGERIAL HONOURS (winners)

1967-1968 First Division title
1969   FA Cup
1970   League Cup
1970   Cup Winners Cup
1981-1982 Portuguese Championship, Portuguese Cup

Big Mal Salutes the Ayresome Park crowd

The only thing missing is the champagne.

Big Mal poses in typical style

Bernie's About 2

'For me making the fans happy was the biggest kick I got and I'm sure other players were the same.
 We wanted to see people go home with a smile on their face.'

On making the fans happy.

DAVID ARMSTRONG

Interview 2 David Armstrong

SPIKE ARMSTRONG was born in Durham on December 26, 1964. He
made his Middlesbrough debut against Blackpool on April 3, 1972.
Armstrong was one of the best left footers in the game, silky skilful.
A player who was very seldom injured who had an eye for goal and could
create them as well.
I met up with Spike at Ramside Hall in Durham.
Spike was quite unassuming but a nice guy and his love of the Boro faithful
was evident throughout our chat .
He is a Middlesbrough record holder when it comes to successive games
played and when you put his stats up against the modern day players there
is no comparison.
In the interview I tease him when I ask the question: 'Is it true your
shirt was never wet with sweat after games?' You can be the judge as to
whether he has a bite!

BERNIE

You came through the ranks and made your debut at the age of 17 against
Blackpool. What were your memories of that debut?

DAVID

Oh, it's a fair way back Bernie.
Obviously you became very apprehensive. As a young lad I didn't have too
many games in the reserves which was possibly a good thing in many
respects. I came more or less through the junior ranks as you said and made
my debut away to Blackpool. It was quite a difficult game because
Blackpool then were quite a good, strong side and I think we got beat 2-1,
so overall it was quite a disappointment. But at the same time very, very
enjoyable to
be in the first team, feeling as though I was good enough to be in the
first team. Which of course, it was very exciting. That was the start of a
great chapter in my life, playing for Middlesbrough.

BERNIE

By all accounts you gave the side a good balance, is that because you were left-footed?

DAVID

Yes, especially when Jack Charlton came. Of course, I was left-footed and Jack was obviously looking for a balance to the side, which was vital in those days, as it is in any era. One or two left-sided players just gives the right balance to a side, which was Jack's biggest thing. When he came he insisted we got the right balance to the side, and of course we did.

BERNIE

What are your memories of that 1973 championship winning season?

DAVID

There's so many isn't there? The biggest memory for me is actually winning promotion with about a month to go and the championship with a month to go as well.
So at every home game there was a great party atmosphere, we could actually go out there and enjoy the game as well and that doesn't happen too many times.
I remember the likes of Willie Maddren, Stu Boam and Jack saying that these sort of things don't happen too often, so go out and enjoy it. We've won the league, we've won the championship.
Enjoy the party atmosphere, turn it on, go out and express yourself because you've got no pressure on you's at all. I think we scored goals for fun in that last month or so, which is very pleasing because I've got a great affinity with the Teesside public and at the time it was nice to see people going home with a smile on their face.
That's what we got paid for and back then we played with a smile on our face the best we could.
For me that's the biggest kick I got and I'm sure the other players were the same - we wanted to see people go home with a smile on their face. They work all week to come and watch us play, we entertain and that's what we get paid for.

BERNIE

How proud are you to be a Boro record holder? Is it seven years without missing a game?

DAVID

For anybody, in any walk of life, to go through 7 seasons or 7
years without having a day off work - I'm sure you've had a headache and
your wife's had a headache many times before Bernie!
But to go that length of time without missing a game or missing a day of
work, it wasn't easy.
Admittedly, tackling wasn't my strong point - attacking was my strong
point. In many respects I was a thinker and I was quick off the mark, so
invariably I didn't put myself in those situations but that didn't stop
people tackling me.
I remember playing with 17 stitches in my ankle, fractured ankles, twists,
and kicks all over the place.

BERNIE

I've heard from certain players, that played alongside you, that after the
games you didn't have to wash your shirt. It wasn't dirty, no sweat on it!

DAVID

You don't score a dozen goals every season Bernie and not get a shirt
dirty and you don't when you're defending either.
I mean, I used to challenge centre halves in the box when we were
attacking, when we were defending and things like that so to go away with a
clean shirt, I'm not too keen on that particular line!

BERNIE

Several guys told me that who played alongside you.

DAVID

I can't imagine who they could be!

BERNIE

I believe that when they wound you up about having a clean shirt you used
to turn around and say: "When you've got as much skill as me you don't
have to tackle!"

Bernie's About 2
28

DAVID

You keep going back to the tackling scenario don't you! Well, that's another thing. I'm a quick thinker. I mean, if they want to go into a 60-40 challenge in the other fellow's favour let them do it.
But I'd be the one that gets the 60-40 and poke the ball away.

BERNIE

These days you do media work, do you keep up to pace with the Boro?

DAVID

Well I look for the results because, as I say, I've got a great affinity with Middlesbrough and I grew up in Middlesbrough from the age of nine. Although I lived in Durham, a guy called George Wall used to take me Tuesday and Thursday nights and he instilled a discipline into me which helped me grow up as a person irrespective.
I was very fortunate to play football at the top level but if I hadn't I would have succeeded in whatever I had done. I felt because of the discipline instilled in me through George and the club - Harold Shepherdson for example - and people at the club was second to none and really that was my education.
So I've been very, very pleased with Middlesbrough. As I say, I've got a great affinity with the Teesside public as well.

HONOURS

DAVID ARMSTRONG

PLAYING CAREER HISTORY

1972-1981 Middlesbrough
1981-1987 Southampton
1987-1988 Bournemouth

3 FULL ENGLAND CAPS

Boro record holder for most consecutive appearances - 305 league games,
358games in all competitions

Spike in action

Spike shows his ball control that the fans became accustomed to.

Bernie's About 2

**'I would have loved to have gone into Europe and won something
or won the First Division,
or the Premiership as it is now.'**

On unfulfilled ambitions.

STUART BOAM

Interview 3 Stuart Boam

STUART BOAM was born in Kirkby in Ashfield on January 28,1948.
He arrived at Ayresome Park for a fee of £50,000 from Mansfield.
As a player his qualities were he was strong, aggressive, good in the air and vocal. All in all he was Captain Courageous, who lead by example.
It's quite clear and evident when you read the interview that he felt he was forced out of Middlesbrough Football Club.
I met up with Stuart at the Blue Bell Hotel in Acklam.
I found him warm, opinionated and charming. I've met him over the years at games and functions and always found him to be a down-to-earth individual with a very dry sense of humour.

BERNIE

You started your career at Mansfield, where you went on to make over 170 appearances. Was that a good place to learn your trade?

STUART

A very good place - start at the bottom and work your way up. I went the right way round this time. (Laughs)
But don't forget it was my local club as a lad as well. I supported them and the next club was Forest of course.
But I found it easier to get into Mansfield and I was with some very good, old, hard players at the time, they taught me a lot.
Start at the bottom and work up.

BERNIE

Stan Anderson signed you for the Boro for a fee of £50,000. How did that come about?

STUART

I was playing in the end of season County Cup game, where Forest, Mansfield, Notts County played three games. One-off things, where it doesn't mean a lot.

But apparently they came up to watch me in this game, although I was being written about at the time.

Stan and some of his mates were at the County Final, which we happened to win 1-0 and I played quite well that day.

It was a phone call the next day in the factory I was working in, because we used to have to have three months break.

I was banging springs in making seats for a bus company to make a few bob through the summer.

I was called up to go to the club and that's where it all started. Very lucky.

BERNIE

You skippered Boro to the Second Division title. What qualities does a skipper need?

STUART

A lot of people think a captain's strength is you toss the coin up and you kick with the wind and the sun at your back.

But as you know very well there's a lot more to it than that.

I felt my job was to pass Jack Charlton's messages - how he wanted to play and everything else - the best way I could to the players and I was responsible for looking after the kids and talking to the young lads and bringing through the new players.

Making sure the tactics were right that Jack wanted to play and of course sometimes it worked out, sometimes it didn't.

Sometimes players pulled out, sometimes they didn't, but it was my job mainly to motivate the players. I felt that anyway.

BERNIE

It must have been a great honour to captain such great players such as Maddren, Souness and Hickton to name but a few.

Did you ever have any backchat during a game?

STUART

Well I always believed that the rules were the same and fairness counts but you speak to everybody differently.

That's how I've been in life, not just in football but in business and at home with the family. Some people need talking to, to get the best out of them differently than others. The rules are the same and what you want out of them is the same.

When I used to get on to Graeme and wind Graeme up, he used to give me a mouthful and threaten me, some players are like that.

I knew I had won the bet because I got him exactly the way I wanted. He would go out there and kill somebody and that's what I wanted.

But with certain players you had to treat them differently, I'm using Graeme as an example. We all know that Graeme was a great player.

He was a bit fiery, but I found him at his best when he was fiery, you know what I mean? And it was my job to get him to that state.

BERNIE

During your time at Ayresome Park you formed a great partnership with Willie Maddren. How good were you as a partnership?

STUART

Considering we all know Willie is suffering from MS obviously Willie was my best friend at the club and I still like to communicate with him now. Getting back to the football side, Willie was also injury prone. I mean, to finish your career at his level, very close to international level, he should have played for his country. Had he played for a bigger club at the time, I've no doubt he would have done. I certainly was a robust type of player, we played well together. As a big lad I used to get in the mixer, Willie would pick the bits up. Basically that's how we played in those days and I was always the one with my nose at the back of my head. Willie got all the praise in the papers (laughs) but considering we didn't see a lot of each other during the week with his injury problems, because his knee would swell up every Saturday night. We would meet on a Thursday for free-kicks and Friday for team talks and we just seemed to gel.

It was just luck, that's it. We hadn't worked on it but I think we were both good readers of the game and readers of people.

Because in my opinion, if I had been Jack, I would have given the captaincy of the club to Willie. I was fortunate Jack just happened to pick on me. But Willie would have been a perfect captain for everybody, any club. Because he was a role model for any player that there's ever been.

He's the perfect person and character and the ability he had was tremendous. I was just lucky that Willie was around. He certainly made my career

.

BERNIE

You did manage to lift the Anglo Scottish Cup but you never lifted a major trophy. How frustrating was that?

STUART

Can anybody remember the Anglo Scottish Cup? (Laughs)

BERNIE

No.

STUART

I can't remember the Anglo Scottish Cup! (Laughs)
But it was a fairly well-known competition at the time. It doesn't mean
anything now but it was nice to win something.
It was nice to win the Second Division Championship in my first season as
captain, everything went right.
Only losing 2 or 3 games in a season, that was a fabulous thing. But I have
to admit it was after that, that we could have improved.
I would have loved to have gone into Europe and won something, or won
the First Division, or the Premier League as it is now.
I mean that was disappointing, but I can't grumble at my career. I had 20
years exactly and never got left out of any side, never got injured.
I was captain everywhere I've been and I'm quite proud of those things. But
it would have been nice to have won something big.

BERNIE

You left the Boro for a short move to Newcastle for a fee of around
£100,000. Did you feel you were you forced out of Boro?

STUART

In a one word answer, yes. I didn't want to go.
I had just over 8 years at Boro and loved it here. I loved the people, it was a
successful club and at 31 I was playing okay.
I was fit and everything was going okey dokey, I wanted to finish and get a
testimonial. I was coming up for a testimonial and that would have done me.
I had opened a business near to the ground on St Barnabas Road, a brilliant
shop. I was made to finish my career at Middlesbrough.
But John Neal bought Irving Nattrass. At the time I don't think the club had
enough money to pay for him.
Newcastle wanted a big lad at the back to sort things out and somebody to
lead the team.
They wanted some leadership qualities up there but I didn't want to go.

I remember going to see Charlie Amer, the chairman, many, many, many a time and actually begged him for me not to go.

Don't forget, the financial rewards for me were a lot of money in those days. My wages were doubled, my bonuses were doubled, financially I would have been secure. But I still didn't want to go.

But you know as well as I do, if your face doesn't fit and you can see the manager wants to change, at the end of the day you'll be left out and things will go from bad to worse. So I went for everybody's interests.

BERNIE

If you could change anything, what would you change?

STUART

I had a wonderful career. I mean I have a shop now in Kirkby where actually I'm living at the moment, people come in the shop and they say:
"Don't you wish you were playing now with all the money they are getting?"
I mean, I was okay in those days, I was well-paid at Middlesbrough. I didn't play for the money as such but you will not take those 20 years off me.
I wouldn't change anything I've done in football and I loved it at Middlesbrough, that's where most of my career was spent.
But no, I wouldn't change anything.

HONOURS

STUART WILLIAM BOAM

PLAYING CAREER HISTORY

1966-1971 Mansfield Town
1971-1979 Middlesbrough
1979-1981 Newcastle United
1981-1983 Mansfield Town
1982-1983 Hartlepool United

PLAYING HONOURS (winners)

Middlesbrough
1973 -1974 Second Division title.
1975   Anglo Scottish Cup.

Bernie's About 2

Stu Boam and David Hodgson proudly show off their awards.

'After three minutes I was told I can never play again.'

On how his Middlesbrough career came to an end.

MARCO BRANCA

Interview 4 Marco Branca

MARCO BRANCA was born in Grosseto, Italy on January 6, 1965.
Marco arrived at the Riverside from Inter Milan for a fee of £1million.
He got off to a glorious start, scoring on his home debut against
Liverpool.
His attributes were he had a good first touch, was fairly strong with good
technique and he knew where the goal was - he was a natural goalscorer.
I met up with the Italian at the Tall Trees in Yarm. He was accompanied by
his interpreter and his team-mate Gianluca Festa.
He was smartly dressed, as most Italians are, and his English was hesitant
but still more fluent than mine!
I found him sincere, warm, cool and likeable.
This interview never made it onto the Boro TV screens - you can make your
own mind up as to why it was never aired.

BERNIE

Marco, you started your professional career in Italy playing for Cagliari,
followed by moves to Udinese, Sampdoria, Fiorentina, Parma, Roma and
Inter Milan. I noticed you played for Udinese on three separate occasions,
why?

MARCO

I think I must start this interview by saying sorry for my English because
in the last month I've forgot maybe my better English. So I will try and
speak my best.

Udinese took me three times because every season I played well and my
behaviour was good. So the club was happy and me too - no problem.

BERNIE

Would you class your move to Inter Milan as the biggest move in your
career?

MARCO

Inter Milan is, was and always will be a team with a great, great history, with great tradition. But I think that Sampdoria, Parma, Roma and Fiorentina are all big teams.

BERNIE

What honours did you win in Italy? Did you win cups, leagues?

MARCO

I won the League Championship in 1991 with Sampdoria, a UEFA Cup with Parma, Italian Cup with Sampdoria and lost the UEFA Final with Italy, so that's it.

BERNIE

When Brazilian Ronaldo signed for Inter were you excited by his arrival, or did that signal your departure? Did you partner him?

MARCO

No, no. I left Milan seven months after his arrival. I met him, I know him very well. He's a very nice boy and he's great, sometimes he's the best in the world I think. That's my personal opinion and so I would have been happy to play with him because he's a mate.

BERNIE

How many caps did you receive for the national team? Did you play international football for Italy?

MARCO

I played just for the Olympic team in Atlanta in 1996 but after three games we went back home. (Laughs) I scored four goals.

BERNIE

You joined Boro in February 1998 for a fee of £1 million. Why did you choose Boro?

MARCO

Because I wanted to try an English football experience. I always saw on TV the great atmosphere here in England so I wanted to try.
I had the opportunity in the same team where my friend Gianluca played. So I thought I would be happy and I thought for my family it would be easier to settle.

BERNIE

You're obviously big friends with Gianluca. Where did that friendship start?

MARCO

He was older than me.

BERNIE

He was never older than you! (Laughs)

MARCO

When I played in the first team he played in the younger team, so maybe he saw me and looked at me with admiration. An idol! (Laughs)
But after I knew him very well at Inter Milan, so we became friends after four or five years.
His presence was important, but the first decision was I wanted to play this football.If Gianluca was here, much better for me.

BERNIE

You made your Boro debut at the Riverside against Liverpool and had a dream start scoring a goal. What do you remember about that game?

MARCO

I remember when the match ended afterwards the supporters demanded the players come back out to do a lap of honour.
It was very, very strange for me because it was just a semi-final match, so I couldn't believe it. It was a great start.

BERNIE

Last season you made 11 appearances and scored nine goals. You must have been delighted with your goal tally?

MARCO

I was happy for all the team for the promotion and for my goals because in my life I have scored many goals.
But the final target was very, very important for all the team so I was happy for that.

BERNIE

Did you find many differences between Italian and English football?

MARCO

Everybody says yes. I think that here there's a different atmosphere, a different culture, so the players that come here must accept this and must strive to do better.

BERNIE

During the close season you had an operation. What was the problem?

MARCO

I had a problem after I twisted my right knee in the summer.
I had an operation to clear inside my knee, because I had a little piece of cartilage around my knee.
And after I worked here in Middlesbrough with the physiotherapist for my recuperation for three months until September, afterwards I played just 20 minutes against Tottenham.
I had two weeks of good training, but after 20 minutes maybe my leg wasn't strong enough so it was a little swollen and the club decided to do another operation to see inside, that's all.

BERNIE

That 20 minute spell at White Hart Lane has been your only appearance this season. How frustrating has that been?

MARCO

No, no, I respect the gaffer's decision every time. I have had an injury for a long time so it was right. No problem, no frustration.

BERNIE

After the operation you decided to stay in Italy, why did you not return to England?

MARCO

Because I had the operation and went to the hospital alone. I've been in my home alone, no-one from the club, just like a mate, he's a player of the club.
And after three minutes the doctor, the physiotherapist and the chief executive said to me that I can never play again in England.
They said my career was finished after the vision of my scan in two to three minutes maximum.
So in that time I tried to ask them if it was possible to see other specialists in Europe, in the USA or elsewhere.
They were very sure of their decision - three minutes and my career was over.
They were so sure that I couldn't understand them.
Because I played for so many years, I won't decide myself about my injury, I want to go to another specialist.
Maybe if all the specialists say you're finished then yes.
But all of the specialists out of England said I could continue to play football, so I tried.

BERNIE

So while you were in Italy did you keep in touch with the club. Were you phoning and faxing the club letting them know your position?

MARCO

Yes, I sent a fax from a Doctor Martins: after a good recuperation on my patella I can play.
But the club disputed it.
But I don't understand English very well but I can read and I must respect everyone.
So I worked very hard and sent the fax about my work, but the club wasn't very happy about my work, my effort.

The club just sent a fax to me about my house, my car here, they didn't ask about me. When I sent a fax to the club saying I was coming back to train with the team, they replied by saying it was useless me coming back. There was absolutely no point in me coming back to train.

BERNIE

When you finally returned you weren't allowed to train with the first team. How difficult was it training on your own?

MARCO

I thought about all the aspects, about my situation, but sincerely I found it fine because I gave so many chances to my club when I came back here. I said to the chief executive and club, I said: "I'm here two months before the end of my contract, so we have time to see together if I can or cannot play.
"So I don't want more money. If the contract is fixed for April 14, if in this time if I can play I will be happy, but if after this date, after my contract another injury, the same injury, I don't want the money."
The club didn't have to pay me, I wasn't expecting the club to. If this injury was very serious I would stop instantly - no money, no contract.
So I thought for me and the club that way would be the right way but I was wrong (laughs).

BERNIE

How many consultants have you actually seen?

MARCO

The furthest I travelled was to Mr Steadman in Colorado, who is one of the best in the USA, maybe in the world.
He said about my knee that he thought I can play with good work.
So I was happy because maybe Mr Steadman's opinion was enough.
After I send, I bring a fax, bring an original certificate to the club and they said: "No, we need an English doctor, a specialist."
So I went to Cambridge - alone again on a train (laughs) - to see the specialist.
I don't want to say, you can say to the supporters what the specialist wrote because you've seen it.
If I say yes Bernie, I'm not the right person to give that point of view.
You saw my certificate, you can explain because I have the confidence in you as an old player like myself.

So you saw Mr Steadman's certificate, you have seen both and I thought the English specialist said "Yes."
But another time I am wrong. So because I am in a ridiculous situation everything I say...
If I speak about weather or water or the flowers, the club say 'You can't play'. But I'm talking about flowers not football.

BERNIE

You're in a no-win situation.

MARCO

So I must go back to my home now because here I'm losing my time. I have to train every day alone (laughs), so I prefer to go back.
I'm not happy but I must go back to train with my ex-team Inter Milan to play little matches, to touch the ball.
But that isn't important to me. I think here is a great place to play football because the supporters have great passion and patience so everybody can work and enjoy.

BERNIE

Some people are saying you're just hanging on for money reasons. Do you need the money?

MARCO

Every person needs the money, every person needs much money, the right money.
But at this moment I didn't ask for the money for my consultations or treatment, for my travel.
I can be happy if I can pay for my training. With a fax from my club in my pocket, with just a little sentence: "How are you?" or "When do you think you can be back?"
But I have been alone in my fight. I was unhappy. The problem wasn't the money, the problem isn't the money, I don't want the money if I can't play. The supporters must know this. It is very, very important for me after everything. Things can happen possibly. I can never play here but I want to leave with respect, with my head held high. That's enough.

BERNIE

How would you describe your fitness level at this moment in time?

MARCO

Yes, yes, I lose my time. Last month I trained alone - consultations, travelling, so a wasted month.

BERNIE

What does the future hold for Marco Branca?

MARCO

I will take my time to train every day with the ball. I will decide with calm.

BERNIE

When you return to Italy, if a player approached you and asked about joining Boro, what would you advise?

MARCO

What do you think Bernie!?
For all the fans, I must say thank you and to the supporters and my ex team-mates I want to say good luck for the end of the season.

BERNIE

Okay Marco, thanks very much.

MARCO

Thanks. Bye, bye Bernie.

HONOURS

MARCO BRANCA

PLAYING CAREER HISTORY

1984-1986 Cagliari
1986-1987 Udinese
1987-1988 Sampdoria
1988-1990 Udinese
1990-1991 Sampdoria
1991-1992 Fiorentina
1992-1994 Udinese
1994-1995 Parma
1995   AS Roma
1996-1998 Internazionale
1998-1999 Middlesbrough
1999-2000 FC Lucerne
2000-2001 Monza

1996 Italy Olympic team

Bernie's About 2

'I think to win something with Middlesbrough would be nice but I can't wait around forever'

On losing patience.

STEWART DOWNING

Interview 5 Stewart Downing

STEWART DOWNING was born in Middlesbrough on July 22, 1984.
He joined the club at the tender age of 10 and progressed through the ranks, playing youth and reserve football before breaking into the first-team.
Not only did he establish himself as a first-team regular, he has also broken into the England squad as a regular.
Stewie is arguably one of the best and most natural left wingers in the country.
He is fairly quick, direct, an excellent crosser of the ball and very seldom gives away possession.
He both creates goals and scores goals.
I've been in Stewie's company several times over the years.
The first time I met him was at the unveiling of the Middlesbrough legend banners in the town centre.
I've sat alongside him flying back from a European game and bumped into him at the Prince's Trust Player of the Year dinner, which he deservedly won.

For this interview I met up with him at Crathorne Hall on the outskirts of Yarm.
I had arranged to meet him at 2pm but at 2.50pm there was no still no sign of him.
Just as I was finishing my coffee, about to head off, in he walks accompanied by his father.
I shouted out: "Have you not got a clock at the training ground?"

Well the words were stronger than that, but not for print!

He apologised - he had been kept back doing yoga and I believe his father was chatting with the Chief Executive.

I've always found Stewie to be a smashing lad despite his fame and fortune.
He is down-to-earth, fairly quiet and loves a laugh. He has never changed to his credit.

Three-and-a-half weeks after this interview, he put in a shock transfer request.

BERNIE

You grew up in Pallister Park. Was it a good upbringing?

STEWIE

Yes, it was a good upbringing. Obviously it was football, football, football on the estate.
We had a good school team; a lot of them went on to play at quite a high level of football.
So in terms of upbringing I wouldn't change anything at all.

BERNIE

As a Boro fan no doubt you went to the games. How did you get there and where did you stand?

STEWIE

I think I probably went with our dad to all of the games. If it was at the Riverside we'd walk because it was walking distance from our house.
I probably went to all of the home games but not the away.

BERNIE

Who where your boyhood heroes?

STEWIE

I used to like Alan Moore actually, considering he played in my position.
I just got a glimpse of him at the end of his career, before I started in the reserves.
He was a decent player, he had a few bad injuries, but I think if I looked at anybody in my position it was him.

BERNIE

You learned your trade in Middlesbrough's academy - who gave you the most guidance?

STEWIE

I think probably David Parnaby and Mark Proctor. They had different styles.
Proc was probably the one that bollocked me more, where as Dave would be

the talker.

They had two different qualities I think but they were the best.

And like you said, they brought many amounts of kids through after me and before me, so I think those two have done the most for me.

BERNIE

As a youngster at Middlesbrough did you have a specific job - cleaning boots, dressing room jobs?

STEWIE

Yes, we did. I think we may have been the last lot. Do the ball, put the right pressure in it, stuff like that.

When it came to cleaning the boots I did them for Jason Gavin and Paul Ince I think at the time.

And they definitely had to be clean with Incey!

BERNIE

Did you get a good Christmas bung?

STEWIE

Yes, I did. I think I got £100 off Jason Gavin. I didn't get anything off Incey, he probably didn't know who I was then.

So yes, we definitely had to do jobs.

BERNIE

In 2002 you made your long-awaited debut in the Premier League against Ipswich. What do you remember about it?

STEWIE

We got beaten 1-0. I hit the post in the last minute didn't I, I think?

I remember travelling down there on the bus and thinking: "I'm in with a chance here."

Looking around at the players that were travelling there was myself, Mark Hudson and Brian Close all travelling, all the young lads.

I thought: "I'm in with a chance here."

We got to the ground and one hour before the game we were still waiting.

He picks the team: Stewie on the left. Sweat on, I didn't even have time to tell my dad or anyone, I just heard I was playing and that was it.

So I didn't have time to think about it really, just an hour before the game. I think Franck Queudrue, Colin Cooper, it was that sort of team. Beni Carbone I think played brilliantly.

Incey was brilliant before kick-off. He told me there was nothing to worry about and things like that.

He just said: "I remember my debut and I thought this is going to be one of many."

So I had a lot of confidence from him, but in terms of the game, I remember nutmegging one of their players once and then him putting me in Row F about two minutes later. Brilliant!

BERNIE

In October 2003 you joined Sunderland on loan and scored 3 goals in 7 appearances. You must have enjoyed it?

STEWIE

I did. I didn't actually want to come back at the time. Obviously looking at the team I was frustrated.

I was only young at the time but (Steve) McClaren wouldn't play me. Even though I was young, I thought at the time I was better than Bolo Zenden. Not being big-headed, just confident enough that I was a better winger than him.

But as you said, that loan spell probably opened McClaren's eyes a little bit. I know I was a division below, but I still proved I could do well and score goals.

I think probably that helped a lot going on loan.

BERNIE

Did it enter your mind that you could be on your way out of Middlesbrough?.

I heard rumours that Steve McClaren was willing to let you go to Wigan.

STEWIE

Well we knew that anyway (Stewie and his dad agree).

I knew that stuff was going on with Wigan, I never made any real contact, but I knew that they had apparently agreed a fee for £900,000.

So from then on I didn't really click with McClaren.

But like I say, that loan spell I forced it on myself because he was looking to send me to QPR, Chesterfield, all these clubs - Swansea.

They're all in the Second and Third Division. I didn't think it was beneficial to me, so I remember Mick McCarthy coming to a reserve game and saying to me: "Do you fancy coming?"

So I jumped at it and said yes.

McClaren wouldn't let Mick take me for ages and ages, then all of a sudden he had no choice.

My dad went in, the old stories came out, he had a go at him and he let me go.

McClaren may have got the credit for me going to Sunderland, but it was me who forced the issue to go there.

BERNIE

You returned to Middlesbrough after rave reviews and established yourself. It must have always been your dream to play for your hometown club?

STEWIE

Definitely, definitely. Obviously it was difficult going to Sunderland on loan, but to come back and to get my chance was what I wanted.

Even then I thought I did quite well but they left me out again.

I was close to the stage of leaving.

I went to see him (McClaren) and told him I wanted to go.

Then I had a little bit of fortune, Mendi got injured with a cruciate.

Bolo was his ideal left winger but I did say he was a better left-back or midfielder, I just didn't think he was a winger. But it turned out very well for me so I was pleased from that point of view.

BERNIE

What would you say your qualities are as a player?

STEWIE

Moaning! Crossing, running at players. I'd like to score more goals. I did that last season, 10 in total.

Hopefully I can get a few more as well. But I think those are my qualities, probably my crossing being my biggest strength.

BERNIE

Middlesbrough won their first trophy in 128 years in lifting the Carling Cup. You were on the bench that day. Were you disappointed that you never got on?

STEWIE

A little bit, a little bit. I remember warming up and he was going to put me on at one point but when I look back, I have to count myself lucky because there was Coops, Andrew Davies, Jon Greening who played in most of the rounds and I'd been on loan and I'd only played in the quarter-final, sub in the semi-final and sub in the final.
So I was lucky to be on the bench but you still don't feel part of it if you don't play.
But nevertheless I've still got my medal.

BERNIE

When you first came into the side you were direct 9 times out of 10, taking the defender on the outside.
In the last couple of years you're content cutting inside and keeping possession.
Is that down to the coaching or down to you?

STEWIE

Yes it is. Obviously you play with no fear when you're young. You've got nowt to lose and you go for it and stuff.
But in terms of the team then you had two up front players filling space and, as you said, Zenden was giving me the ball.
I think as we got older McClaren got a bit more defensive - 4-5-1 - and sometimes I couldn't do that because I had nowhere to go.
I thought I had gone back-over on my game, but I don't know what that was about actually.
Over the years I have been coached to keep the ball at the right times in the right areas, defend in the middle third, keep the ball in the last third free to do what you want.
Obviously fans will look at that and say: "Oh, he's not doing what he did before," which was running at players.
I understand that possession is key in the last third, but a lot of people say: "Oh, he's changed his game, it has been coached out of him." Obviously you learn a bit of that from England of course.

BERNIE

You played a major part in getting Middlesbrough to the UEFA Cup Final in 2006.

Unfortunately we got walloped by Seville. How disappointing was that?

STEWIE

Very disappointing. We underestimated them a little bit and we didn't know anything about them.
We saw a couple of video clips of them and the best information I got was: "The right-back is crap."
Before kick-off - this was 10 minutes before kick-off - McClaren and Steve Round said to me: "We've watched the right-back. He can't defend, can't do this, can't turn, can't do anything."
It turns out that he (Daniel Alves) was one of the best right-backs I'd ever played against.
On the day we were defensive. Once they scored I think we didn't look dangerous going forward.
We had a few penalty claims and a chance, but apart from that they outclassed us.
But it was disappointing. After the way we got there it was disappointing to finish like that.

BERNIE

In February 2005 you were called into the England squad by Sven Goran Eriksson and came on as a substitute against Holland. How big an honour was that?

STEWIE

It was brilliant. I had heard rumours that I might be in, but I thought they were just saying that because I was a left winger and they needed a left winger. I remember McClaren pulling me one game and saying: "They are looking at you. You've got to keep it going, keep doing well and they will pick you."
They left me out of the Spain game, they lost 1-0 in Madrid. I think that was a good game to miss.
Then they called me into the next friendly - Holland at home. It was a shock but I was over the moon.

BERNIE

What was Sven Goran Eriksson like?

STEWIE

He was totally laid-back, even when under pressure. Even in the World Cup big games with pressure, he never shouted.
I think the only time the lads said when he shouted was when they lost to Northern Ireland 1-0.
But apart from that he was calm. He was different from a lot of managers I've had before. I couldn't believe how quiet he was as a manager, but he was good with the players.

BERNIE

He was good getting those birds!

STEWIE

He was. (Laughs)

BERNIE

In 2005/6 you made the World Cup squad and made 3 appearances as a substitute.
Could you believe that 4 years after your Middlesbrough debut you were playing for your country on the biggest stage in the world?

Bernie's About 2

STEWIE

When you put it like that, no, I didn't. I didn't actually think that at the time, but ahead of the World Cup waiting to get into the squad I didn't think I'd done enough.
I sat down with Steve Round coming back from injury. He said: "You've got 25 games, can you get in the squad?"
And I saw a little bit of light. That UEFA Cup run probably helped me. Sven was at the games and I played in some big games and did quite well.
So I thought in the 23-man squad I wouldn't play that much, but I was first sub in the first couple of games, so I was over the moon with that.

BERNIE

You've played under 3 managers so far with England - Sven, McClaren and Fabio Capello. What's Capello like?

STEWIE

I like him. I think he's probably what the England team need. In terms of young lads coming through like me and Wheater and that, he will give youth a chance if they're good enough.
He's not bothered about names or egos or who you play for. If you're doing the job you'll play and in terms of the other managers - without criticising them but for me he has probably been the best.

BERNIE

Do you call him boss?

STEWIE

Boss yes, or don't say anything when he walks past.

BERNIE

Do you call Gareth boss?

STEWIE

Yes. Obviously now and again you slip up and say Gar or Gareth but he doesn't mind. I played with him for a long time.

So gaffer or anything like that.

BERNIE

You played alongside Gareth Southgate and now he is your boss. How difficult is that?

STEWIE

Yes, a little bit because if we had problems as captain we would go to him. He was first class.
But now it's different. Obviously you've got Pogi as captain now and he knows if you're down or not or if you've got a problem and how he deals with it. He's now not your friend, he's your manager.
In terms of me, I can get on with it, but in terms of him it must be harder for him.

BERNIE

You've received some unfair criticism with England, just like Lampard, Cole and McClaren. How do you cope with that?

STEWIE

Not well. I don't like all the attention that goes with it but it's part and parcel of what you do.
I think with the media and that they bring it on more than your own local media.
But in terms of living in Middlesbrough I never get any hassle if I'm out and about in town or anywhere.
I get people saying: "Well done." Or: "Keep it up."
I have never really had any criticism.

BERNIE

Had any photographers outside your door?

STEWIE

A few times, a few naughty stories. But no, not really. My dad would probably chase them!

BERNIE

What do you enjoy best as a winger? Creating or scoring a goal, or both?

STEWIE

Obviously scoring goals is brilliant. But I think in terms of where I play, I think it would be probably creating them.
If I'm creating a goal for Afonso Alves and he is scoring goals then everyone is happy - I'm creating and he's scoring. But at the minute I'm creating and no one is putting them away. (We all laugh).

BERNIE

When you played alongside Jimmy Floyd Hasselbaink you were forever getting an ear bashing.
I never once saw you retaliate. Why was that?

STEWIE

I did one day. I remember when we played Charlton, we played in the cup and it was 0-0 away.
And we played them in the replay here and Luke Young always reminds me of the story.
He pulled me at half-time, he was yelling: "Don't you tell me to f*** off again or I'll f***** do you!"
"Come on then," I replied.
It was Coops who actually stood in the way and said: "You f***** won't, you should be proud of him for what he has done for you, setting your goals up."
But off the field Jimmy was probably one of the nicest guys I've ever met.
He just said: "Obviously I need you, sometimes I'm out of order, but I need you because you set my goals up."
But I've heard from Ross Turnbull that when he was at Cardiff he was a good player and a good lad, so I never really had any problems with Jimmy.
Sometimes I thought he went over the top with how he did it.
Remember Ravanelli used to do the same to Mikkel Beck?

BERNIE

How was your relationship with Steve McClaren? He had the psychologist Bill Beswick at the club.
Did you ever go to see him?

STEWIE

No, no, I've not got a problem with Bill Beswick. Obviously people used him but in terms of me I just get on with my own job. I don't need psychologists and all that.

BERNIE

So the door was always open but you never got dragged in?

STEWIE

No, but I felt he had more influence on the team than I would have expected. But obviously my relationship was probably the classic working relationship.
You know, obviously he was... I just wasn't into all the psychology thing.

BERNIE

You've had a couple of agents over the years. Is it important in the modern game to have an agent?
Do you get involved with the contract talks?

STEWIE

Not really. I think that obviously when you're young you think: "I need a agent, I'm getting a new contract and it's something they can help with obviously on contracts." You can focus on the football. But I've had my problems with agents, which has been sorted.
If you get a good one then fair enough, there are some goods ones out there. But there are also ones that are in it for themselves I think.

BERNIE

Do you go and see the manager before the agent?

STEWIE

Yes, I think if it has been offered to me and if I've got an agent he'd say: "It's not good enough" and you can get round it that way.
I never went in for a contract and said: "I want a contract, I want this, I know what he's on."
I have gone in and said: "This is what I think I am worth."
I'm not bothered what other people are on. They could be on more than me

or less than me, I'm not bothered.

When I was in the last time he said: "As long as we get this we are happy."

I have never been one to say: "Well he's on so-and-so, I want more than him because I'm better than him."

As long as I'm happy with my contract I would sign it.

BERNIE

Have you been disappointed to see the departures of Yakubu, Viduka, Schwarzer and company?

STEWIE

I've been surprised at a few of them - George (Boateng) and so on.

Maybe we could have had another year or so out of them. Maybe they wouldn't have played every week, but when you're struggling you need experienced guys like George, who is ideal.

Obviously the squad's a little bit young at the minute, I'm probably one of the oldest. But I do think at times when you're down at the bottom you rely on the new lads to get you out of it.

George probably played his best football in his last season before he left. The Duke on his day was probably one of the best players I played with and Yak, he's a proven goal scorer.

So I think I'd be lying if I said we didn't miss them.

BERNIE

On February 26, 2008 you signed a five-year contract until 2013. Was that a difficult decision?

STEWIE

Well yeah, probably the biggest decision I've had to make in terms of contracts.

Obviously its a big contract and a long one that could take me through to age 28, 29.

But I always hope for European football in that five years. I'd like it to be this year if possible because I think that it's our third year without it.

So it's a big year for Gareth and a big year for the players and hopefully we get into Europe and we'll be happy, but we'll see how we go.

BERNIE

Every time you lift a newspaper you're linked with clubs like Liverpool,

Tottenham and several others.
Is that upsetting or flattering?

STEWIE

I think it's flattering. I'm obviously aware of how the press work. If someone
needs a left winger there's not many of us about so I'll be linked. If they
need a centre half it will probably be Wheater or someone like that.
I mean, you can obviously find out if a club is interested in you.
Every time someone makes a bid for me I've been told by the manager,
which is quite good.
But I think it's a bit flattering and upsetting unless someone makes a final
bid.

BERNIE

You have played in several derby games. How much do they mean to you as
a local lad?

STEWIE

Well if you look at our team there are five, six or seven of us all from
Middlesbrough, so it means a lot.
Even the foreign lads understand. Tuncay understands because he has
played in derbies and they know it's big for us.
I don't know what it's like for other clubs, but I still think it's big for us and
to lose is not good.
It's for local bragging rights isn't it?

BERNIE

England caps. Is your target 100-odd, like David Beckham?

STEWIE

Yes, well as many as I can get really, more than probably winning
something. If I can only get 30 caps and win something, that will be
remembered more than me getting 70 caps or 100 and not winning anything,
so it would be nice to play in the European Championships and a World Cup
again, so I can always say I played in the biggest tournaments.
But I'd like to do well on the big stage as well.

BERNIE

When you were first selected for England Beckham was captain. What was he like?

STEWIE

He was brilliant. Very quiet, a different captain to what I've had in the past. But in training with the lads he was first class, he was all for them.
 He got them a lot of merchandise and suits, he was brilliant that way and obviously on the field as well. In the World Cup he took a lot of stick but he was our top goal scorer I think so I mean, I liked him. I thought he was a nice lad.

BERNIE

Best moments with England so far?

STEWIE

Best in terms of producing and scoring goals, that was the best yeah.

BERNIE

In your spare time I believe you do a bit of DJing. What kind of music do you play?

STEWIE

R & B. A bit of house, funky house electro stuff. Not too tough - it has got vocals and that in it.

BERNIE

Do you not play any Smiths, Morrissey or Bowie?

STEWIE

I'm sick of hearing Frank Sinatra in our house?

BERNIE

Your worst moment?

STEWIE

There's been a few. Probably missing the penalty against Sunderland away.

BERNIE

I called you that day Stewie!

STEWIE

I think I called myself! It was a big game.

BERNIE

Best moment?

STEWIE

I think it's got to be, if I'm looking at games, I've got to look at the England-Germany game.
That pleased me most because I was probably thinking I'm in the last chance saloon maybe.

BERNIE

Tell me your match day schedule.

STEWIE

Nine o'clock I get up and put on a bit of Soccer AM. If I was at home I'd be chilling out eating scrambled egg on toast. I don't like pasta or spaghetti before a game, its too heavy. Just chilling out, especially if I'm at home, just flicking through the TV to see if there's any football on. If there's an early game on watch a bit of that.
I'm probably one of the first to get to the stadium, I don't know why, it's probably just a ritual just to get there early at 1.15pm. I just chill out and read the programme.
I'm quite relaxed on match day because I think you've done all your preparation, you know what you have to do on match day.

You don't really need anyone to tell you what to do, I'm just totally chilled out before a big game.

BERNIE

After the game do you go out or does the result dictate if you go out?

STEWIE

I think the result dictates it, especially where we are living. I mean, I've been out in the past when I was younger and we've lost or drawn and you get a lot of stick.
But I tend to go out of the town a lot because a lot of the Middlesbrough fans there have a good drink after the game so I tend to go out of town a little bit more than I stay in Middlesbrough.

BERNIE

Your ambitions for the future?

STEWIE

Like I said before, play in another World Cup, European Championship, hopefully win as many caps as I can.
I would like to win something with Middlesbrough if I could.
I know we won the Carling Cup but I didn't play and we lost in the UEFA Cup final.
I think to win something with Middlesbrough would be nice but I can't wait around forever.

BERNIE

Do you watch Jeremy Kyle?

STEWIE

Yes.

BERNIE
Dark hair, left peg, scored a few goals - we need a DNA test. You could be my love child!

Stewie's dad shouts: "Well Bernie, if you want to pay his maintenance you can!"

HONOURS

STEWART DOWNING

PLAYING CAREER HISTORY

2001 Middlesbrough
2003 Sunderland on loan
2009 Middlesbrough

PLAYING HONOURS (winners)

Middlesbrough
2003- 2004 Carling Cup

23 FULL ENGLAND CAPS

Stewie represents his country against Spain

'Some players had left the club and spoken out against Middlesbrough in the press, but I never had a reason to do that.'

Reflecting on his time at the Riverside.

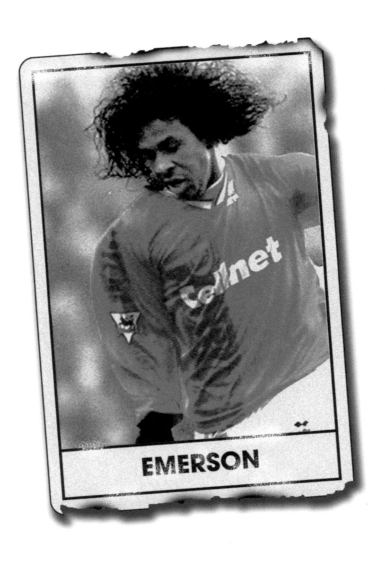

EMERSON

Interview 6 Emerson

EMERSON MOISES COSTA was born in Rio de Janeiro, Brazil on April 12,1972.

He signed for the Boro in 1996 from FC Porto for a fee of £4million.

With his long black curly hair, he looked like a throwback to the 70s and was certainly a colourful character as well as a fantastic player.

Strong as an ox and very skilful, he also scored some spectacular goals but hit the headlines for the wrong reasons a couple of times when he returned without permission to Brazil.

That, along with his trademark flamboyant dancing celebrations after scoring, was one of the many things I asked him about when I travelled to Leeds and met up with him at a posh hotel.

Emmo was in England because his Spanish club Deportivo La Coruna had a game against Leeds at Elland Road in the Champions League.

I did the interview outside the hotel as it was quite a pleasant day.

Zalia Knight, the interpreter who he had at Middlesbrough, travelled with me to make sure there was no language barrier or slip-ups.

Emmo's usually wild, bushy hair was in dreadlocks and he was wearing his club tracksuit.

He came across as very laid-back, warm, passionate and funny.

BERNIE

What attracted you to Middlesbrough when you were playing for FC Porto?

EMERSON

I was 24-years-old and attracted by the idea of playing football in England. It was also important to me that players like Juninho, Ravanelli and Branca were at the club.

They were all good players and I knew with other foreign players at the club I would find it easier to settle.

BERNIE

How much did you enjoy playing alongside the likes of Juninho and Ravanelli?

EMERSON

It was a very good experience and I enjoyed it very much.
They are both very good players and playing with good players enriched my experience of playing at Middlesbrough, which was very important.

BERNIE

You had a great start and scored some great goals. How did you adjust to life in the Premiership?

EMERSON

To begin with it was difficult, but because of my style of football and physical presence I was able to adapt quicker than others.
Some players, some foreign players, take two or three months to settle.

BERNIE

On a couple of occasions you returned to Brazil. Everybody wants to know why?

EMERSON

The first time I went back to Brazil it was because my wife couldn't settle in the UK, which was very unsettling for me.
However, when Zalia was brought into the club it made things easier for us.
The second time I went was for a different reason.
I didn't think the team were striving enough to compete for titles and cups.
We made it to two cup finals at Wembley but didn't win anything and we were relegated, so the main reason was because the team didn't win anything and wasn't strong enough to challenge for titles.

BERNIE

When you returned from Brazil did the lads give you a bit of stick?

EMERSON

No, no when I came back there was no aggression in the dressing room from my team-mates. They all supported me.
I know I caused problems for my team-mates but both my team-mates and the fans always supported me.

BERNIE

You played in two major cup finals at Wembley. How disappointing was it to not at least win one?

EMERSON

I was very disappointed not to win anything, but I was also disappointed for the fans. It would have been good for the supporters to see us win.
The expectations were so high it would have been wonderful, but to get to Wembley was good for the supporters and an achievement. To experience playing at Wembley is something you'll always remember, but the memory would have been better if we had won.

BERNIE

When you returned from the FA Cup Final you grabbed the microphone and stated you were going to stay with Middlesbrough
even though they had been relegated. What was that all about?

EMERSON

(Laughs) I stayed for six months, but what made me leave in the end was although we were top of the First Division, I wasn't sure we would be promoted and if we weren't promoted, I thought that staying in the First Division could limit my chances to progress to a bigger club or a Premiership club.
I was only 24-years-old and I was worried about playing in the First Division for too long, so in the end I was transferred to Tenerife.

BERNIE

Juninho left and Paul Merson, an England international, arrived. Did you enjoy playing alongside Paul?

EMERSON

Yes, I enjoyed playing with Merson. He was a good player and a good team-mate, even though when he left I heard he made negative comments about the club. I don't know if that was true or not because I had gone.

BERNIE

During that season you scored a great goal against Sunderland. Was that one of your best?

EMERSON

I'm not sure. I think the one I got against Huddersfield or Sunderland in the Premier League was the best goal.

BERNIE

What was that goal celebration dance you always used to do all about?

EMERSON

(Laughs) Brazilian people have samba in their blood and when they are happy their first expression of that happiness is to dance. Scoring goals makes me happy and gave me the desire to do the samba.
Also it encourages the supporters to show their joy as well.

BERNIE

Does it disappoint you that you haven't represented your country Brazil?

EMERSON

No, I'm not disappointed. I still have a lot of time to play football, I think that my international future is in the hands of the gods, but I wish and think that I will be given the chance one day.

BERNIE

Who were your idols as a youngster when you were growing up in Brazil?

EMERSON

Pele of course. I only watched him on video and on television but Zico was the player that I saw playing in The Maracana and he was my idol. Zico is the player that most Brazilians of my generation admire and look up to.

BERNIE

In that First Division season you got yellow-carded against Bury, which meant you missed the Christmas period through suspension. Was that pre-planned? A lot of people said that it was and I was one of them!

EMERSON

(Laughs) I don't think so. I was yellow-carded but it was not intentional at that time.
Because we were in the First Division and the players had a long weekend off and we went to Ireland for some rest and relaxation.
It was only after that weekend that I went to Brazil.
I stayed in Brazil for New Year's Eve because New Year's Eve is a very important time for me, but I came back after New Year's Eve.
When I was in Brazil all my family were pressurising me about playing First Division football and it was then that I made my decision to leave Middlesbrough and I was transferred to Tenerife.
After a year with Tenerife I regretted that decision despite the good weather - although the weather was never a problem for me in Middlesbrough.

BERNIE

After the Christmas period you failed to turn up yet again, which signalled the end of your Middlesbrough career. Were you disappointed or did you expect it?

EMERSON

To begin with, yes. I was very surprised because I had been used to behaving that way, because it had never been
difficult for me I'd always been able to make that spur of the moment decision and I was very young at the time.
At the end of the day, I would have liked to have stayed. And I had already agreed with my wife that we would start to learn English, so I was a little bit upset. But I understood that the club were tired with me and the way I behaved.

BERNIE

How did you get on with manager Bryan Robson?

EMERSON

Wonderful, it was a great experience for me working with Bryan Robson.
I never had a manager before who had so much patience. Bryan always
supported me even through the difficult times.
I understand that when I left Bryan needed to make a difficult decision to
transfer me, he had to make the decision for the club and I never had a
problem with Bryan or his decision.
Some players had left the club and spoken out against Middlesbrough in the
press but I never had reason to do that.
I was very well treated by the club and never, ever had a bad word to say. In
fact, the complete opposite.

BERNIE

When you left you were quoted as saying the club treated players like
slaves. What did you mean by that?

EMERSON

Who said that?

BERNIE

It was quoted in the national newspapers when you left, you didn't say it?

EMERSON

No, never. No, no, I never said that - like a slave? No, I swear to you I didn't
say that and I'd like to set the record straight.
I never said anything like that against the club, the journalists can sometimes
put words into your mouth.

BERNIE

Do you keep in touch with any of the players?

EMERSON

At first I tried keeping touch with the players but my English wasn't very
good and when I went to Spain, I had to learn Spanish very quickly and I
lost touch with them.
My wife and I still keep in touch with Zalia and her family.

BERNIE

What were your highs and lows during your time at Teesside?

EMERSON

The high point of course was going to Wembley for two cup finals, the Coca Cola Cup Final and the FA Cup final.
It was wonderful to play at Wembley and the low point was obviously being relegated. It was bad for the club, the players and the supporters. Everyone felt bad about relegation, especially the supporters.

BERNIE

Your friend Juninho has returned to Middlesbrough for a second time. Would you consider it?

EMERSON

Of course.

BERNIE

Would you like to end by sending a message to the Middlesbrough fans?

EMERSON

Finally, I would like to apologise to the fans. I know I caused a lot of problems during my time at Middlesbrough and I blame a lot of that on my age because I was very young at the time.
But I would like to apologise and secondly I would like to say a big thank you to the supporters for the way they treated me and made me so welcome in the area. They treated me with such warmth and kindness.
I always say to this day that anyone who speaks badly about Middlesbrough obviously has not been there.
I was always treated wonderfully and the people of Middlesbrough are wonderful people.

HONOURS

EMERSON MOISES COSTA

PLAYING CAREER HISTORY

1990-1992 Flamengo
1992   Coritiba
1992-1994 Belenenses
1994-1996 FC Porto
1996-1997 Middlesbrough
1998-2000 CD Tenerife
2000-2002 Deportivo La Coruna
2002-2003 Atletico Madrid
2003-2004 Rangers FC
2004-2005 Vasco da Gama
2005-2006 Skoda Xanthi
2006-2007 AEK Athens
2007   APOEL FC
2008   Madureira

PLAYING HONOURS (winners)

1995, 1996 Portuguese Championship
1996   Portuguese Super Cup
2002   Spanish Cup

First ever Brazilian to play for Rangers.

Bernie's About 2

Brazillian in full flow

'Gazza could have and should have been the greatest player in the world.'

On Paul Gascoigne's ability

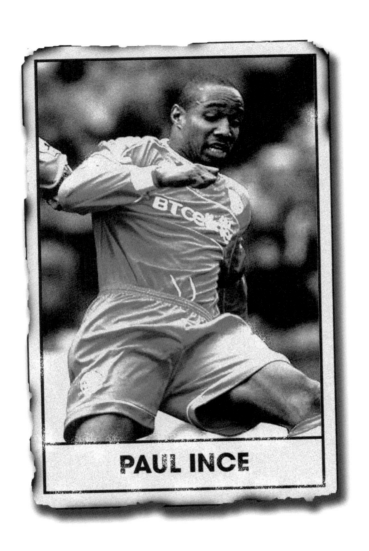

PAUL INCE

Interview 7 Paul Ince

PAUL INCE was born on October 21, 1967 in Ilford. After playing with some of the biggest clubs in the world he arrived on Teeside from Liverpool for a fee of £1 million.

I had played against Incey on several occasions while he was at Manchester United and I was at Middlesbrough.

I always found him a great competitor - tough in the tackle and a good distributor who chipped in the odd goal.

I met up with him at the training headquarters at Hurworth in Darlington. He was suffering from flu virus but to his credit the interview continued.

I found him to be witty, straight-laced and honest. In the interview he indicates that some of his career moves were dictated because of the love of his family.

BERNIE

You started your professional career at Upton Park. How did you enjoy your time there at West Ham?

PAUL

Obviously I was at Fulham and West Ham when I was 12 or 13, I had a choice of signing schoolboy forms for one of the two clubs.

And I decided to go to West Ham because at the time they had the indoor astro turf! I don't know if you can remember it? It was kind of cool.

I liked that, so that's originally the reason I signed for West Ham basically.

And from age 14 until I was about 20-odd I enjoyed my time there under John Lyall, who was more of a father figure to me.

He looked after me not just on the pitch but off the pitch, finding me digs and that kind of stuff, because my mum went to Germany when I was 10.

I was kind of on my own, you know what I mean? So I struggled for a bit, then he took me under his wing and looked after me, so I enjoyed my time there.

Obviously when the truth about Man United came out it became a bit nasty.

BERNIE

You joined Man United under a tide of bad publicity. What was that all about?

PAUL

It was funny see, because no-one actually knows the full story.

BERNIE

Are we going to hear it? (Laughs)

PAUL

Basically to cut the story short, I was living in a place in Dagenham, where I came from, and I had a car that kept getting ripped to pieces.
It was an XR3i cabriolet and it kept getting ripped to shreds by idiots outside my house.
So I went to see John Lyall just before the end of the season and said: "Listen John, I need some more money. I want a rise in my wages because I want to buy a house. I've got a girlfriend now and we want to settle somewhere nice. People keep ruining my car, that kind of stuff.
So I want to sign a new contract so I can afford to buy a bigger house."
So he said: "Yeah, yeah no problem, fine". So he sorted out the contract.
We sat down and negotiated the contract, sorted it all out and I said: "I will leave it until next season."
Obviously I wasn't to know that John Lyall was getting the sack.
So I came back that pre-season and Lou Macari was manager and I sat down with Lou and said: "I agreed with John Lyall to sign this contract, blah de blah. Is it okay?"
He said: "No, no, no that's just too much money. For someone your age you should be on the same money as you originally were."
Which I wasn't happy about as you could imagine. So with that happening and John Lyall getting sacked, I just thought maybe it was time for me to go.
Then Man United came in and we negotiated. I was going away to Malta on holiday with Claire, my wife.
The deal was close, so they said: "Right, we'll do a picture with the Man United shirt to save you from coming back from your holiday."
To do all that rubbish that you do when you sign for another club.
So I remember it, I did a picture with the Star I think. He took the picture, it was all confidential, no-one knew anything.
He put the picture in his library.
I think the Star at the time were linked with the Express, something like that.

Bernie's About 2
93

So obviously the Express was on to the story.

They went to the library to find a picture of me with the West Ham shirt on, to put in the paper saying I could be on my way to Man United, and they found the Man United picture. So clever that they are, they ran it in the papers and then it all started.

When I returned everyone went mad. I played a couple of pre-season games, a couple at home. Half the fans were saying stay, half were saying go and it came to a head.

When I was sub one game and Claire was sitting in the stand, they started abusing her, so she left at half-time.

I left with her and for me that was the bottom line, for me to say: "I've got to get out of here."

BERNIE

Would you describe your move to Old Trafford as a dream move?

PAUL

Yes, definitely. As a kid as I've publicised a lot of times I was fully aware of Bryan Robson as a player. I thought he was a fantastic player and I wanted to base my game on the way he played. So when United came in at 20 years of age, you cant turn it down, you've got to go, ain't you?

Of course you're a bit scared because you know it's a big club.

They were going through a period where they hadn't won anything for a while, so for someone so young to go there was a bit daunting but very exciting.

BERNIE

You played over 200 games for Man United then headed off for Inter Milan. Why did you leave?

PAUL

I just didn't feel wanted at the time. Once Inter showed an interest and the club said that they had accepted a £7.5 million bid, which they accepted from them, to come to me and say: "Hey, we've accepted a bid from Inter Milan, the ball's in your court."

It wasn't like: "We've received a bid for £7.5 million but we've turned it down because we want you to stay for another three or four years."

It wasn't on that wavelength. So the feeling I got from the club and from Alex Ferguson and the chairman was that it's a good deal now, you're getting on a bit. You're 27,28, we've got Nicky Butt coming through, we

feel that you're stopping him coming through, so it's up to you.
So it happened in a matter of two or three days. One minute I'm playing for Man United, the next minute I'm packing my bags for Inter Milan.

BERNIE

You returned to England and joined Liverpool. Was that the right move?

PAUL

Yes, definitely, because I always wanted to stay up in the North. I spent my life in London, I spoke to my wife and I could have gone to numerous clubs in London at the time when I left Inter Milan. But at Liverpool I had a lot of friends there. Steve McManaman and Robbie Fowler were good mates of mine, so I thought it would be easier for me to settle down in a club like that and we could stay up in the North, which we wanted.
Looking at it, yes, it was the right move, definitely.

BERNIE

You've gained 49 caps for England at this moment in time. The highlights so far have been what?

PAUL

I think Euro 96 and the game against Holland was probably the best game, not just for myself but the best game an England team has played against a World Cup side like Holland.
They had fantastic players and we went on the pitch and absolutely slaughtered them. All the euphoria, every time you went to Wembley the streets would be full of people and the further we got, the more people there was.
It was a shame the way it ended, but for me it doesn't really matter that we lost in the semi-final, because I believe we were the best team there.
I believe that we should have won the tournament at the time.
I honestly believe that we were the best team in the tournament.
It doesn't matter that we lost to West Germany, the fact that it was a great experience for me, to do so much in your home country, in such a big tournament.

BERNIE

Talking about Euro 96, in the semi-final you faced Boro team-mate Christian Ziege. Some say he's still got the bruises!

PAUL

Yes, he was playing left-back. As you know, Christian likes to get forward.
He happened to wander just into my area. (Laughs)
Then I thought: "What are you doing here son?" It was in the first five
minutes and when he came to Middlesbrough, he reminded me what I had
done to him.
He's told me he's going to get me back, but I can't see it somehow.

BERNIE

Leaving Anfield you joined Middlesbrough. What swayed your decision? I
heard you had several clubs wanting your signature?

PAUL

It was the case. I'd settled at Liverpool, just bought my house. Thomas, my
son, was eight and I'd spent the last three or four years travelling around.
He has been to Manchester, he has been to Italy and he has been unsettled
with his life. So I thought, he's at Liverpool, he's settled with his life, he's
got his school friends and everything's just right and there were clubs in that
area I could have gone to.
I could have gone down to London but I think it was the fact that obviously
for me, Bryan Robson, as I've said, I worked under him in Euro 96.
The passion of the Boro fans I remember playing here in the League Cup
semi-final when we lost, I just remember how passionate the fans were and
how they loved their football and those two combinations work.
So the Bryan Robson factor and the fact that the club wanted to get into
Europe - I feel that I've got another couple of years in me and I feel I want
to prove people wrong. Because some people criticised my hunger to still
want to win things and play well. Some people said that's why I went to
Middlesbrough. That's not the case the club wants to progress, look at the
training facilities, look at the money in the club, 30,000 odd fans every week
I know this club is going in the right direction and I just feel I want to be a
part of it and help the gaffer succeed and get into Europe.

BERNIE

You've teamed up with Gary Pallister and Paul Gascoigne, how good are
those two?

PAUL

Pally's fantastic. I think Pally should have got a lot more caps than he
actually did. For me at the time, apart from the first year or so which we
struggled at Man United, after that, for me he was the best defender in
Europe without a doubt at absolutely everything.
He had pace, was great on the ball, six foot four, got the odd goal every two
or three years. (Laughs)
But he had everything, he could read the game and not many people beat
him. Let's just say he didn't get as many caps as he should have got.
Gazza on the other hand for me could have been and should have been the
greatest player in the world.
Obviously at the time he got a bad injury which cost him because he went to
Lazio.
But I remember playing against him for West Ham and there was me and
Billy Bonds in midfield. You know what Bondsy was like! (Laughs).
He was a bit of a mad man and we played Newcastle at Upton Park and
Gazza was playing in there.
He just ran riot and he megged Bondsy and Bondsy lost his head and chased
him all around the field to try and do him.
Gazza chipped the ball past him and Bondsy fell on the floor.
Gazza turned round and said: "Oh, get up you old man" and all that lot. So
for 90 minutes Bondsy just chased Gazza around, chased Gazza the whole
game.
I remember it well and I said to myself: "Phwoar, this kid's a player. He
doesn't care who he's playing against, he's going to be a player."
And he still is a great player. Obviously through injuries and lapses in his
life he has lost a bit.
But I still believe that if he really puts his mind to it, it's not too late. Even
though I'm the same age as Gazza and I still feel good, obviously you've
got to look after yourself off the field. Gazza knows that and I've told Gazza
that. We are close friends so I tell Gazza how I feel.
I say to him: "You've got so many doubters out there, it would be nice to
prove so many people wrong. You've got to get your head on."
We need him. If he is sharp and fit he is a fantastic player to have in your
team. But if he isn't then he is a liability and I've told him that.
So I just hope at the end of the season he chooses to go away and get
himself fit and makes sure he returns as the real Paul Gascoinge.

BERNIE

You were voted Supporters' Club player of the year. Are you happy with
that?

PAUL

Delighted, absolutely delighted. You know, I've won numerous medals, as you well know - FA Cups, European Cup, Cup Winners', League cups and that.
But to be recognised by your own fans is the biggest of them all. To have recognition that you've been the best player in the side, to me it's the greatest thing ever. To me it's better than winning all the other medals. It's great and I would just like to say: "Thank you very much."

BERNIE

Looking to next season, are we realistically looking to a European spot?

PAUL

Yes. Depending on the players that we bring in, we've got to be looking at Europe next year. You're looking to fourth place for the Champions League. This year would have been ideal, we had a chance of Europe in the cup game against Tranmere. That would have been ideal for us to get into Europe and we failed. If we have a good cup run, or we do well in the league, we have every chance. This club needs to be in Europe, it's a big club now.
Now we are stabilised in the Premiership we should be looking to progress into Europe and we need to do that Bernie.
We need to be there, because to attract great players or big name players you need to be in Europe, otherwise you ain't going to attract them.

HONOURS

PAUL INCE

PLAYING CAREER HISTORY

1984-1989 West Ham United
1989-1995 Manchester United
1995-1997 Internazionale
1997-1999 Liverpool
1999-2002 Middlesbrough
2002-2006 Wolverhampton Wanderers
2006   Swindon Town
2007   Macclesfield

MANAGERIAL CAREER HISTORY

2006-2007 Macclesfield Town
2007-2008 Milton Keynes Dons
2008   Blackburn Rovers

PLAYING HONOURS (winners)

1989-90 FA Cup
1990   FA Community Shield
1990-91 Cup Winners' Cup
1991   UEFA Super Cup
1991-92 League Cup
1992-93 Premier League
1993   FA Community Shield
1993-94 FA Cup
1993-94 Premier League
1994   FA Community Shield

Wolverhampton Wanderers First Division play-off winners

MANAGERIAL HONOURS (winners)

Milton Keynes

2008 Football League Trophy
2008 Football League Two

53 FULL ENGLAND CAPS

Bernie's About 2

**'I didn't feel the pressure at all to be honest. It was a sense of pride
for me, as to looking back to where I'd come from.'**

On being Britain's first half million footballer.

DAVID MILLS

Interview 8 David Mills

DAVID MILLS was born in Whitby on December 6, 1951.
He became a full-time footballer at his hometown club in December 1968
and made his debut in a 3-2 home defeat to Bury.
In two spells at Middlesbrough Millsy clocked up 398 appearances and
scored 111 goals.
I met up with him at Central Park restaurant in Middlesbrough, facing
Albert Park.
When I first arrived at Middlesbrough back in the 1984/85 season he was on
the coaching staff and stuck out with his long blond shaggy locks.
Millsy's qualities as a player were he was very quick and direct. He
created and scored goals and had a phenomenal workrate.
As a person I found Millsy a likeable, straight-laced personality, someone
who knew his capabilities and loved the game of football.
He definitely wore the shirt with pride and it's amazing in the interview
that he doesn't regard himself as a goalscorer despite his goal tally.

BERNIE

Millsy, you were a schoolboy international who attracted interest from
several clubs, including Hull City, Man Utd, Stoke and Burnley, as well as
Boro. Why did you choose Boro?

DAVID

I think it was circumstances more than anything else, Bernie. I had a pick
of a lot of clubs when I was 15 and scheduled to leave school and was really
looking forward to it.
Unfortunately I picked up a back injury and you know all about back
injuries Bernie, so you know the suffering I went through. I was out of the
game for 12 months.
In simple terms, I twisted and fractured my vertebrae, which meant I was
in a plaster cast, then a corset.
I had three or four months rehabilitation and in that time a lot of clubs
lost interest because I wasn't playing.
Middlesbrough, in fact With Stan Anderson as manager and Harold
Shepherdson as his assistant who looked after the schoolboys at that time,
still Showed an interest.

They said: "Look, come and watch the first team play, come and watch us train, come and watch the Northern intermediate side play," because I knew a few of the kids that play there.

Because I came up with them through schoolboys level I did that.

Then when I was finally passed medically fit if you like, although I hadn't played when the specialist said, "It's okay to give it a go," Middlesbrough said:

"Well we will sign you, providing you're okay and fit we'll take a gamble and we won't have to see you play again."

My father and I felt a sense of loyalty and the rest is history, as they say. I signed for Middlesbrough and on it went from there.

BERNIE

You scored 111 goals in 398 appearances, a ratio of one in four.
Would you describe yourself as more of a team player, than an out-and-out goalscorer?

DAVID

Without doubt I never classed myself as an out-an-out goalscorer.

BERNIE

What were your qualities?

DAVID

Well, I was never a box player, I was never a clinical finisher and I suffered accordingly for it.

I was criticised, which you accepted. You play the game, you pay the price, you take the credit and you get the criticism when you don't produce.

I think I was a team player. I had a good work rate and I wasn't bad particularly at anything.

I could do my fair share of chasing around, fair share of tackling.

I wasn't bad in the air, my touch and control wasn't bad but I was quick and I would get about.

I could put defenders under pressure, I could create things for other players, I could create chances for players playing who were more clinical finishers.

Of John Hickton's 200 goals or near enough for Middlesbrough, I probably made 150. (Laughs).

BERNIE

You got capped several times at Under-23 level. You were called into the full squad for Scotland but you failed to gain a full cap. How disappointing was that?

DAVID

A huge disappointment. I mean, it was a big year for me 1974. We had got promotion under Jack (Charlton), I'd been capped at Under-23 level that year, I'd gone on tour with the Under-23s and I got married that year.
I came back from the Under-23 tour and was picked to go with the full squad and never got a game.
So it was a huge disappointment, having had such a tremendous season up until that point and obviously I felt that I had been playing well enough to maybe justify a chance.
But there was Tommy Bould, who was the-ex Man City centre half, and me and we were the only two that didn't play under Joe Mercer on that European trip. Of course we came back, Joe was only caretaker, he'd taken over from Alf Ramsey and of course they appointed Ron Greenwood as full-time manager.
Then of course, different managers have different opinions about players and I never got back in until Don Revie took over.

BERNIE

You were Britain's first half million footballer when you left and big Ron Atkinson signed you for West Bromwich Albion. Did you feel the pressure of that fee?

DAVID

I didn't feel the pressure at all to be honest.
It was a sense of pride for me as to looking back to where I'd come from and the problems I'd had getting to where I'd got to. I always felt going as Britain's highest paid or highest transfer, if you like, was quite a prestigious thing and I knew it would only take a matter of weeks before somebody went to somewhere higher.
You look back now and there was the likes of Steve Daley, they all went for a million quid.
Trevor Francis was the first one actually who went shortly after me from Birmingham to Notts Forest for a million.
So I always felt that it wouldn't last long. For all the disappointments and maybe I didn't have the success at West Brom that I would have anticipated,

I couldn't really use them as an excuse that I felt the pressure of the fee because I didn't to be honest.

BERNIE

Who were some of the players at West Brom at that time?

DAVID

Well we had a good, solid team. Derek Statham. Bryan of course, Bryan Robson. Cyrille Regis, Peter Barnes, Alistair Brown, Tony Brown with 200 goals throughout his career.

BERNIE

Willie Maddren brought you back to Ayresome Park. How did things go second time around at Middlesbrough. Did it come as a surprise?

DAVID

Yes, because I hadn't planned on it. I planned on staying on at Newcastle but circumstances ironically changed there. We'd got promotion but Arthur Cox, instead of taking the team into the First Division had contract problems and left and I'd still been commuting from Sheffield to Newcastle.
He said to me: "If you stay, obviously there's a new contract there.
"If you don't and are unsure because of what's happening, I'll let you go on a free."
That was great in the circumstances. Of course, he left, I left on a free back to Sheffield and in that period of time Willie took over as manager of Middlesbrough.
He said: "Will you come back and get involved in the coaching side?"
I quite fancied it, it was an opportunity for me to do that and it was a path I wanted to go down anyway at the time.
So I came back here as player/coach. Playing-wise started off quite brightly.
I ended up with a few goals by Christmas time and that was the best stat I'd had in my career, ending that season top scorer.
In many ways I was a better player then. Maybe not quite as quick but I wasn't slow.
I'd got a better understanding of the game probably than what I'd had first time around and I was probably more of a clinical finisher at that time. I'd learned by then.
I picked up an achilles injury after Christmas and that kept me out and to be fair to Willie, I always felt that maybe if I hadn't got that injury, at that time maybe we wouldn't have been in a relegation fight at the end of

that season because we had to go to Shrewsbury and get a result and the boys did that to be fair.

But maybe if I hadn't picked up that injury, maybe it wouldn't have got to that stage.

Maybe we would have had a bit of breathing space and that would have been needed.

BERNIE

How was your relationship with Willie?

DAVID

Great. We go back 30 years.

You've got to remember we played at Stockton Boys Under-15s together.

We joined Middlesbrough at similar times, played in the intermediates at similar times, the reserves, and went into the first team and Under-23s together.

So our careers go back a long way. Obviously he suffered an injury at 26,27 which finished him.

I went off to West Brom and obviously our paths changed course then but I think there was a fair amount of respect for each other.

It was an unbelievable experience to come back at that time, in the most difficult time.

I mean, you went through it, you know what it was like, but coming back to start with no money, lack of personnel, no training facilities.

The road was a shambles, the training ground there was cockroaches in the roof, the whole thing was an absolute shambles trying to get finances for anything.

I mean, we went up to Scotland pre-season, which was before you arrived. I drove the mini bus! I came back as a coach but I didn't realise it meant driving a bus!

I drove the mini bus, played in the game, put the kit out, collected the kit and now I was a first-team player.

That summed it up and I loved every minute of it. Don't get me wrong, I wouldn't have changed it. It was a great experience but when you look back at the hours we put in under such circumstances and you look at what they have got now, you think modern day players are spoiled, in as much as a lot of them don't know any different.

I think what they have got now is absolutely out of this world and great, I would have loved to have had that.

I wouldn't particularly have changed anything I had. It doesn't make you a better player and at the end of the day, you have to have self discipline and the drive and desire to want to be the best.

BERNIE.

The club was struggling financially and you were shown the door. Where did you end up?

DAVID

I went to Darlington part-time. I took employment outside of football because I needed a job at the end of the day and Cyril Knowles was manager of Darlington and he was struggling.
He must have been struggling to be fair! (Laughs)
Let's be fair - if he came for me, 15 months out and then another six months out and asked me to play, not being disrespectful to any of the players that were there but he must have been desperate! (Laughs)
Because I was 36 and he said: "Will you come and play and do a job for me?"
What I had wanted to do, rightly or wrongly, there had been the possibility of getting insurance for me and I didn't want to do that.
I didn't want to just fade into obscurity having had 15 months working my socks off to try and get fit and then another six months to just walk away and turn my back on it for a few quid, which is all it would have been.
I thought: "I want to play again." And that's what I did.
I had six months at Darlington, possibly a little less.
I played first-team football and enjoyed it because I was playing.
I wanted to play, that was all I wanted - to play at pro level. I wanted to finish as I had started, if you like.
I didn't want to finish as a result of an injury having spent such a long time getting fit and having had injuries playing a significant part through my career.
I suppose I just wanted to go out physically playing, even though I might not have been playing well or at the highest level.
I wanted to play and that's always been my philosophy. I've just loved playing.

HONOURS

DAVID MILLS

PLAYING CAREER HISTORY

1968-1979 Middlesbrough
1979-1982 West brom
1981-1982 Newcastle (on loan)
1982-1983 Sheff Wed
1983-1984 Newcastle
1984-1985 Middlesbrough
1986-1987 Darlington

PLAYING HONOURS (winners)

Middlesbrough
1973 - 1974 2nd division championship.

Mills in full flow

'If I can be successful enough to prove them that I can do the job well enough, I could come back to Middlesbrough.'

On managing Middlesbrough one day.

TONY MOWBRAY

Interview 9 Tony Mowbray

ANTHONY MARK MOWBRAY was born in Saltburn on November 22, 1963.

He joined Middlesbrough in 1981 and left in 1991 to join Celtic for a fee of £1million.

Mogga's status on Teesside was greater than any other. He was bold, brave, passionate, a natural leader and captain who led by example.

During his stint at his hometown club he very seldom missed a game.

Manager Bruce Rioch was his biggest fan and even went on record as saying if you were on a rocket going to the moon, the man you would want sitting next to you would be Tony Mowbray.

I met up with Captain Fantastic in a hotel in Sunderland while he was playing for Ipswich Town.

I asked Mogga if he would like to manage Middlesbrough one day. Find out what he says.

BERNIE

Mogga, you signed schoolboy forms for the Boro in 1978, was it always an ambition to wear the red shirt of your hometown club?

MOGGA

Definitely. I remember playing at the age of 11, playing for the Lakes estate primary school and there was a scout called Ray Grant, who I've spoke to recently on his 90th birthday believe it or not. I remember him coming to watch me at the age of 11, I scored a hat-trick. (Laughs)

I was a midfield player then. From then it hit home that you possibly could make the professional grade, when a professional club, my local team came to watch me. It always was a big ambition.

BERNIE

Before you became a player, you used to cheer the lads on from the Holgate End and John Hickton was your idol. Why John Hickton?

MOGGA

He was every young player's idol I think. He was the man who scored the goals, he was dashing, he was courageous and he smashed penalties in like you never saw anybody smash penalty kicks. John was just very direct and bustling through and smashing one in and there's that feeling of any young kid. You still have those memories of being in the Holgate when it was terracing and a goal goes in and everybody rolls to the front and you get taken back on this wave, a big wave of emotion. I've got some great memories.

BERNIE

You made your debut against the old enemy Newcastle in 1982. What do you remember about that game?

MOGGA

The game, I think obviously the build-up to it. It was a big, big game for the football club and I think Paul Ward made his debut on the same night, so whether we were struggling with injuries at the time I'm not sure.
But the night itself was a fantastic occasion. Keegan was playing for Newcastle, I played right side of a back three, centre back Mick Channon played that night also. He scored the goal, he was there on a month's loan. It was just a fantastic occasion. I think any night game adds to the atmosphere of football and it was a night game at St James's, 33,000 or something there.
We came away with a 1-1 draw, so you're left with the euphoria in the dressing room of getting a good result away at Newcastle and being my debut it was a great occasion.

BERNIE

When Bruce Rioch took over at Middlesbrough he made you captain. It must have been a great honour with being a local lad?

MOGGA

Yeah of course. Goodness me it was one of my biggest honours I suppose. You captaining Glasgow Celtic Bernie, could you imagine that?
It was a huge honour and at the time we were all young boys. I was probably one of the oldest in the team at 22 or 23-years-old and allied with the

success we had over the next few years, I think they all went together in a nice heap sort of thing.

I was captaining a very young team which was very successful and we achieved great things together. Maybe my role was over-defined possibly because I was just doing what came naturally.

BERNIE

And you were Captain Fantastic. (Laughs)

MOGGA

I was just doing what comes naturally to me on a pitch.

BERNIE

Bruce Rioch was quoted as saying if he went to the moon he would take you with him. What did he mean by that?

MOGGA

I think he meant that I would try and put across his ideas and discipline he instilled in the team through the week come match day.
I was like his right-hand man. I think I was trying to put across the things and make sure the plans that he had laid out throughout the week went according to plan on a Saturday and he would give me the licence to change things along the way.

BERNIE

You scored some fine goals. One against Aston Villa, one in an FA Cup tie against Everton and what about that one against Newport when you put your head in?

MOGGA

When it comes to one important goal Newport sticks in my memory, because it was my birthday and it was away.
It was an important game. Sometimes you think at that stage in the division, we were playing at the time Newport away, it's not a very nice place to go and play. Especially that day when it was hail stoning, it was freezing cold and the pitch was poor.
To win 1-0 at places like Newport was ultimately what got us out of that division and kept the progress of the club going, you remember it.

All goals are important to me.

BERNIE

Was bravery a big part of your game?

MOGGA

I like to think so - bravery or stupidity! I don't know, there's a fine dividing line. I've got a few scars and stitches around my eyes and on my forehead to say that if the ball is there and there to be won I feel one of my strengths in the game is attacking the ball.
I like to think in both penalty boxes if attacking the ball means putting your head in, that's fine. And bravery, it's not something you throw yourself at. If somebody's got that in you then that's fine.

BERNIE

You left Middlesbrough in 1991 and signed for Celtic for £1million. How difficult was it leaving? Who was the manager that let you go? (Laughs).

MOGGA

Lennie, your mate Lennie Lawrence, and the timing was right possibly. I had another picture at home of waving goodbye to the Boro fans at Barnsley away. But going to Celtic, you know what a football club that is. It's a massive, massive club. It was in turmoil at the time, there were boycotts and everything over sacking the board. It was a club that was looking to change and I had four fantastic years there. I liked the European nights, big European games. I remember being down 2-0 in the away leg to Cologne and winning 3-0 at Parkhead in front of a full house. An amazing, amazing night. And scoring against Rangers in my first Old Firm game at Parkhead on New Year's Day.

BERNIE

You've had problems on and off the park, it's been well documented. How did you cope with that?

MOGGA

I think you just get on with them. We are talking about the loss of my wife and her going through a cancer ordeal and I think while you're living it you live each day as it comes. Looking back in hindsight it was very, very hard and very hard to keep my career going. Trying to be there every moment I could for my wife, it was an ordeal. It was something that's built me and made me a better and more courageous and thoughtful person I think in life. Bernadette was a really, really, really special person and her family surrounding her were a special unit. A very close Roman Catholic family of 10 kids.

It was something, again, it's a part of my life that's never ever going to go away. I still go to Glasgow frequently and see the family up there and visit the grave but you get on with life Bern. You do what you can, you deal with it and you try and rebuild and I've rebuilt in my football.

Not long after I left to go to Ipswich Town, as you know, and I tried to rebuild my career and focus totally on football and what I wanted to do in the future.

BERNIE

You left Celtic and joined Ipswich. Was it the right time to move?

MOGGA

I'm not sure whether it was to be honest.

It was eight months after I had lost my wife. I don't know whether eight months is long enough to leave the close family which I left that were there supporting and always there for me.

I went a long, long way South to East Anglia and felt very, very alone and isolated for a long time. I think I possibly left too early.

I think maybe I should have spent another year in Glasgow either playing or just being in the environment, a loving environment.

Basically my first year in Ipswich was difficult because of being on my own. I picked up some injuries as well which was very frustrating, but I didn't really do myself justice on the football field.

I think now looking back because of my emotional state and possibly that's a major factor as to why I didn't really perform in my first year at Ipswich.

BERNIE

What are your ambitions for the future? Managing, coaching? People on Teesside say one day you'll manage the Boro. I certainly think you will.

MOGGA

My ambitions lay there. I think, like yourself, I've done coaching courses

and stuff recently. Whatever you think of them I've never been a great admirer of coaching badges and certificates and I've never put much stock in them. I see it possibly reading stuff that Howard Wilkinson writes.
I've felt if somewhere down the line there's going to be legislation that you possibly need, you need these badges to get the jobs in management.
Like in Italy, obviously pushing the issue with the David Platt story at the moment in Italy. So, I mean, that's why I've done coaching badges - to make sure if you need that ammunition it's there for you, But I see my future in coaching and managing and I've got my own ideas and you pick up things along the way.
To be honest, you pick up most of the stuff not to do I think, rather than stuff you would do, over the years.
The future in the next few years is hopefully going to be coaching and managing. And regarding ambition, whether it's five years or ten years down the line,
hopefully some day if I can be successful enough to prove them that I can do the job well enough I could come back to Middlesbrough.

HONOURS

ANTHONY MARK MOWBRAY

PLAYING CAREER HISTORY

1982-1991 Middlesbrough
1991-1995 Celtic
1995-2000 Ipswich Town

MANAGING CAREER HISTORY

2002-2004 Ipswich Town
2004-2006 Hibernian
2006-   West Brom

Bernie's About 2

121

Mowbray salutes the Holgate End

Bernie's About 2

'I was a bit upset when people started talking of selling players who were very valuable to me.'

On players leaving without his consent.

JOHN NEAL

Interview 10 John Neal

JOHN NEAL was born on April 3, 1932 in County Durham. After nine
Years at Wrexham he was persuaded to join
Middlesbrough in 1977.
When he arrived on Teesside as manager he decided to sell one or two of
the big name players and replace them with a couple of younger starlets.
During the interview he reveals how players started to leave without his
consent.
I travelled to his home in the Midlands to interview him. I found John to be
a gentleman, very softly spoken, and he relished talking about the past. A
lovely guy.

BERNIE

You moved to Middlesbrough as manager in 1977. What attracted you to
Teesside?

JOHN

First Division football was the main thing. Things had happened at
Wrexham which had upset me a little bit.
Middlesbrough came along and asked me if I would do the job and they
were in the top league. As a player your ambition was always to play in the
top league.
Now as a manager automatically your ambition then is to manage in the top
league and that gave me the opportunity.
I thought I'd had a crack at it as a player and that was great, I'll have a go as
a manager.

BERNIE

Who was it that approached you? Did you get a phone call or did someone
come to talk to you?

JOHN

I had an indirect phone call. Harold Shepherdson used to do a lot of that work didn't he? Old Harold God bless him, he died didn't he, God bless him. He contacted me and wanted to meet me and everything.
I said I would do and then decide. So I finished off the season at Wrexham, met them and I decided to have a crack at it.

BERNIE

Did you enjoy that side, the wheeling and dealing?

JOHN

I did yeah. I learned it at Wrexham paying the odd few bob, here it was bigger money. People like Souness went, well that was circumstances.
It was disruptive. You tried things, but you found out at the end of the day he'd be better out of the club and we did, we shifted him out finally for a record fee. Then later on David Mills, who had done a great job at Middlesbrough.
But I thought with people like Proctor, Craig Johnston, David Hodgson, young lads Bobby Murdoch had brought through from the youth team, I thought we could
introduce them. No good holding them back for another two or three years.
I believe in giving them a head start, getting them in early so they learn and we did this by getting rid of people like Souness, David Mills and that upset a few people. But at the end of the day it proved right.

BERNIE

Were the players you took on board better than the players you let go?

JOHN

I think in terms of value for money, I got a lot of money for them. So the club financially was secure and by bringing in the younger players like Mark Proctor, young Craggs and David it was tremendous, it evolved with the rest of them. Along with Craggsy, I kept good pros so we were developing into a very good side. I think we were two players short of being Championship contenders when I left. People didn't realise that because when I left they flogged David Armstrong and there was no better left-sided midfielder in the country. Not only did he do the left half's job, he did the outside left's job and was capable of going forward and getting goals. Craig Johnston got double figures, David Armstrong got double figures and I think Proc got nine.

I nearly sold Proc because he never got double figures (laughs) and that was from midfield. Up front we had Jankovic and the Irishman Terry Cochrane. Terry was a character, he was a personality. Things could happen and a lot of things did, so it was exciting, entertaining and we were developing on the right lines. At least I thought so until the board decided to go over my head and sell one or two, which I objected to.

You know, I sold quite a few but there was a reason behind them. But when they just started selling my players that I wanted to build into a Championship side, there was no way people like Craig should have gone. They sold the lot didn't they? Craig went to Liverpool, Proc went to Forest, Cloughie was after him. It was sad because it was hard work and we were very close. Teams didn't like coming to Ayresome Park, Spurs and people like that.

Chelsea we beat six or 7-1 and that was the potential. We weren't quite there but we were very close.

BERNIE

You left Middlesbrough in 1981. Was it down to the selling of the players?

JOHN

No, I think it was a parting of the ways, that the chairman and them didn't really see eye to eye on what was happening.

BERNIE

Who was the chairman?

JOHN

Charles Amer, and the directors. I wasn't happy and they weren't too happy about me. I think directors have got their place in football and their place is what they contribute to the club. I was a bit upset when people started talking of selling players who were very valuable to me.

You can refer back to when I sold David Mills and people like that. That was in my building process and that was an important part.

But once you've got your players you can't sell your best players when you're in the top division and expect to win things.

That's what I was in the game for, to achieve and get as high as possible and win things and if you're going to sell the best players you've got no chance, as it proved later. I left and they suddenly sold the kids. The future of the club rested on their shoulders and as you know they went down and down, very sad, but it was a parting of the ways. It was sad for me because we had worked hard. Jonny Coddington and people like that, there was a nice family atmosphere like I had in Wrexham. That's what I tried to create and it was nice until it was spoiled.

BERNIE

You had a reputation throughout your career of being a quiet man. How did you motivate players?

JOHN

You can't buy respect. People try. Nowadays they pay a lot of money and bring a player in, give him a lot of money. That isn't buying respect, you've got to gain respect by getting into players, taking an interest in them, be prepared to do a little bit extra for them. Look into their home life. If things aren't right, look after their finances. In the afternoon when everyone's gone home, bring a couple in and work with them, they appreciate that.
Hodgy (David Hodgson) loved that. I'd say: "Come back, I'll get a goalkeeper and we'll do a bit of shooting," and the players appreciated that. I think that's how it's done - a lot of work done in the background without the big mouth.

HONOURS

JOHN NEAL

PLAYING CAREER HISTORY

1949-1955 Hull City
1957-1958 Swindon Town
1959-1962 Aston Villa
1962-1965 Southend

MANAGERIAL CAREER HISTORY

1968-1977 Wrexham
1977-1981 Middlesbrough
1981-1985 Chelsea

PLAYING HONOURS (winners)

1960 Second Division Championship
1960 Inaugural League Cup
1974 Welsh Cup
1984 Second Division Cup

John Neal overlooks Terry Cochrane signing his contract.

**'I don't see any problems with buying players over the age of 30.
I think what you do need in the Premiership is experience.'**

Defending the age limit.

GARY PALLISTER

Interview 11 Gary Pallister

NOT a lot of people know this, but Pally was born in Ramsgate on June 20, 1965 and as a youngster was a Leeds fan.

He joined Middlesbrough in 1984.

No fee was involved, instead Billingham Town received a set of strips for his signature.

His debut was against Wimbledon.

He left Middlesbrough in 1998 and moved to Man United for £3 million.

I know more than most about Pally as I roomed with him for years before his move to Old Trafford.

I also socialised with him and taught him everything he knows outside of football!

Pally was originally rejected by Middlesbrough manager Malcolm Allison before Willie Maddren signed him up.

He was a perfect foil for Tony Mowbray.

Pally's qualities were that he was an elegant, stylish and composed player. He read the game well, was a good distributor, excellent in the air - all in all a great defender.

I travelled to the theatre of dreams (Old Trafford) to meet Pally in one of the boxes. I've always found him to be laid-back, funny and at times aloof. From the interview you realise how successful he was.

The second part of the interview was conducted after he had rejoined the Boro.

BERNIE

Obviously you've had a great career. Looking back, when Boro loaned you out to Darlington did you ever think that one day you would be playing with the biggest club in Britain?

PALLY

No. I mean, obviously when I went to Darlington Willie Maddren actually did tell me it was just for the benefit of the experience and getting toughened up against league opposition.

He told me not to worry about it, he wasn't getting rid of me.

BERNIE

It didn't toughen you up did it? (Laughs)

PALLY

I got a few kicks and I think I got a few bruises from that division. It was a great experience.
Cyril Knowles was the manager at the time and I met a few good lads there and enjoyed my time at Darlington.
Fortunately, when I came back Willie put me straight back into the team. I think it was against Southampton, in the Cup and we got a good whupping that night.

BERNIE

A lot of talk over the last year or two has linked you with a return to Boro. Is that just speculation?

PALLY

I've read a couple of headlines. I suppose with the club bringing in a couple of centre halves in the last couple of years, Henning Berg and Ronny Johnsen, and with Steve Bruce leaving, people thought my time was coming to a close at Old Trafford.
Plus, obviously, the tie there with Robbo being the manager at Middlesbrough and us being team-mates here.
I suppose it's a big rumour factory at the Cellnet so that's one of the questions I've been asked many times.
But at the moment I'm still enjoying my football here. It has been a fantastic move for me and with the European occasions we have got this minute I don't want to leave at the moment.

BERNIE

I've heard a rumour that you're United's most decorated player ever in terms of medals?

PALLY

Yes, I believe so. It's nice to have won so many things. It's nice to have earned the most I suppose, but there has been a lot of great players here and they have probably not won as many medals as they probably deserve.
It's a nice position to be in, I guess.

BERNIE

Go on then, tell us all the medals - go through them!

PALLY

(Laughs) Well, I haven't got a Full Members Trophy medal (Laughs) or an Auto Glass Trophy medal! (Laughs)
So far, four Championships, three FA Cups, a League Cup, a European Cup Winners' Cup, a European Super Cup and I believe four Charity Shields.

BERNIE

What do you think the secret is behind United's success?

PALLY

I think obviously the manager has to take a lot of the credit for it.
He came into the club and he turned it upside down, in the sort of respect Bruce Rioch tried to do at Middlesbrough.
He changed everything. It wasn't just what you saw on the football pitch, it was everything - the structure of the club, everything.
A manager changes things. As soon as he came in he saw it didn't match with what he wanted and he set about changing it.
He changed the youth system, he changed the scouting system.
He had his fingers in everything that had a pulse really.
It's just down to sheer hard graft. Eventually that put the club on the right track again, I think.

BERNIE

How did you and your old team mate Steve Bruce get the nicknames Dolly and Daisy?

PALLY

I don't know, you'll have to ask the manager that one! I don't know where they came from. I've been asked that a few times now and I still don't know where he digs that up from.
I think it was just a throwaway comment that he used in a press conference once and it seemed to have stuck.
So I don't know whether it's a cartoon character or what it is, or something from one of his bedtime stories as a youngster. You'll have to ask him.

BERNIE

At Boro you were by far the laziest player I have ever seen. Has anything changed?

PALLY

People have told me a million and one times that I look knackered on the football pitch and they say: "Why do you look so knackered?"
And I say: "That's because I am!"
It's simple and straightforward. It's hard work out there and that's the way I look.
But I still pride myself to match people's run and things like that.
The lazy thing is just a thing that's stuck with me over the years, I guess.

BERNIE

Yes, but I look back and we used to go on a long run and I would put my money on you that would come in last every time. Yet on the pitch you were quick.

PALLY

I think you were misjudging it. Me and Archie Stephens used to come in hand in hand didn't we? (Laughs)

BERNIE

Yeah, the difference was Archie was 45 and was smoking 60 a day and drinking two bottles of whisky!

BERNIE

You left Man United after nine glorious seasons to return to your hometown club. Did you have to give it a lot of thought?

PALLY

Not when I realised that United had agreed a bid for me.
That came as a bit of a shock in the first place, I think I didn't expect that.
But once they had done that I realised that I had seen players be hurt at United, left out of big games.

I always promised myself that that would never happen and once United had made that decision and as soon as I realised it was Middlesbrough, it was, I suppose, quite an easy decision for me.

BERNIE

People have questioned and criticised Bryan Robson for signing players over the age of 30 like Cooper, Gascoigne, Townsend and yourself. What do you think of that?

PALLY

Well, I think you have just got to look at the results. We were into last season and people were wondering if we were going to survive in the Premiership.
We did more than that and that was after the manager was criticised for buying players that were over the age of 30.

I think that it's irrelevant, you get a balance. I certainly don't see any problems with buying players over the age of 30 because I think what you do need in the Premiership is experience and we certainly had that in abundance.

BERNIE

Do you feel any added pressure second time around? Are the expectations greater?

PALLY

The expectations are certainly greater than they were when we were first playing at Middlesbrough. We were at a club that was struggling to survive at the time.
Now it's a club that's really looking to make great leaps and trying to build towards a really big future.
The chairman's got some tremendous ideas. He has backed it with his cheque book and the fact that we can go out and buy quality players like Gazza and Ziege, bring Juninho back, I think it's a great testimony to the club and the way it's performing now.

BERNIE

What do you think of Man United winning the treble while you're here at Boro?

PALLY

I think I cast a little bit of an envious eye over there. For certainly the last four or five years I was there, it was the Holy Grail for us to win the European Cup.
But I'd be lying if I said I wasn't a little bit envious. I'm delighted for the lads, they have been under so much pressure to emulate the team of '68 and win the European Cup.
That pressure was never going to go away until they had actually won it so I was delighted for the team and obviously delighted for the manager. It's what he desperately wanted.

BERNIE

Have you read Sir Alex Ferguson's book? I've not had the chance to, I'm not much of a reader. But reading between the lines, you're pretty boring according to Sir Alex!

PALLY

Well, I'll have to read it myself, you'll have to fill me in on that one.
(Laughs)

BERNIE

What was it like winning the Premier League title at the Riverside?

PALLY

I didn't know how the fans were going to react to it at the time because Manchester United weren't one of the most loved clubs in the country.
So to go there and win the Championship, I just really didn't know what to expect.
But in the end it surpassed all my expectations.
It was one of the best feelings I've ever had in football because as we went around with the trophy after the match and most of the Boro fans had stayed there and they were all chanting my name.

BERNIE

They didn't chant it when you were here first time around! (Laughs)

PALLY

It was nice to know that even though I had left under a bit of a cloud that the fans still appreciated what I had done in football.

HONOURS

GARY PALLISTER

PLAYING CAREER HISTORY

1984-1989 Middlesbrough
1985   Darlington (loan)
1989-1998 Manchester United
1998-2001 Middlesbrough

PLAYING HONOURS (winners)

Manchester
1990   FA Cup
1990   Community Shield
1991   UEFA Super Cup
1992-1993 Premier League
1992   League Cup
1993   Community Shield
1993-1994 Premier League
1994   FA Cup
1994   Community Shield
1995-1996 Premier League
1996   FA Cup
1996   Community Shield
1996-1997 Premier League
1997   Community Shield joint holder

22 FULL ENGLAND CAPS

Pallister clears the danger

'Ugolini brings new Dior look to football.'

Headline in national papers.

ROLANDO UGOLINI

Interview 12 Rolando Ugolini

ROLANDO UGOLINI was born in Lucca, Italy in June 1924 but moved to Scotland at an early age.

As a youngster he played for my boyhood heroes Celtic.

I met up with the former goalkeeper at Marton Country Club. I have to say, he turned up looking like a tailor's dummy!

He was very smartly dressed and his shoes were gleaming.

He was certainly a character, warm and very funny, probably the funniest guy I've interviewed over the years.

He oozed charm and charisma and I was under his spell for the duration of the interview.

Rolando reveals some of the tricks he used to get up to as a player and how one day it went wrong in a hotel.

During his time at Middlesbrough he clocked up 335 games between the sticks.

BERNIE

I noticed you had a chance to join Blackpool. Why did you turn them down?

ROLANDO

Well, Blackpool and Middlesbrough came in and I just decided Middlesbrough was the better deal.

BERNIE

You eventually moved south and joined the Boro for a fee of £7,000, in May 1948. Was it always your ambition to play in England?

ROLANDO

It was always an ambition to play in England. I always wanted to travel because I lived in little village called Armadale between Glasgow and Edinburgh. It's a little mining village, but my ambition was always to travel, so I thought going down to England was something I should try.

BERNIE

People over the years have described you as an eccentric dressing room character. Would you agree with that?

ROLANDO

Well, Micky Fenton was our coach, he was a great Middlesbrough forward and he was our coach at Ayresome.
He was always playing gags on us, running into the shower room with someone else's shirt on and everybody would start throwing water on him.
The time he got a brand new car, I think it was a Vauxhall, a beautiful red car, so everybody, we were at training and messing about and Lindy Delapenha and I said: "Right, we'll catch him."
So we went to Atkinson, who was the groundsman then, and he gave us a bucket of whitewash that you did the lines with and we painted his whole car all whitewash. So we never said anything, so we all got out quick and had to wait about 10 minutes while he put all the shirts away and everything.
That was part of his job and he came out and saw this car.
He nearly went berserk and of course what happened then is we painted Atkinson's car. He had a black car and we painted it all white.
The things we used to do were horrendous!

BERNIE

What about the one with the stocking over your head?

ROLANDO

Oh yeah, yeah, well that was a bit naughty really. I used to dress up and do things. I used to do Frankenstein, turning my jacket inside out and frightening people and it worked.
Anyway, this time we were staying in the Gresham Hotel and the manager was a Scotsman called McKenzie.
We knew him very well and I said: "I'll give your girl a fright at the reception."
So I had an old stocking and I pulled it over my head. I always used to carry my old trilby and I put the trilby on, wrapped my collar round and I said: "Oi, this is a stick up, I want the money."
And the poor girl fainted! She actually fainted! I was so cut up about that, I didn't mean it that way.
The boys used to egg me on and I'd do things like that.
I mean, one time we were at Bristol and there was a bus. Every time we went away to play they took us away on the Wednesday and on the Friday

night we went to a show, always before the game on a Saturday.

We were passing this bus stance and there was a bus, an empty bus behind a bus right in front and we were all passing.

And I said to the boys: "Watch this!"

So I went on and started shouting: "All change, onto the bus at the back please."

And everybody came running out of the bus and changed to the bus at the back and we were off our mark. (Laughs).

BERNIE

I'm glad I wasn't in the same team as you!

Do you find a difference between Scottish and English football?

ROLANDO

Without a doubt. Down here now it's the opposite to when I came down.

It was much quicker, more competitive, more people playing for places and it was quick and smart and sharp.

But in Scotland it was a wee bit sluggish then, but now it's the opposite up there. I feel they run about with their heads cut off every game. You can see it's bang, bang, bang, and down here there's more skill.

BERNIE

Were the strikers better in those days in England?

ROLANDO

Oh yes, without a doubt. Great strikers.

BERNIE

Is it true you were the first keeper to use the drop kick?

ROLANDO

I was, yeah. What happened was when I was playing for the reserves for Celtic, Jimmy Mallon brought the Daily Record in and said: "Look at that Rolando.

It says: 'Le Genard of Partick Thistle brings new kick to football, drop kicking a ball'."

He said: "You've been doing that for two bloody years." He said: "come on with me."

And we went up there and it was, I forget the reporter's name. We told him the next day and it came out that Ugolini actually was the first to use the drop kick.

It was effective because I used to get Johnny Spuhler here to come back into our circle and I would drop kick the ball over his head and the centre half's and he used to run past him and often got a goal that way.

And it went so quick, the ball.

BERNIE

Tell us about the time you pulled the strand of wool from your goalkeeper jersey.

ROLANDO

That was a real embarrassment. (Laughs). In those days they used to have the old fashioned polo neck.

It was uncomfortable at times and I said: "I'm going to take this off."

So I took it off and it was a wee bit ragged, but I sewed it up so it was just like crew cut neck.

We played at Tottenham and at the end of the game it was hanging down below my chest, just a big blob of wool and the headlines the following day were Ugolini brings new Dior look to football with goalkeeper's jersey and that's when they did start playing with those wind cheaters.

Remember the wind cheaters?

BERNIE

I don't remember.

ROLANDO

They went up to the neck with a V. We used to use them for golf as well.

BERNIE

You were Boro's first Italian signing, followed years later by Ravanelli and Festa.

How highly do you rate those two?

ROLANDO

Ravanelli for me is a worker, a good goalscorer and I like his enthusiasm for the game.

The only downside is at times he's a bit moody. If things aren't going well he doesn't want to know.

But otherwise I thought he was a good player. I've not seen enough of Festa.

BERNIE

What do you think of the foreign influx. Is it a good thing?

ROLANDO

I don't know. I think it's bad, certainly for Scotland.

I don't know about England, but England's got plenty of players that can play international now.

Who have Scotland got? There's no young boys coming through. Rangers and Celtic have got all these foreign players.

How are the young boys going to get a chance to become a Scottish international?

The other young boys that are any good want to go to Rangers and Celtic.

BERNIE

I must finish off with the tale about the carrots.

ROLANDO

(Laughs) Oh, the carrots. There were so many good memories.

David Jack was our boss and Harold Shepherdson says: "David Jack wants a word with you."

I go into his office and he says: "Rolando, I here you have been having tests for your eyesight?"

I said: "Who has told you that?"

He said: "Peter McKenna."

"Och, I said. David, he's having you on."

He said: "I'll tell you what I want you to do Rolando. I want you to eat some carrots in the morning and first thing at night when you go to sleep."

I said: "You're joking. Don't be silly David, they're having you on!"

And that was the kind of carry on we had.

I was 24 at the time and the whole thing was a joke.

BERNIE

Rolando, some great stories.

ROLANDO

Thanks Bernie.

HONOURS

ROLANDO UGOLINI

PLAYING CAREER HISTORY

1946-1948 Celtic
1948-1957 Middlesbrough
1957-1960 Wrexham
1960-1962 Dundee Utd
1962-1963 Berwick Rangers

Rolando shows a great example of meeting the ball at the highest point

Dressed to kill

Smile you're on camera

Rolando and team mates during training session.

Bernie's About 2
157

'I loved my time there, my problem was with an individual, which was sad.'

Viduka on why he left Middlesbrough.

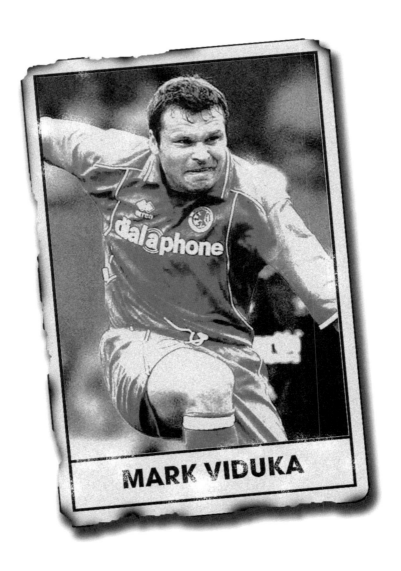

MARK VIDUKA

Interview 13 Mark Viduka

MARK VIDUKA

Mark Anthony Viduka was born in Melbourne, Australia on October 9, 1975.

He arrived on Teesside from Leeds for a fee of £3 million before departing for Newcastle in the summer of 2007.

His qualities are an immaculate first touch, he is great at holding the ball up, has good body strength, scores and creates goals and brings team-mates into play - a very talented and skilful player all round.

I travelled to the Newcastle training ground in Benton to interview Viduka. It was February and the snow was four inches deep, with blizzard conditions.

As I jumped out of the car, I headed for the main reception only to be told by several Newcastle employees that the interview was taking place elsewhere.

I was directed back out into the Arctic conditions, went right and right again only to find myself at the back of the building.

There was a massive glass window and the first person I clapped eyes on was caretaker manager Chris Hughton, who I knew from my Ireland days. He looked in disbelief and shouted: "Come around the front to the reception."

It was then I knew I had been stitched up - Geordie bastards!

I did the interview with the Duke in a small room. I found him warm, straight and funny.

On the way out I had a word with Chris Hughton, who said: "You did well getting Viduka, he's a complex character."

BERNIE
You were born in Melbourne, Australia, but are also of Croatian and Ukrainian descent?

MARK

To be honest my parents were both from Croatia but they emigrated to Australia in the 60s, in 1964. My dad's from an area in Croatia which is called Dalmatia. It's on the coastline. And my mums from Bosnia, but she lived in a place called Slovenia, but her background is Ukrainian. So it's quite complicated. She's from the ex-Yugoslavia but her generations were Ukrainian, you know what I mean? But my dad was Croatian.

BERNIE

Could you have played international football for the Ukraine or Croatia?

MARK

Probably not the Ukraine because that's sort of like, down the lines. For example, my mothers grandparents moved from Ukraine to the ex-Yugoslavia.
Her and her mother were born in Croatia or Yugoslavia. At the time I could have played for Croatia though.

BERNIE
You started your career with Melbourne Knights in 1993. What kind of standard was that?

MARK

Well it was semi-professional at the time. I was professional - most of the players were semi. Most of them had jobs and they'd do that on the side. The standard wasn't too bad to be honest.
We had quite a good league at the time, very competitive. Some very good players came out of that league.

BERNIE

A couple of years later you moved to Croatia Zagreb, now called Dinamo Zagreb. How did you enjoy your time there?

MARK

It was mixed. It was good and it was different. It was a big difference for me having lived in Australia, which is a democracy.
At the time I moved it was war time there, so everything was chaos at the time. Half the country was occupied and stuff like that.
They won the territory back, there was a lot of political problems but I enjoyed the time there.
I liked learning about my background a little bit more. I mean, I won four

league titles, I won three cups and played in the Champions League, I played in the UEFA Cup.
So it was a great stepping stone for me, a great, great experience.

BERNIE

Looking back, is it true that Melbourne Knights named one of the stands The Mark Viduka Stand?

MARK

It is, yeah (Laughs). To be honest I was overseas, I don't know why.

BERNIE

Were you that good?

MARK

(Laughs). Well for two years in a row, I was named Australia's player of the year. I was top goal scorer, player of the year and Under-21 player of the year.
I won everything that you could win in Australia and we won the league for the first time as well in the history of the club. I think I wasn't bad.

BERNIE

In 1998 you left Zagreb and joined my boyhood heroes Glasgow Celtic for £3.5 million. A month after signing Celtic announced you had quit the club. What was that all about?

MARK

What happened was Bernie, it was towards the last three or four months of my time in Croatia. I had a bad time, I had a very difficult time with the fans, with the club and the press, I had big problems with that.
When I came to Glasgow it was in the winter transfer window, it was 98 going on to 99 and I came then and I went to Joe Venglos at the time and I said to him: "I need a bit of a break, I've had a hard time there."
I just wanted to have a bit of a break and then come back and start again. That was basically it.

BERNIE

As clean cut as that?

MARK

Once the press got wind of it, it wasn't clean cut.

BERNIE

In your first full season in Glasgow you were voted Scottish player of the year and scored 27 goals. You must have been delighted?

MARK

Well yeah, I was very happy. After the difficult start I had there was a lot of negative press about me.
There was a lot of rumours made up which were all untrue really. I can't remember all of them but 99.9 per cent were untrue.
There were stories of me going to a mental hospital, there was everything, and I was really determined to prove everybody wrong.

BERNIE

You were on the receiving end of a bit of stick from the Celtic supporters after you claimed to be only playing at about 75 per cent of your capability. Why did you say that?

MARK

I didn't say that. No, see what happened, I went to Leeds then I think an article came out in the Scottish newspapers saying that I had said that I played at 75 per cent in games, which I never have. Whoever got that article or whatever I would love them to show it to me because I never said that to anybody.
You can't if you're playing 75 per cent, it doesn't matter what league you're playing or whatever, you can't be voted player of the year if you're playing at 75 per cent and be a top goal scorer.

BERNIE

Ex-Arsenal player Ian Wright claimed that during half time in Celtic's
Scottish cup defeat against Inverness Caledonian, that an unnamed striker
refused to go back out for the second half. Was that you? If so, why?

MARK

You've got all that stuff off Wilkapedia! (Laughs)

BERNIE

Yes, I saw it on Wilkapedia. Was it you? Because he didn't name you, did
he?

MARK

I don't know which striker he's talking about because there was a bit of a
ruckus going off in the dressing room at the time.
So there were a few players that were a little bit upset at the time
because we were losing at half-time to Inverness in the Scottish FA Cup and
nobody was in a good mood, put it that way. Nobody likes to be losing.

BERNIE

So there were a number of candidates, not just you? He could have been
talking about a number of centre forwards?

MARK

I was the only one who didn't come out but yeah, it was me yeah.

BERNIE

You left Celtic and joined Leeds for a fee of £6million. How did you enjoy
your time at Elland Road?

MARK

It was excellent, really good at Leeds. We had a great environment, great
atmosphere, we got to the semi-final of the Champions League and I think
we finished fourth or fifth in the league at the time.
It was just a great atmosphere, good times and really positive. We had good
players and I loved it, I really loved it.

BERNIE

In your first season you scored 22 goals, including four against Liverpool in a memorable 4-3 victory. That must have been a highlight?

MARK

Yes, definitely. I mean, that game is a game where everything went right. Basically I remember saying in an interview after the game that I didn't play exceptionally well but I got four chances and I put them away.
I've played in games where I've played unbelievably, took on players and set up chances and did all these great moves and whatever but I never got on the goal scoring sheets.
But in this game it was one where, you know, four times the ball came to me in positions and I finished them.

BERNIE

As a striker what would you rather do - have a great game or score goals?

MARK

See I'm a little bit different, I'm a little bit picky probably, a little bit of a perfectionist.
A lot of times people say just shoot, just score, but I like a little bit of finesse - that's what fuels me.
I remember one of the best games I ever played for Leeds was when we played in the Champions League against Lazio away and Alan Smith scored and we won 1-0.
I set him up with a back heel and it was a beautiful move. It was one of the best games I've ever played in.
So if somebody said to me four goals against Liverpool and that game, I think they are on a par.

BERNIE

Unusual for a striker - I just wanted to score. (Duke laughs)
After a couple of years with Leeds the club hit off-the-field financial troubles and started selling their key players.
Could you believe that after Champions League football the club was struggling?

MARK

It was devastating for everybody who was involved in the club.
We were in administration for a while, you're in the club and you know
what it's like, you get used to the kit people, you're friends with the people
in the kitchen, you're friends with everybody, the cleaners.
And you get to know everybody and everybody was just unsure of their
jobs, nobody knew what was going on.
Whether the club would be bought, whether the club wouldn't be bought.
It was just a big shame really, it was very difficult to take as a player
and also as a person who was working at the club at the time.

BERNIE

You joined the Leeds exodus and signed for Middlesbrough - why
Middlesbrough?

MARK

What are you laughing at?

BERNIE

I have to ask the question

MARK

Well at the time they were very interested in signing me and it was a good
option for me because I had lived in that same place for four or five years
at the time.

BERNIE

Where was that, Harrogate?

MARK

In Linton, which is Wetherby. They made a good offer for me, they
approached me and it looked like they really wanted me.
Steve McClaren at the time was a good manager and I was on my holidays
and Keith Lamb came out to see me.
It was really nice, it was a good move for me, you know?

BERNIE

Your debut season at the Riverside was impressive but disrupted by injuries. Was that frustrating?

MARK

Yes, I mean it's always frustrating. The first season was my worst season at Middlesbrough. If I look back nobody likes to be injured, everyone likes to be playing.

BERNIE

On the subject of injuries, the critics would say you're injury prone. Do you agree or disagree with that?

MARK

I disagree.

BERNIE

Why would you disagree?

MARK

I disagree because for 10 years I hardly ever had any injuries.
I played for Melbourne Knights, Dinamo Zagreb, I played for Leeds almost every game, I played for Celtic almost every game as well.
Once I got to Middlesbrough a little bit less, but for many years, I mean you get players who get injured at 19 or 20-years-old and it takes them two or three years to get over it. For example look at Jonathan Woodgate - he's had a very hard time with injuries.
But for a good 10 years before I even came to this country as well I was playing every game.

BERNIE.

I mean, it's a bit of a myth because until I looked it up, I was astonished at the amount of games you've played and the goals you've scored as well is second to none.
But there is a myth that goes about that Mark Viduka is always injured.

MARK

Yes, because as you get older you get more prone to injury don't you? And after playing that many games and training sessions and whatever it takes its toll after a little while.
But because it's now they want you to be playing and that's the case usually.
In football people have short memories, you know?

BERNIE

In the 2005/6 season you were in sensational form in all competitions for Middlesbrough. What happened in the UEFA Cup final against Seville?

MARK

The UEFA Cup final was a big, big disappointment. It's all well and good saying we got to the final.
Yeah, we did get to the final in a very unbelievable way. That lead up to that final will remain something, that's the best memories of my football career.
It was ridiculous the way we got into that final. That final for three weeks after I was a wreck, because I wanted to win - everybody wanted to win.
I remember after that final I had to go and play in the Confederations Cup and I just remember I was devastated for three weeks after.
But I had to pick myself up because first of all I was disappointed in myself.
I had a good chance to score a goal and the goalkeeper saved it.
Also, obviously, there was a penalty decision that should have been given and things didn't go the way we would have liked and we didn't play particularly well.

BERNIE

Leading up to that final you were rested along with two other players. Was that your decision?

MARK

No, no. The reason I was left out was because I had played against West

Ham and either had got a knock or a calf strain. That was the reason why I wasn't playing, because I was rested.

BERNIE

Throughout your career you've worn the number nine jersey. Are you superstitious?

MARK

Not really. At the minute I'm 36. I had 36 at Celtic - I was either 9, 10 or 36.
I don't know why when I got to Celtic that was halfway through the season. That was the number that was free - 36.
So I had no option. Six and three adds up to nine. I don't know. (Laughs)

BERNIE

Have you any superstitions?

MARK

Not really, no. I'm not superstitious at all.

BERNIE

You played alongside Gareth Southgate. Did he portray leadership qualities in terms of becoming a manager?

MARK

Yes, I think for Gareth, for me it was a natural progression for him to go into management. He's that type of person I think. First of all he's very well respected in footballers' eyes, everybody liked him.
He has got those people skills, he's a genuine type of person, he's not going to go behind your back trying to do things.

BERNIE

A lot of them do.

MARK

Some of them do. He did have the qualities, yes.

BERNIE

In your third and final season for Middlesbrough you scored 19 goals and Gareth expressed his interest in keeping you. Why did you leave?

(MARK laughs)

BERNIE

Come on, why did you go?

MARK

Well because, the reason why I left was it was Christmas time, I had six months to go on my contract which is four months of the season.
No-one had come to me with an offer. They said: "When we get safe from relegation, we'll make you an offer."
In the mean time we kept playing, I was playing very well, I was scoring a lot of goals towards the end of the season, doing really well, and still nobody had come to me.
The first offer I received from them was when I was on holiday, so no-one had said anything to me.
Other clubs started to show an interest, there were seven or eight clubs who were already showing that they wanted me to go to their teams and I'd got no response at all from Middlesbrough.
It was like, not even an offer. Listen, they made me an offer - I don't even recall how much it was.
It was the same money that I was on and I was a free agent at the end of the season. The other clubs were showing a lot of interest in me.
I was on my holidays and they sent me an offer by mail here to England.
When I came back I didn't even know that they had made me a better offer, they sent it by mail in my post.
When I came back to England I had already signed for Newcastle.
I opened up my mail box and there's an offer from Middlesbrough.
So it's just the way that they treated that whole matter.
It was like, you're our player, you have to sign for us, you understand?

BERNIE

Yes

MARK

As I had other clubs, other managers who were desperate to ring, I know
Gareth wanted me to stay but it was the people who were in charge, whoever
it was didn't make any effort at all to sign me and I was a free agent, you
understand?
I liked Middlesbrough, I loved being there, it was ideal for me. I had been
there for three years, I enjoyed the fans, I had a great relationship with
the fans, I had my house that I have lived in for seven years.
I was in the same house, my kids were starting school, it was ideal for me.

BERNIE

On the last day of the season against Fulham I walked past you and the
chief executive Keith Lamb on the stairway. Was Keith trying to drag you
into a room to sign?

MARK

Sort of, yes.It doesn't have to be money, do you understand?
If you feel that they appreciate you, it's the same as every job. You know,
you've been a footballer.
If they say to you: "Don't worry Duke, we'll look after you, you've done a
good job for us, we'll look after you."
But nobody contacted me or my agent or whatever for months.
The end of the season was coming and they knew that I was free.
Then they expected me to sign it, almost as if they don't want you to sign
but they do. You don't even know.
So I had to make a decision whether or not I'm going to.
I couldn't make a decision at Christmas time when legally I could have
signed for somebody, which I didn't because I was waiting for them coming
with a decent offer.
The first offer they made me was the same money I was on and I was a free
agent. It doesn't make sense.

BERNIE

What was Steve McClaren like?

MARK

Steve McClaren, I think tactically he was good. On the field, coaching and
organising the team and stuff like that.
I think his man management skills were his weakest point. That was his

first managerial job and it takes time.

I look at Gareth and I think: "F**k, that's a hard job."

Playing with a team and then becoming manager - very, very difficult.

I personally don't think I could have done that, which is a big, big thing for him because you've played as mates, you've done things together and all of a sudden you're the boss. Very difficult.

BERNIE

McClaren got the England job, where you surprised?

MARK

Was I surprised? Well, we did really well in the UEFA Cup and they were desperate for a new manager, people were calling out for an English manager. I wasn't really surprised, no. I remember Steve Harrison was make jokes all the time about that after the UEFA Cup Final.

Bernie's About 2

BERNIE

I thought the timing was awful. Did McClaren have to announce the England
job before the UEFA Cup final?

MARK

Awful, no. It's awful when you get beaten 4-0, you look for excuses. But if
we would have won nobody would have said anything.

BERNIE

That's true. (Laughs)

MARK

Someone would have said: "He was going to England anyway, he didn't
give a shit."

BERNIE
Yes, you can't win either way.

BERNIE

When you left the Riverside one or two people criticised you, saying you
never played enough games or scored enough goals. What would you say to
that? You must have read the articles criticising you?

MARK
No I didn't. I think I was disappointed. Well if it's Keith Lamb who said it
he knows why because I told him straight to his face with me and the
chairman as well.
You can tell the chairman I was very disappointed, very disappointed. I
thought he was a gentleman. I thought he was a respectful person and he
rang me when I was in Australia.

BERNIE

I've heard that.

MARK

He rang me when I was in Australia. I was in a car park.

BERNIE

Were you eating an ice cream?

MARK

I was in the car park.

BERNIE

You weren't dogging were you?

MARK
I wasn't dogging (Laughs).
I was in the car park.
I remember that conversation and I told him the exact reason why I'm not
going to re-sign, because at the last minute they made me a ridiculous
offer. They wanted to make me the highest paid player in the club's history
and whatever.
I told him that the reason why I'm not going to sign, and it was because of
the fact of, the way I was treated.
They weren't f*****g getting a whip out but its those things. Football is a
different business from any other business it's not the same as running a
factory.
Footballers are specific people I think and that's probably how they get to
that level.
If it was that easy every man and his dog would be a footballer.
So to get to that level you have to have something in you. But most players
just want, as I have said earlier its not always about the money.
He offered me to be the highest paid player in Middlesbrough's history but
I told him it's not about the money it's the way you feel wanted to stay.

BERNIE

Is it not the manager's job to deal with contractual stuff?
In that situation I would be going and fighting on your behalf if I was a
manager.

MARK

Gareth probably was and I know he wanted to keep me.
He definitely wanted to keep me. Whether he did or didn't I still respect
Gareth as a person and as a manager as well.

BERNIE

Did you enjoy your time at the Riverside?

MARK

I did, I loved it. I'll remember some fantastic games, especially in Europe
and that's how I will remember Middlesbrough.
I loved the time there. My problem was with an individual which was sad. I
made good friends at the club, as I said.
The kit lady Elaine and all the people who worked at the club, they were
very nice people. I enjoyed coming to work there.

BERNIE

Did you ever see Bill Beswick?

MARK

I spoke to Bill a few times, that's when Steve McClaren was there, but not
too often.
I went in now and again and he did everybody, he took the whole team for a
session.

BERNIE

You joined North-east rivals Newcastle on a free transfer. How did that
move come about?

MARK

They were desperate for me to come. I had a choice of four clubs and Big
Sam (Allardyce) was desperate for me to come and I thought he'd bring a bit
of stability to the club long-term.
He'd done a great job at Bolton and like everybody thought he'd be there
long-term and that was that.

BERNIE

Could you believe it when he left? You were his first signing.

MARK

I didn't think it would be that quick. I thought it was a long term kind of thing but as soon as he signed a new owner came in as well who had their own thoughts on the team and ideas. It was a funny sort of a situation.

BERNIE

You scored your first Newcastle goal against Middlesbrough. How sweet was that?

MARK

Well it was sweet when it hit the back of the net.

BERNIE

What did you think of when you hit the net? Who did you think of?

MARK

No, no. Listen, I don't hold any grudges, I've got nothing against Keith Lamb either.
There's no doubting he was the biggest reason why I left but I've nothing against him.
I like Steve Gibson, I think he's done really well for the club. I think he's done a good job keeping them in the Premier league and it's not an easy job keeping a club like Middlesbrough in the top flight.
It hasn't got the revenue of a Newcastle or a Chelsea. It's not an easy job and I understand they have to do that and I respect them, it's just that I was a little bit disappointed with Steve Gibson.
Because I had the vision of somebody who wouldn't do that, I've had those sort of instances in the past where managers are under pressure, then they go and blame it on a player to deflect it from themselves.
I didn't expect Steve Gibson to do something like that.
I know it was a difficult situation for him because he lost one of his best strikers to the rivals and maybe he had to make the club look good and himself look good with the way he came out with that. But it was still disappointing.

Bernie's About 2
177

BERNIE

Could you believe both you and Yakubu left?

MARK

Yes, I could because of the reasons I just told you.
Well, let's look. Why did Woody go? Why does Stewie Downing want to go?
Stewie's a great player, one of the best players I've played with definitely as a striker.
He set up many goals for me and for other players. He is a very good player and he loves that club, he was born there, he lives there. But... (Shrugs his shoulders)

BERNIE

Keegan comes across as charismatic, was he?

MARK

He was charismatic, he was good. I liked Kevin because he loves pure football and I love pure football. We got on really well to be honest. I liked him, I really did.

BERNIE

Keegan changed the formation to 4-3-3, with you, Michael Owen and Martins up front. Which formation do you prefer?

MARK

Oh, I loved it. That was my best period for sure. I really liked that, you know? I wasn't sure whether or not it would have worked at first with the three of us but we were unbelievable.
We played some really good games and we felt confident as a group going into those games.

BERNIE

What about lone striker - do you like that role?

MARK

I don't like that, I prefer to play with somebody. When you play up front
it's much easier for the defenders to defend against you because they can
put one on you and let one drop off a little bit.
If you have somebody else like a Yakubu or whatever, two up front, at least
you're taking one player away from you and if you get the ball and turn
around you can see somebody else.
Whereas when I was younger I was a little better, quicker. (Laughs).
But as you get older your pace disappears and you need someone to play off
I think anyway.

BERNIE

Keegan walked out and Joe Kinnear filled in. What has your relationship
with Joe been like?

MARK

Yeah, good. He seems like a decent bloke, I've had no problems with him at
all.
He keeps himself to himself, he's a quiet type of a person.

BERNIE

Reading the reports, he's far from quiet! (Laughs)

MARK

Oh, to you guys he's different (laughs) but to the players he's a decent
guy.

BERNIE

Obviously Joe has a heart problem at the minute.

MARK

I wish... Listen, these things are more important than any football game,
people's health and I wish him and his family all the best.

BERNIE

Off the field the club has been put up for sale by Mike Ashley, the owner.
Do off-the-field things affect the players?

MARK

Well, you like to say that it shouldn't but it does. Like it or not, it
does.
I mean, it's just the stability and the instability of the whole thing.
Every day you read something else and nobody knows whether...
You look at the Man Uniteds, the Arsenals and the Chelseas, you've got Sir
Alex Ferguson, sir Alex has been there for 100 years. (Laughs)
And that is the reason why they are so successful. That is the reason they
are always stable.
If you look at how many managers this club has had in the last I don't know
how many years, it can't be a good thing.

BERNIE

Looking back at Middlesbrough, they are second bottom of the Premier
League as we speak. Can they escape relegation with 13 games left?

MARK

Can they do it? Of course. I think to be honest I'm surprised at the
situation how it is now because the way that they started off the season
was very good.
I mean, 13 games ago they were flying. They were doing very well, playing
some good football.
They have brought in some good players as well.

BERNIE

In my opinion we let yourself Yakubu, Cattermole and Young go and
brought
in inferior players.

MARK

You brought in Tuncay.

BERNIE

I would pay to watch him - a good finisher.

MARK

But up front Alves, he's alright. Wheats has stepped up and done well.

BERNIE

But you still think we'll get out of it?

MARK

I hope so.

BERNIE

Would you put your money on it?

MARK

I don't gamble mate. (Laughs)

BERNIE

You've gained 43 full caps for Australia. Was captaining your country in the 2006 World Cup the highlight?

MARK

It was unbelievable. You know, it was the second World Cup we played in and it was just something special, unforgettable to be honest.
I was watching pictures last night of my family which we took in the World Cup.
My kids, all my family came from Australia and stayed in Germany.
The way that the tournament was organised was unbelievable.
The Germans did such a good job over there, we had such a great time and played some big teams.
We played Croatia obviously, who are close to me and we got through to the next round.
It was very disappointing, again the same thing as the UEFA Cup final.
It took me three weeks to recover. I didn't want to watch the rest of the World Cup after we got kicked out in that manner.

If you remember the game, Italy got a penalty in the last second of the game against us.
Do you remember that? It was definitely not a penalty and very disappointing.
After that, just the whole experience was unbelievable.

BERNIE

Your career highlights are what?

MARK

The high point would have to be the World Cup and also there have been plenty.

BERNIE

More highs than lows?

MARK

Oh, there has been a lot of lows mate.

BERNIE

Give us some of them.

MARK

Lows would be getting booed off personally in front of 40,000 of my own fans in Croatia.
Scoring a goal away from home getting abused by the fans in Croatia, very low points.
The low point was when I went to Celtic. At first when I went back home it was a very difficult time for me to get through.
The high points, I'll tell you something.
We got a bottle of scotch. I won Scottish player of the year and top scorer and I went home and got a bottle of scotch, nice Scottish whisky.
And I just sat there on the couch, a rented couch (laughs) and started drinking it.
I was so happy at that moment, very happy, and then somebody goes and writes I only gave 75 per cent of my capabilities.
Oh, a big high point as well was winning the title with Melbourne Knights.

That was the biggest thing.

BERNIE

As it stands today, you have played in 489 games and scored 237 goals. More to come?

MARK

I hope so mate.

BERNIE

There was recently talk that you could retire. Is that true?

MARK

I don't know, I don't like being injured. I love playing and for me I would rather somebody pulled out my tooth without an anaesthetic than go on a f*****g tread mill every day or in a weights room or something like that.
I love the ball, I love playing and if I can't do that properly... This year has been a big testing year for me because I haven't been able to do what I love doing.
You know yourself, players who love physically playing that love running all day, they're players that love to play.
If they loved strength work they'd be in the gym all day.
I just love the ball, that's all. It's a good habit.
I'm not physical, I'm not one who loves running obviously! (Laughs)

BERNIE

I've noticed.

MARK

I don't mind a bit of gym work, I love doing something. I love setting up players, I love scoring goals, I love anything to do with the ball and when that's taken away from me it's no fun.
So this year has been a really testing year for me. I'll have to see.

BERNIE

How long is your contract?

MARK

I'm finished at the end of this season.

BERNIE

How old are you now?

MARK

33

BERNIE

A couple of years if you want it left?

MARK

Maybe, I don't want to be playing if I'm in the physio room.

BERNIE

And when you retire in years to come will you retire in England or Australia?

MARK

Probably Australia.

BERNIE

Have you been able to get a bond with the Newcastle fans?

MARK

Well listen, I think that while I've played I've probably done quite well. Last year I went through a patch when I did quite well and I combined well. Obviously it's frustrating for the fans and frustrating for me, especially

now we have a lot of injuries.
They want to see you playing and I want to see me playing as well.
To be honest, they've been very supportive of me.
There's 50,000 people at a game and not everyone's going to have the same opinion.
They are entitled to love me or hate me but in general they have been very good.

BERNIE

Duke, thanks very much.

MARK
No problem, Bernie.

HONOURS

MARK VIDUKA

PLAYING CAREER HISTORY

1993-1995 Melbourne Knights
1995-1998 Dinamo Zagreb
1998-2000 Celtic
2000-2004 Leeds Utd
2004-2007 Middlesbrough
2007-present Newcastle

PLAYING HONOURS (winners)

Melbourne Knights
1994-95 NSL title

Zagreb
1995 League
1995 Cup
1996 League
1996 Cup
1997 League
1997 Cup

43 FULL CAPS FOR AUSTRALIA

Bernie's About 2
187

'I just want to play centre half and that's it, Train there every day and play there every game.'

Wheater makes it clear where he wants to play.

DAVID WHEATER

Interview 14 David Wheater

DAVID JAMES WHEATER was born in Redcar on February 14, 1987. He joined Middlesbrough as a scrawny teenager and developed his skills progressing through the youth team and reserves, finally gaining his first team debut with a run-out from the bench against Sporting Lisbon in the UEFA Cup.

Wheats at one time thought his days were numbered at Middlesbrough, when he was sent out on loan.

I met up with Wheats at Crathorne Hall, on the outskirts of Yarm.

The only way to describe Wheats is on the pitch he's a man, off the pitch he's a boy.

To his credit, he's a very down-to-earth, fairly placid lad, cool and relaxed.

Yet on the field he's a totally different animal.

As a player he reads the game well, is good in the air, composed on the ground and has an eye for goal.

His qualities haven't gone unnoticed at international level.

BERNIE

You were born in Redcar, were you always a Middlesbrough fan?

WHEATER

Well, when I was really young it was Man United, because they were winning trophies.

Once I realised what football was all about, I went to a few games at Ayresome Park then I got a season ticket at the Riverside for the first season, then I realised I was a Boro fan.

BERNIE

Was it always an ambition to be a footballer?

WHEATER

Yes, definitely. From that first season just seeing Juninho, I realised that's what I wanted to do.

When I saw him the fans were going crazy for him.

BERNIE

Who were your favourites as a youngster?

WHEATER

It was Eric Cantona. I've always admired him, he was fantastic. And since I've become a centre half, Rio Ferdinand has been the best player I've seen.

BERNIE

You are a product of the academy and you played in the FA Youth Cup winning side. You played all eight games and scored three goals. Was that a highlight?

WHEATER

Oh, it was fantastic, the best night of my life so far because it's all your mates really.
All my family were there, all my mates as well, it was just fantastic.
My first proper trophy as well. Once you win a trophy you just want to go on winning them all the time.

BERNIE

You came through the academy. Who nudged you along?

WHEATER

My mam and dad, they have been fantastic all the way through.
My granddad's been there at every game I've ever played.
In the academy, Dave Parnaby and Peter Hood the sports scientist have been unbelievable for me, both of them.
I used to be a bit of a daft lad when I was in the academy but those two guys stuck with me.
They could have quite easily let me go but I've matured and it's all come to this and I have to thank them really.

BERNIE

You made your first team debut as a substitute away at Sporting Lisbon in the UEFA Cup tie in March 2005. How big an honour was that?

WHEATER

There was about two minutes left, Steve Round shouted me as I was warming up and within 10 seconds I was standing next to him. Once I got on I couldn't believe it really.

BERNIE

You went on to make a number of impressive displays in the latter stages of the 2005/6 season as Steve McClaren rested some of his experienced players. Did you enjoy that experience?

WHEATER

Yes, I loved it. I was quite skinny at the time and I thought the opposition would batter me all over but they didn't and I did enjoy it. That's how you need to improve yourself, playing against top players in the Premiership.

BERNIE

The same year you went on loan to Doncaster Rovers followed by Wolves and then to Darlington. Did you think your Boro days were numbered?

WHEATER

When I was at Wolves I wasn't even playing. It was Gary Breen and Jody Craddock who were the centre halves.
I hated it so much that I wanted to quit football.
It was about 3.10pm, the game had kicked off and I was on my way back to the car because I wasn't involved, wasn't even on the bench.
I was just thinking what else I could do in life but I just stuck with it and Dave Penney took me on loan twice.
He was manager at Doncaster and Darlington and whenever I've been with him I've loved it.

BERNIE

Do you think that matured you?

WHEATER

Darlington definitely, because it was a grind with three games in a week in
a first-team situation and I loved it. And of course they are a local team.

BERNIE

The following season you were well down the pecking order at Boro. Huth
arrived for £7 million, with Woodgate and Pogatetz also ahead of you.
Injuries occurred and you got an unexpected opportunity. Could you believe
it?

WHEATER

Yes, it was before the very first friendly. When we were in Austria all
the centre halves got injured and I knew I was going to get a chance. But I
thought as soon as they declare themselves fit they would be back in.
But the manager stuck with me and I have to thank him for that because it
takes balls really when there's Riggott, Pogatetz and Woodgate coming
back, but he stuck with me.

BERNIE
Your form was so good that Gareth cashed in on Jonathan Woodgate and
sold him to Spurs. Were you confident you could hold onto the number one
spot?

WHEATER

Yes I was, because my confidence was sky-high because I was doing so
well.
I felt like a proper first team regular. I knew I wasn't at that point and
only had a few games really. But to let Woodgate go gave me a massive
confidence boost.

BERNIE

Away from football you were used to front an iconic video campaign to help
sell season tickets. How did you get involved in that?

WHEATER

I don't know, I think it was PR man Dave Allan who asked me to do it. I
thought it was just going to be done on a small scale but then he told me
it was getting sent out to season ticket holders. It has gone on You Tube as

well, I couldn't believe it.

BERNIE

Where did you do it?

WHEATER

It was done at the Riverside, just behind the reception. There was a room full of make-up and it was like a proper studio.

BERNIE

Were your nerves going?

WHEATER

Yes, a little bit. It was worse than playing in front of thousands of people! I don't like small, confined spaces.

BERNIE

Any ambition to go to Hollywood like Brad Pitt or Vinnie Jones?

WHEATER

I wouldn't mind! There's a few nice birds in Hollywood. (Laughs)

BERNIE

You signed a new three-and-a-half year contract in February 2008. Surely you deserved it?

WHEATER

I felt like I did. The club offered me a five-year deal but I wanted to sign a three-and-a-half year just to keep me on my toes and make sure that I can get a new one.
Not just sit there getting the money, I want to better myself all the time.
I think my dad wanted that for me as well. I was playing well and the manager stuck by me so it was nice to sign that.

BERNIE

Have you got an agent?

WHEATER

Yes, he's one of the good ones.

BERNIE

Do you think that's important in the modern game?

WHEATER

You don't really have to have one if you know that kind of thing yourself.
I would have signed a five-year, not on very good money just because I
didn't really have a clue. But my agent has been excellent to me over the
years and he has sorted me out very well.

BERNIE

Apart from your contract, do you have any other deals?

WHEATER

Yes, I've got a boot deal with Puma, he has got me all sorts. I also have
to sign from time to time 1,000 stickers and get paid in return, so it's
not bad.

BERNIE

Is it an advantage having a manager who played in the same position as
you?

WHEATER

Yes, definitely. After training he knows the stuff that he has done, like
extra stuff.
And there is also Colin Cooper who helps me as well. It's probably the best
club to be at for a young centre half.

BERNIE

Last season you scored several quality goals. Where did you learn how to put the ball in the net?

WHEATER

I came here as a striker. When I was younger I played for Marton. I was scoring 80 goals a season - three, four, five or six a game.
Then I got pushed back one time at Middlesbrough, Laurie Pearson was coach.
Someone came off and he said for me to go centre half and I got man of the match and I've remained there since.
I always stay behind with Stewie Downing, just striking balls at the goal every day.

BERNIE

Does the whole team stay behind after training? I used to stay behind myself most days.

WHEATER

There's only ever me and Stewie. Johnno comes now and again. For me, the strikers should be staying back.

BERNIE

So when you stay behind as a centre half, what do you do?

WHEATER

I always do finishing with Stewie or some heading, some long passes most of the time. It's just shooting because we do defensive stuff during training.

BERNIE

And you think its important to stay behind on your own?

WHEATER

Yes. There's nothing else to do but go home and sit watching TV, so you might as well stay behind and polish up your ability.

BERNIE

You've played every level for England. Were you surprised to be called into
Fabio Capello's senior squad?

WHEATER

Yes I was. It was all in the papers the day before, which took away the
surprise a bit. I don't know how they find out, but once you read it in
every paper you think you're going to be in it.

BERNIE

Where were you when you officially heard you were in the squad?

WHEATER

I was just reading the paper, then I ran out to my car just to check my
phone and I'd got a text off the woman.
I walked back in and it was on Sky Sports News.
I couldn't believe that I was in contention for it, the full England
set-up.

BERNIE

Have the England lads welcomed you?

WHEATER

Yes, they have been fantastic. The things that they say about all
footballers being big time is not true.
Beckham's a great lad, Lampard and Gerrard are fantastic. They are world
superstars but you can just talk to them like normal lads.

BERNIE

In the modern game the majority of managers rotate the team. How do
players cope?

WHEATER

I don't know, it's hard. When I went right-back and the two centre halves
were doing well and he didn't put me back to centre half I couldn't believe
it.

They were playing well and I couldn't complain but you just want to play every game.
I think Martin O'Neill's played the same team every game. I think it helps if you keep the same team but sometimes you can't with injuries and other people playing well in training.

BERNIE

Would you rather play every game than be rested? Have you ever felt tired or fatigued? Do you hear your team-mates mentioning it?

WHEATER

Not any of mine, only when they are injured. Personally I want to play every game.
I said to the manager that's my aim - to play every game this season.
I only missed two or three last season, I wanted to play every game.
This season obviously I haven't but that was my aim - you should want to play.

BERNIE

Of course you should. Getting called into the England squad, how much did it help with Stewie being alongside you?

WHEATER

Oh it was great having him and Woody around, just to have them there.
Stew looked after me, made sure I was there on time at every meeting.
So it was great having someone that you know to get you settled and it was great for me as well because Woody is mates with Becks as well.

BERNIE

Recently you were put on standby for England by Capello and flew to Minsk in Belarus just hours after you had played 90 minutes for the Under-21s against Wales. Gareth had a moan, how did you find that?

WHEATER

I thought it was great getting called up because obviously you're in the manager's thoughts. But when I got back I was knackered.
I only trained on the Friday, then we had Chelsea on the Saturday and that didn't turn out too well - 5-0.

So I was shattered after that. The thing was we were supposed to fly after the 21s game but there was fog in Minsk so we couldn't fly until five o'clock the next morning. So we had a five o'clock wake up call and I couldn't sleep much after the game anyway. Then we flew there and we had only done like a few stretches and then we went to the game.
So we had a whole day and went to the game and flew back. I had no sleep for nearly two days.

BERNIE

What about the flying? Is that a problem, do you enjoy it? I have a phobia!

WHEATER

I'm not sure after watching that film Lost! (Laughs) You get used to it, I'm on a plane every other week.

BERNIE

Is it true when you joined England that George Boateng told you to leave your autograph book at home?

WHEATER

It's not just me, it's everyone else. He just said it for the craic.
There's worse people than me in the dressing room chasing autographs! (Laughs)

BERNIE

You have been left out, played right-back and centre-back and been suspended. That must have disrupted your season?

WHEATER

Yes I think so, definitely. I enjoy playing right-back but it's not my position and then I couldn't get back into the centre.
That was important if I wanted to kick on and be a regular member of the England squad.
It hasn't turned out as I wanted as yet. I just need a run of games. The thing is I'm suspended now and the other two are in and if they play well I'll be back on the bench.

BERNIE

Would you rather play in one position?

WHEATER

Yes, I just want to play centre-half and that's it. Train there every day
and play there every game.

BERNIE

A normal day's training is what?

WHEATER

I start at 9.30am in the gym because I have to do weights.
I've had a lot of back problems since last year so I have to do squats with
big heavy weights and train from 10.30am to midday.
Then me and Stewie do a bit extra. I also have to do yoga in the afternoon,
that's why I was late for this interview!

BERNIE

Who gives you that?

WHEATER

Frank Nuttall, the new sports scientist. In its defence it's not too bad.

BERNIE

Is there just you that does it?

WHEATER

No, no there's a few of us - the stiff group!

BERNIE

You don't you wear a leotard and that do you?

WHEATER

(Laughs) No!

BERNIE

What's your match day build-up?

WHEATER

I'll get up about 11am because I like to sleep.

BERNIE
Do you set the alarm?

WHEATER

I just set the alarm but I usually wake up and I get Red Bull just to wake
me up. Then my girlfriend does me scrambled eggs, I love scrambled eggs.
Then I pick up my mate and my granddad to go to the game.

BERNIE

Do you stick to a diet?

WHEATER

You have to eat healthy at the training ground because that's all there is,
it's just health stuff.
But I don't think I could go home and eat pasta and stuff. Now and then
I'll go and get a Macdonald's or something. You train hard the next day -
you just burn whatever you've had anyway.
Before training I'll go upstairs and have a few slices of toast. There's
only about five of us do that, most of them have their own routines.

BERNIE

Who is the biggest joker in the dressing room?

WHEATER

I think I might be up there. Yeah, I'm up there. Just the English lads I'd
say, especially the local lads.

BERNIE

Talking about jokes, you were dressed as an elf at Christmas time!

WHEATER

I posed. I was messing about and they go and put it in the Gazette! Every other player dressed up and looked normal except me! People realised it was all a bit of fun but I still looked better than Johno!

BERNIE

Best moment so far?

WHEATER

Obviously my debut and my England call-up. But I think just scoring at the Riverside. My first goal in front of the North Stand with all the fans singing this season against Tottenham, that was brilliant. Just to celebrate in front of them, it was great.

BERNIE

Do you like scoring goals?

WHEATER

Yes, there's no better feeling than scoring a goal.

BERNIE

Worst moment so far?

WHEATER

Just when you make mistakes. But I had an Under-21 game before I went away with the England squad to Trinidad.
I had a stinker. Capello was watching as well. It was straight after the season had finished, I was knackered and Capello and his assistant witnessed it.
It was the worst game I had ever had. Then I went away with them and didn't play.

BERNIE

Were you aware they were watching?

WHEATER

Yes, I was captain as well and I was just looking up towards the stand when the national anthem was on and I saw him but you don't remember that in the game.
But I just had a horrendous game, I was tired. Maybe if I had performed I may have gained another cap.

BERNIE

Away games - how do you travel to them?

WHEATER

I think anywhere past Birmingham you get the plane but our coach is comfortable anyway.

BERNIE

What are the comforts on the coach these days? In my days we only had a microwave and a TV.

WHEATER

We have a few TVs but I don't think anyone has them on because we've all got iPods and DVD players. There is a microwave, fridge, all sorts really.

BERNIE

Recently you were voted player of the year.

WHEATER

Yes, fantastic but it's just the start really. I want to win more awards. It's nice to get awards in your first season but I need to do it this season and in seasons to come.

BERNIE

How do you see this season going?

WHEATER

It's not going too bad, I just need a run at centre-back.
This suspension hasn't helped me. I had a couple of decent games against
Newcastle and Hull but who knows, people might get injured again and I'll
be back.

BERNIE

Wheats, thanks very much.

WHEATER

Cheers Bernie.

HONOURS

DAVID WHEATER

PLAYING CAREER HISTORY

2004-present Middlesbrough
2006 Doncaster Rovers (loan)
2006 Wolverhampton Wanderers (loan)
2007 Darlington (loan)

PLAYING HONOURS (winners)

Middlesbrough
FA Youth Cup winner

Bernie's About 2

■ Meeting Mark Viduka at the Newcastle United training ground.

■ Sharing a joke with Marco Branca.

■ Meeting Stewart Downin

CHRISTCHURCH
Curiosities

W.A. Hoodless

The
History
Press

*This book is dedicated to the extraordinarily interesting people
of Christchurch, past and present – without them, it would not
have been possible*

First published 2010

The History Press
The Mill, Brimscombe Port
Stroud, Gloucestershire, GL5 2QG
www.thehistorypress.co.uk

British Library Cataloguing in Publication Data.
A catalogue record for this book is available from the British Library.

ISBN 978 0 7524 5670 6

Typesetting and origination by The History Press
Printed in Great Britain
Manufacturing managed by Jellyfish Print Solutions Ltd

Contents

Introduction   4

1. Christchurch Nelson – a Fund-Raising Dog   5
2. Saxon Wall Controversy   7
3. Bow House and a Nightclub Under the High Street?   10
4. Pig-Killing and Life Between the Wars   13
5. Flambard – The Hated Founder of Christ's Church   16
6. Remarkable Mudeford Family   19
7. High Price of Leather and Hobble-de-hoys!   22
8. Henry VIII's Last-Minute Reprieve   24
9. Unique River that 'Freezes the Wrong Way Round'   29
10. Pipe, Boot and River Keeper   33
11. Why is the Town Called 'Christchurch' Today?   36
12. Invasion Scare of 1539   38
13. Some Ancient Decisions of Christchurch Corporation   41
14. D-Day from Hengistbury Head   42
15. Can the Priory Church Endure?   43
16. Humour and Hardship at the Petty Sessions   46
17. Second Miraculous Beam   49
18. Eels of Christchurch   51
19. Mudeford in 1900 with Florence Hamilton   55
20. Normans, Weather Vanes and Salmon   57
21. Astonishing Catches and the Royalty Fishery   60
22. From Helping the Poor in 1372 to Helping the Traffic Now   63
23. Stocks and Ducking Stool – For Visitors   64
24. King Canute, Climate Change and Christchurch   68
25. Now We Have Trams!   70
26. England's Last Surviving Bus Turntable   74
27. Oliver Cromwell and the Salmon Thieves   80
28. Wartime Evacuation to the Cadburys   83
29. Childhood Memories of a Victorian Mayor   85
30. Town That Should Not Be Here   88
31. Railway Workers' Rescue Boat on River Avon   90
32. Did the Priory's Old Tower and Spire Collapse?   92
33. Billy Combe's Last Fight   94

Bibliography   96

Introduction

My intention has been to convey some surprising stories about the background of Christchurch and its surrounding area. Admittedly, the choices were without much rhyme or reason – the deciding factor has generally been how unusual and/or unknown they might be. But just what is curious? We can certainly say that the town itself is attractive for both visitors and residents and well able to justify the council's catchphrase of 'Where Time is Pleasant'. After all, the rivers, the Priory Church, the general quaintness and so forth speak for themselves. You might say that these things are not 'curiosities', but rather they create attractiveness through a fortunate combination of environment and over 1,000 years of development with character. I would agree with such sentiments but also say that the more you research, the more unexpected things emerge from the fabric of the town, well beyond matters of local interest. For example, the Priory Church was saved from demolition by a hair's breadth in 1540 by a decision of Henry VIII and, very recently, the congregation has benefited from a Second Miraculous Beam (*see* Chapter Seventeen).

Sometimes, the locality provides only part of the explanation. For instance, a broad look at the life of the eel is needed in order to give an adequate account of those in the town's rivers. The same applies to the 1539 invasion scare and the unique Christchurch bus turntable. Perhaps there are no hard and fast boundaries in such matters. I hope that the reader will agree with my way of trying to provide a fuller picture of some topics and endure the occasional expression of a personal view. The intention has indeed been to separate each curiosity by making the chapters self-contained and not in any specific order. There has also been a lot of reliance on what people have said and recollected, to try and give a feel for times past.

Many people have helped greatly in my research for this book. In no particular order, I would like to thank David Eels for his help concerning the de Redvers family history and the gifts of salmon to the Christchurch canons; Roger Castle regarding the eel runs in the Stour and Avon; the British Library and National Maritime Museum for the supply and interpretation of Henry VIII's map of 1539; David Bowler, David Bradley and the Christchurch Museum of Electricity regarding the trams and trolleybuses; Michael Hodges, Michael Tizzard, Michael Andrews, Jane Rutter and others from the Christchurch Local History Society; the National Archives for the copy of Prior Draper's petition; John Lewis at the Red House Museum; Harry Manley of Bournemouth University about the town's Saxon wall; Durham Cathedral Library concerning Bishop Flambard's effects; Tony Timms at the Royalty Fishery; Mike Parker regarding salmon netting technique; Heather Coleman and the RAOB to do with the clay pipe at the Fishery; Ian Jessopp, Tony Ruth and Barry Beesley concerning the Church of the Holy Trinity, Christchurch; John Sheppard and Richard Keith in relation to Bow House; Ian Stevenson (historian), John Elliott (Permanent Way Institution) and the Railway Benefit Fund for the railway stories; and Ted Baker for transcriptions.

W.A. Hoodless, 2010

ONE

Christchurch Nelson – A Fund-Raising Dog

In the nineteenth century, working for the railways was a hazardous occupation, with many sad cases of deaths at work and bereaved families left to fend for themselves to the best of their ability. Out of 400,000 railwaymen in 1900, some 500 were killed each year. In true self-help Victorian style, some alleviation was found in charitable institutions. Fund-raising by collecting-box dogs was a most appropriate scheme that encouraged people to recognise the dangers which lay behind the enormous improvement in long-distance transport. The first one was reportedly London Jack, who frequented Waterloo station until his death in 1901. By 1916, there were fifteen dogs collecting money for the London & South Western line's orphanage. Altogether some eighty dogs and their handlers, often retired railway staff, were involved over the years, including the town's very own Christchurch Nelson.

Not only were they trained to avoid the railway lines, but they also learned to perform a variety of tricks. For instance, a dog might be able to sit up and beg, take a bow, climb a ladder, play leapfrog and even sit in a chair with a pipe in its mouth and cap on its head! On occasion, a collecting dog would move between stations. These movements would take two forms – the official transfers of stuffed dogs and the unofficial ones where a live dog got on a train and had to be returned to his station of origin! Here, as so often when looking at social history just a few generations ago, there seems to have been more individuality and humour in daily life. Yet the dogs were important in a different fashion – they raised awareness and gained publicity for

Christchurch Nelson
The railway company's dog at the front of Christchurch station – in 1908, he raised £17 10s for the orphanage. *(Courtesy of Ian Stevenson)*

the orphanage. Although hard to measure, it is possible that this function was indirectly a bigger fund-raiser than the dogs' money boxes.

The photograph of Christchurch Nelson shows him well-placed to collect money from the travelling public. The front main wall of the station facing the car park is the same today as it was then, with one main difference – a ticket machine has replaced the trolley. In 1908, public donations totalled £17 10s; this was Christchurch Nelson's share of almost £500 raised that year for the railway line's orphanage. It is very likely that Christchurch Nelson is the dog on the postcard image, sent as it was in January 1910.

After a dog died, he might be stuffed and thereby continue to raise money for charity from the confines of a glass case. There were several dogs called London Jack, one of which was stuffed and continued his work in this way at Bournemouth Central station. His 1916 takings after death were reported at slightly above those of Christchurch Nelson eight years earlier, in the sum of £17 17s 2d. In 1908, Bournemouth Central was patrolled by Bournemouth Bob, who raised £20 in that year, and Wimborne station was patrolled by Wimborne Nero, who amassed £2 12s 10d.

The London & South Western Railway Servants' Orphanage was founded in 1885 and opened the next year at Jeffreys Road Clapham for the 'fatherless children of Railway Servants of every grade at all stations served by the London & South Western line'. The first intake was of ten fatherless girls. Demand grew and, by 1895, there were some fifty girls and twenty-six boys cared for in three converted houses in the same road. They were all housed, clothed, fed and educated by the charity. Later, another house was bought in Lambeth and converted. Eventually, the chance arose to acquire a 7.5-acre site in the country. A generous legacy enabled a replacement home to be opened for more than 100 children in 1909 at Woking, a site that became a hospital in the Second World War and now, known as Woking Grange, provides for retired railwaymen and their spouses. Over the years, more than 3,500 children have been helped. This was the excellent cause for which Christchurch Nelson and all the other dogs were working.

TWO

Saxon Wall Controversy

A prominent Christchurch local historian has voiced the opinion that if you place two people in the same room, they will arrive at three opinions on the same subject matter! Seeming to prove this theory, there is a section of old walling in the town centre that has yet to have an undisputed and settled provenance. But first, some background.

Since the Domesday Survey of 1086 refers to less than forty messuages (dwellings), the Saxon burgh (fortified settlement) of Twynham must have been little more than a hamlet by today's standards. The burgh was almost certainly designed as a place of refuge in times of crisis for up to several thousand people, because the protected area was so large for such a tiny population. In a very short time, Twynham would have occasionally experienced a sea change from being sparsely occupied to being overcrowded. The whole of society must indeed have been conditioned by the regular need for protection against foreign raiders within a defended wall, or behind a natural obstacle such as a river.

So what did the town look like in Saxon times when it only had two main routes, High Street and Castle Street? The first road is in line with the natural direction of access from the west, i.e. straight to the town and church between the two rivers. Castle Street, however, runs towards the river for the use of anyone travelling to or from the east. To imagine a typical dwelling, think of a simple single-storey wooden building with a thatched roof, and the family living together in the one available room. The hearth fire, a constant safety risk which did not have the benefit of a chimney, provided a facility for cooking, heating and lighting at the same time.

Otherwise, apart from the church and monastery, Twynham is likely to have had a hall, stores and workshops of similar construction. Despite the deprivations, there were advantages. The saying 'everybody knew everybody' would have rung much more true than it does today. There would have been extended families, a real sense of community and a very strong focus on the Church, agriculture and especially fishing. In such a place, it would have been difficult enough for the Saxons to envisage the population explosion and modernisation of the last 1,000 years, but utterly impossible to visualise their wall taken over by the food supermarket Marks & Spencer (M&S) and accessed courtesy of the internal combustion engine!

It is known that the line of the north-west section of Saxon wall ran across the main road from Bank Close car park to the Mill Stream. We must imagine that the wall contained a fortified entrance to the High Street by what is now M&S. The present road name of 'Bargates' may be derived from 'burgh gate', meaning the gateway into the Saxon burgh from the dangerous area outside the town. But whatever its derivation, at that time, the Bargates road ended at the gate and the High Street one began on the other side. If in 1066 we were standing on the old wall at the M&S location and looking north-east, we would see mainly open, undeveloped land on our left. On that side, there are also the remains of two large ditches that could have been part of the Saxon defence scheme. Straight ahead would be a side view of the main wooden gates to the town and, beyond them, a continuation of the fortified boundary up to the Mill Stream, where the boundary would turn a sharp right. To the right of the wall, the main street of the town would run in a straight line south-east until it reached the priory and church, but with large open areas due to the very sparse population.

In what way was the Saxon wall constructed and what did it look like? A reasonable answer to these questions can be derived both from Wareham and from certain 'Christchurch digs' in recent years. The latter indicate that the wall may be dated to the tenth or eleventh century, whilst the structure is believed to be very similar to the defensive system at Wareham, where a stone crest was added before the twelfth century. Hence, by considering the enormous existing remains of Wareham's large Saxon wall, we can have some idea of Christchurch's defences before they were levelled.

A stone crest, i.e. a substantial stonework finish to the top of the wall, was quite likely at Christchurch, since the ancient ditches were in-filled with that material. However, a stone revetment, i.e. masonry facing of the bank, was added after the original construction as a defence improvement. It is indeed probable that, over the years, the defence banking was variously fronted with turf, timber and stone, including ironstones from Hengistbury Head. The 'Saxon wall' referred to in this chapter may have been simply an earth bank, with some stone facing added at uncertain dates. Equally, it could have been a major effort, including double ditching and a high bank topped by a stone fighting platform and palisade fence.

One feature has been identified with some precision – the 9 to 10m width of the earth bank at ground level. But it is difficult to visualise such a bank with stone walling (estimated at 1.4m wide) on the top of it – even more so when it is suggested that much of the bank was formed by scarping, or cutting into, the natural sand dunes! Although not clearly dated, there were two (probably turf-lined) parallel ditches (2 to 2.5m original depth) about 9m apart and well in front of the wall. The bank's width certainly indicates a considerable wall height.

Data derived from airborne laser scanners has provided a detailed topographic map of Christchurch and the surrounding area. It is interesting to see that through Druitt Gardens, the defensive circuit proposed by Jarvis (author of *Excavations in Christchurch 1969-1980*) follows the break of slope between the surrounding marshland and the higher ground of medieval Christchurch. The positioning of the walls would have enhanced the defensive capabilities of the burgh, as well as creating a strong impression when viewed from the surrounding marshland

Ancient wall remnant
Although this surviving section of wall looks forlorn and insignificant today, it may indeed be a unique heritage feature from the time of King Alfred.

and harbour. Hence, whilst there are some problems of interpretation and dating, the main point is that Saxon Christchurch was a small but well-defended settlement with a landscape so moulded by the defence needs of the day that we would not now recognise it.

Having briefly looked at the Saxon town and wall, let us move on to the controversy. Recapping, it is known that the line of the wall ran through the present retail area of M&S and the rear car park. Amazingly, the latter retains what may be a section of it on its south-western boundary, just about visible through the undergrowth and adjoining a recycling bin. At this point, the wall remnant turns through 90° and proceeds towards Wick Lane, roughly parallel to Creedy Ditch. The photograph of the wall shows what is left of this sadly deteriorating, but unique, part of the town's heritage. The ironstones in the picture would probably have been added after the original construction as a facing to the earth bank for extra strength. Almost certainly, they were gathered from the beach below Hengistbury Head, being that much more convenient than the other source of supply at St Catherine's Hill. But is it a Saxon remnant?

Since the woodland to the rear (Druitt Gardens) is well below the level of the tarmac car park, the wall appears from the car park side to be much lower than its original height. Strangely, the same might be said of the view from the other side. Jarvis records that the upper fill of the ditch discovered in the excavation, known as Trench X5, was 1.5m below the ground surface. Therefore it is possible that since the construction of the defences, the ground surface of Druitt Gardens may have been raised, so giving the false present-day impression that the wall is quite low.

Many hope that the feature can be given the recognition it deserves with renovation, a proper setting and interpretation panel, as has been done for a Saxon wall in Hereford city. However, at the time of writing, there is debate about whether it really is a Saxon remnant, because that has yet to be formally pronounced by a qualified archaeologist. Although a geophysical survey has been produced for the council by Bournemouth University as part of the planning stage for Druitt Gardens, there is no dating evidence available from it in respect of the remnant. Local opinion has it that any investigation must go down at least 2m and, since the survey was much less than this, we are no wiser. Moreover, English Heritage has not permitted an excavation, despite the considerable interest that was expressed by the Christchurch Antiquarians in assisting such a dig.

Consequently, Christchurch Council has yet to receive professional confirmation of the wall's Saxon origin, and what could be about the only visible Saxon remnant of the town is still shrouded in mystery.

THREE

Bow House and a Nightclub Under the High Street?

Since the violent days of Saxon England, perhaps Bow House provides the most intriguing history of land use near to the burgh gate in the town wall. The building is shown in Fig. 1, a recent photograph taken during a busy Monday market. Unfortunately, the story of just how and when the wall was removed, and what was built over it, has been lost in the mists of time. But about seven centuries after the Norman Conquest, we can pick up the threads again with a brewery. Bow House was erected as part of the extensive Aldridge Brewery and a photograph exists of the brewery tower marked in painted lettering – 'established 1783'.

Moving to 1866, Bow House was converted to a museum. By then, the young taxidermist, Edward Hart, had made a sufficiently large collection to do this, although he was only nineteen years of age – even at the age of ten, he had shot and mounted three birds. Certainly, his work proved to be of better quality (including backgrounds of great realism) than the taxidermy of his father William, who became mainly involved in his Fusee watch chain factory in Bargates. The museum business had been passed to the son under the title William Hart & Son, Preservers of Birds and Beasts, with displays running to thousands of items. William's Bridge Street taxidermist's shop had opened in 1834, in the part known as Rotten Row opposite the Water Course. This stream, which has now disappeared due to water engineering improvements, ran adjacent and parallel to the street on its south side. The area was, for many years, notorious for flooding by the river Avon. Later, William opened a new taxidermy shop near the Fusee factory, where the son worked for some years before the Bow House enterprise. A notice from that era when the premises were in West End, now Bargates, advertises, amongst other things, work on 'stags heads, fish and foreign skins'.

William's son's 'escape' to fresh premises and independence perhaps had the not uncommon element of a young man's rebellion and re-invention. Apart from his skill at taxidermy, Edward was excellent at presentation, being talented at both painting and

Edward Hart
Hart was a very talented taxidermist with an enormous and popular display at Bow House until the 1920s.
(Hampshire County Council Museums and Archives, Red House Museum, Christchurch)

modelling plants. One museum visitor felt as if he was looking at a living bird in its natural surrounds, when he was simply viewing a stuffed bird in a cabinet. Fig. 2 is a photograph of one of these exhibits, well justifying the comment – it is an Alpine Accentor shot in 1885 in the grounds of Christchurch Castle by W. Humby. The high quality of his displayed work would have been a big help in getting orders from sportsmen to have their kills stuffed. As ever, before we try and judge this aspect of Victorian culture, it should be remembered that times were very different and people were merely keeping to the norms of the day. In some contrast to those norms, Edward Hart was noted for his strong belief in protecting rare birds and conserving wildlife where necessary. Indeed, he became somewhat fed up with the public, especially the visitors from London, saying: 'Decency should compel them to leave their brazen-throated gramophone and music hall songs in their own homes, and not intrude on the lonely reaches and quiet creeks of our rivers.'

Bow House was described as 'the ideal of a private museum', with bird cases running to a length of 270ft and a height of 10ft. Apart from stuffed birds and animals, there was a host of other exhibits including fossils, butterflies, skulls etc. In 1903, Bournemouth Council almost bought the whole collection for £4,000, but the money could not be raised. It remained at Bow House until sold a few years before Edward's death in 1928. Since then, it has been broken up and much lost through neglect. Luckily, Hampshire County Council managed to obtain twenty-two cases, chosen partly for the Christchurch backgrounds to the exhibits – the Alpine Accentor illustration is one of these.

By 1930, the museum had gone. The buildings between Bow House (a listed building) and what is now the HSBC bank were redeveloped as a garage, the Excelsior. From 1951, the Keith family occupied both the house and garage. While the house may still be there, the garage has long since been redeveloped and occupied by Iceland, followed by Marks & Spencer. When the family moved out of the whole premises in 1974, the Bow House part was sold to the Portman Building Society, which converted it to office use for their Christchurch branch. Finally, it was sold to Christchurch Carpets, who, since 2003, have made it into a showroom specialising in oriental rugs and carpets. Towards the rear of the property is a room with a most attractive inglenook fireplace. That is still there, although conversion works have meant that the beams are mostly no longer visible. In addition to some domestic utensils from a bygone time, an old pistol is on display, pointing at an LP by Anita Harris called 'Just Loving You' – a far cry indeed from the harsh environs of being close to a Saxon defence structure!

A most fascinating aspect of the comparison with Saxon Twynham concerns the space below ground. Richard Keith, the former occupier of the house, has kindly let me record his

Keith Motors has become Marks & Spencer
The Saxon wall of Twynham ran across the present High Street approximately where Bow House abuts the garage in this photograph. *(Hampshire County Council Museums and Archives, Red House Museum, Christchurch)*

Inglenook fireplace at Bow House
This most attractive scene from a different era was evidently still being appreciated some time after 1967, the issue date of Anita Harris's twelve-track LP in the picture. *(Courtesy of John Sheppard, Christchurch Carpets)*

recollections. There were apparently very large cellars under it, long since sealed off and now inaccessible. Entry was either from the rear garden or by the spiral stairs which still exist inside the property. Once underground, a well-built tunnel travelled through the old brewery site to Creedy Ditch and possibly even further. Although he does not personally recall going beyond the ditch, the story is that it continues all the way towards Wick Ferry – for the benefit of the smugglers of old. The implication is that, like most people, the Aldridges brewing family were directly involved in receiving contraband. Whilst that is likely to be correct, the same cannot be said of the tale that the tunnel continues from Creedy Ditch to Wick Ferry.

Of particular interest to the Keith family in the 1960s was the chance of creating a cellar nightclub, using both the tunnel and the vaulting that went about two thirds of the way under Christchurch High Street! At the time, it was considered that the underground structure was 250 to 300 years old, i.e. going back to the smuggling era, and might be ideally suited for conversion. The damper and poorer section was under the High Street and, being so large, it would have become the club floor after first being 'shored-up'. Years before the nightclub proposal, the children of the Keith family were understandably discouraged from visiting the cellars for safety reasons – presumably, that made it all the more attractive to them. The better-quality part was the fairly dry tunnelling running towards Creedy Ditch – every 10ft or so, there was a section wide enough to allow a table and four chairs for potential clubbers. The tunnel began broad and high but became much smaller towards the south-west. In addition, there were underground connections along the High Street towards the Fountain public house on one side and beyond what is now the HSBC bank on the other side. It was not, however, feasible to include these in the scheme.

Clearly, major expenses would have included the need to ensure structural safety, fitting out and damp-proofing. By 1964, the specification was done and the plans drawn – costs were estimated at around £17,500 for the whole project. In the event, the fairly marginal business decision was taken not to go ahead – it was too costly. Sadly, after all this time, the plans no longer exist and, due to the cancellation, never did progress to a planning application. When the matter was reported to the council for reasons of current road safety, it transpired that, some time ago, another cellar had been found running under the road near to its junction with Millhams Street. The ceiling of that cellar had to be strengthened, although it is a small fraction of the extent of the one formerly accessed from Bow House.

Hopefully, the High Street will not collapse one day under a heavy vehicle.

FOUR

Pig-Killing and Life Between the Wars

elow is a slightly gruesome description concerning the everyday reality of life for many – this kind of pig-killing is certainly alien to us now. It derives from a booklet by Reg Kitcher of his early years at Highcliffe and Hinton Admiral, 1910–39.

Nearly every working family needed to rear and fatten a pig. I know my father had one either in a sty or hung up indoors before having it treated by smoking at one of the accepted preparation centres at Christchurch; after which it was salted down and put in the meat tubs all families had in those days. We had large bowls of lovely white lard as well as plenty of scraps and chidlins. Whenever any of these pigs were killed it was always a harrowing time for me; I hated the screams of the victims, the shouts of the men and the light of the bonfires in the eerie light of a winter evening. Mr. George Barnes … was the recognised official pig killer for the district and he was also part of the set-up of which I was terrified. With his knife in his mouth, a rubber apron on and all the other tools of his trade was enough to make me take refuge around my mother's skirts to hide. She, for her part, had to have ready a copper of boiling water so necessary to scraping all the hairs off the dead pig whilst it was warm before bringing it indoors to hang. Some people preferred singeing the hairs off by a bonfire of straw being lit around the victim.

The second eyewitness account is by Jack Hake, who was born in 1920 and talked in 1998 with John Lewis at the Red House Museum. Although we are only harking back some eighty years, his childhood memories still paint a picture of a world that could scarcely be more different from that of today. Broadly, it is the same world that produced the pig-killing experience. These extracts are courtesy of Hampshire County Council Museums and Archives, Red House Museum, Christchurch.

My mother originated from Sopley and her father was an undertaker and wheelwright. In those days there was no electricity and the five sisters, after they came out of school, used to go to a wheel that was set up in the yard and they used to walk round with the wheel, and there was a belt coming from under the wheel and used to be over the top of the lathe, and my grandfather and uncle used to turn the felloes out. The felly is the centre part of the wheel and it goes on to the axle and the spokes go on to the felly …

On Saturday morning, it was my mother's duty, with her sister, to come into Christchurch for the week's provision and they used to ride in from Sopley to Christchurch, bareback on a pony with two big carters' bags on the front of the horse. That was the means for getting our provisions for the week and my uncle always said that by doing this and not being near the shops, you only bought what you wanted … The cost of a funeral in 1925 to 1930 was £12 10d and if you wanted an extra car, that was £2 10d from Mr. Harris who kept the garage in Sopley …

When the beach huts were occupied, Mr. Cutler who lived in what they were called 'up the steps' one of the Dutch cottages on the harbour, he used to row thirteen buckets of water across to the other side, and the occupants of the beach huts used to collect the water from him at 1*d* a bucket … Where the motorists' centre is, on the corner of Purewell, that was all open and it was full of pigs and it was quite common to see pigs wandering all over the road … My uncle said: 'Every trap that I make, the horse is always measured and the reason for this, they have a piece of timber, half inch timber, and they place along the side of the horse and with a pencil they draw the line, the shape, of the horse because each horse has got a different flank, and so that, when the shafts are made, they are made in such a way that the shaft doesn't rub on the back of the horse.'

When a crab is dead, it's not fit to boil so they used to be buried in the garden and, for entertainment, we used to put a piece of black cut line, that's fishing line, on the legs of these big crabs and walk across the road to the Catholic Church and put them by the wall and bring the string across the road under the gate and one of us used to sit on the wall at the top and when the old ladies used to come by, the one at the bottom used to jerk these crabs across the road and 'course, the old girls used to scream and jump and tear off down the road. This is our only entertainment … Used to make the dough for Shirvells – all kneaded by hand – and I used to pull those bags, or with a pair of sacktraps if they were too far away – flour used to come down into the bin. Reg Andrews, one day, was kneading the flour, and he coughed, and his ash in his tobacco flew out of his pipe and I called down the shute: 'Mr. Andrews, your tobacco has gone in the dough.' He said: 'That's all right, boy, it will give it a bit of flavour!'

Opposite the Wesleyan Church, there is the Star public house. When the pub opened for trade, they used to open the doors and you could see the stone floors with a brass foot-

Ye Olde Starre Inne, Purewell
Here is the bay window through which, according to Jack Hake, the town's first fish and chips were served.

rail along and big brass spittoons but, also beside the counter, there used to be a trough full of sawdust and the people who used to frequent there were from the Crispin, a common lodging house in Bridge Street. Most of them were partial tramps or knife-grinders and the sawdust was used to spit in. As you look at the public house now, you'll see a bay window, and in that bay window, Mrs. Stride had the first fish and chip shop and there was two big gas stoves with two very big oval frying pans, chips in one and fish in the other, and that is about the first fish and chip shop in Christchurch. Now called Ye Olde Starre Inne, the bay window is still there but now used only for lighting the Saloon Bar …

As we move down to Stony Lane, the top of Stony Lane was a Romany encampment, the Whites, and they were true Romanies, and when the Hay's Wharf lorries used to come through Purewell at night, they often killed hedgehogs, and we would go with a sack in the morning up the Street Lane and collect these dead hedgehogs and take to Mr. White. We got one and a half pence for a hedgehog and he used to make up mud and press on the spikes of the hedgehog until it was a circular ball and then cook them in a fire of wood like a camp fire. When it was really hard, he used to hammer the clay off with a stick and the bristles used to stick in the clay, and I'm told it tasted like pork.

There is a curious postscript to the fish and chip shop recollection – perhaps it is all a mistake. Having called at the public house, it was unsurprising that the relatively recent landlord had no knowledge of the town's first such shop, but the same cannot be said of the resident opposite. He has lived there continuously since 1920, still appears to have a good memory, and knew nothing of a fish and chip shop on the other side of the road!

FIVE

Flambard – The Hated Founder of Christ's Church

The Priory Church (Fig. 3) is a magnificent monument to Christ and the town itself. The beautiful building and its setting has perhaps one distraction – the recent residential marina scheme. Even that is only a blemish when viewed from downstream of the meeting point of the Avon and Stour, whilst some will argue that such a visual loss is more than outweighed by the attraction of the scheme. Suffice it to say that this remarkable church has been built and maintained against the odds for over 900 years – in other words, it has led a charmed life. Whilst one is tempted to the conclusion that God must have been on its side, many have felt that the same could not be said of Flambard, the unpopular founder of the Norman building.

It is possible that the first Saxon church was erected on the site of a pagan shrine. At the time it was built, believed to be in the seventh century, this was a common early Christian practice in order to remove any pagan influence. The strategic location of the settlement was excellent, providing some control over the two rivers that would otherwise have been attractive to the marauding Danes. Indeed, this benefit may have prompted the Saxons' decision to make it a 'burgh' or fortified settlement. By the time of William the Conqueror, a main church and nine other churches existed within the grounds of the site, including the existing Priory Church curtilage and extending to the Saxon borough boundary of the Mill Stream. The nine minor churches are likely to have been monastic cells. In 1997, Professor Martin Biddle of Oxford University investigated the location of the Saxon church, concluding that it is likely to be under the western part of the present nave. This would have allowed the crossing, and two or three bays of the new nave, to be built before the old church was dismantled.

Whilst as far as is known there were no threats to the church before the Conquest of 1066, we now come to the great new Norman rebuilding project – a difficult task begun by the badly-regarded Ranulf Flambard. Despite his unpopularity, Flambard's building ambitions for what was then Twynham (and later Durham) certainly bore fruit. Flambard means 'fiery', an adjective consistent with adverse comment by chroniclers of the day. He was also described as 'violent', 'ruthless', 'dangerous', 'evil', 'a rent collector of the worst possible reputation' and so forth. Having such qualities as these and, reportedly, a scant regard for justice, he seems to have been well-suited to his position as administrator and tax collector for King William Rufus. The king needed someone of great efficiency at raising taxes, running the country in his absence and, like him, having little time for the Church – Flambard was that man. Or was he? It should not be overlooked that although his management of at one time sixteen bishoprics and abbeys made him generally hated in Church circles, his own chapter held him in high esteem for upholding the rights of his see. In later years, he was also generous to the poor and recent historians have been much less critical. Was he indeed an early victim of spin?

In 1093, the king granted a royal charter of patronage to Flambard of this minor religious community of twenty-four canons. He seems to have persuaded the king to do so simply to have the opportunity to build, i.e. for reasons of ambition not piety. The serving elder, Godric, did not accept his new master and was accordingly dismissed and, when a canon died, Flambard would automatically take over his income. Soon enough, he was able to rebuild in grand style for the time. The new church, begun in 1094, was to be about 24 yards wide (and wider at the crossing) by 69 yards long. It is extremely likely that there were Norman twin towers at the location of the present west tower and Norman apses around the eastern end of the present sanctuary. In other words, only the main central part of the original Norman cross-shaped building now survives. Taken together with the new timber castle, moat and ancillary buildings, Twynham would have been in no doubt that control had passed from the Saxons.

Flambard became Bishop of Durham in 1099 but was imprisoned the next year by King Henry I in the Tower of London. Many approved this action by the new king, who had been swiftly crowned after the fatal arrow wound to Rufus in the New Forest. Even now, some consider that Flambard murdered Rufus. However, the reason for Flambard's punishment was the extortionate taxation he had implemented for Rufus. When a rope was smuggled to him in a gallon of wine, he allegedly invited his guards at the Tower to join him for a great banquet. Once they were completely drunk and snoring, he tied the rope to a column which stood in the middle of a window and, holding his bishop's staff, climbed down. At the foot of the Tower, his friends had horses ready and they galloped off to safety – a skilfully executed and bold escape.

Probably in recognition of his great skills, King Henry later decided to overlook the breakout and restored Flambard to the Bishopric of Durham. He died aged about sixty-eight years old in 1128, two years after a heart attack. Although he flagged in mind and body over these two years, at death he appears to have been a 'powerful old man' of 5ft 9in. A month beforehand, he had had himself carried into Durham Cathedral and made public restitution to his prior and monks of the offerings and fees which he had diverted to the completion of the cathedral.

Amazingly, Bishop Flambard's crozier head (which 'saw action' when he escaped from the Tower of London) and signet ring have survived to this day and are on display in the cathedral library at Durham. These two items (shown in Fig. 4) were found in 1874 when his tomb in the Chapter House was opened. The crozier head, that would have been on the top of his staff, was of iron, covered with silver sheet. It is decorated in silver niello (a black metallic substance) with animal interlace on the socket. The ring is gold with a pyramid faceted sapphire.

One interesting aspect about such a chequered career, was Flambard's continuance with the church here, the construction of which he directed from a distance. A building emerged that was similar to the cathedral in Durham. Despite being much smaller than that cathedral, he still managed to begin what is now believed to be the longest parish church in the country. When entering the Norman nave of the present church, one is met with the 900-year-old handiwork of the famous (or more likely, infamous) bishop. However fair the negative comment on Flambard, he must be given the credit for starting the superb church we have today. Luckily, despite the founder being imprisoned, what became Christ's Church had been 'launched'.

Before moving on from the redevelopment of the Saxon church, an alternative view by the architect, Eric Cockain, should be mentioned concerning dates. He disagrees with the 'official' view that the structure of the present Priory Church, above ground level, is fully Norman or later, and feels that much of what we see today predates 1066. That opinion is not, however, accepted by Professor Biddle. It is strange that we can have this profound disagreement between professionals as to the age of a large part of the church structure – will the received wisdom stand the test of time?

BUILT IN THE 'WRONG PLACE'

Quite aside from the unpopular and perhaps unreliable Flambard, there is a second main reason to regard the church as having a charmed life – it was never supposed to be built where it now stands. It appears that Flambard's instruction was to erect it on St Catherine's Hill. Although the location was outside the town, it would certainly have been seen very well and would have provided him with plenty of prestige, rather like Durham. It is easy to understand how few would have approved such a choice of site; it was a long way from the existing church, housing and community, and the journey alone must have seemed like a 'penance in waiting'. The setting might have suited the ambitious Flambard, but people also knew there was no water supply for the monks up there. Besides, they were well used to the convenience of worshipping in the town centre.

Guile was clearly needed to have the decision reversed. Moreover, immediate action was called for, because if the job made any real progress, the reversal would become difficult, if not impossible. At the very start of the works, in accord with the official plan, materials were duly transported to St Catherine's Hill to begin the job on the next day. However, when the men arrived in the morning, they discovered that these materials had mysteriously been transferred to the old church site! How could this be? After this had happened several times, Flambard apparently concluded that it was divine intervention, providing a strong signal about where to build. There would have been great relief at the outcome, and much local satisfaction as the church began to be erected on the old site. Were the materials shifted under cover of darkness by those against the new location, or was it indeed the work of God? Flambard may have belatedly realised that the best method was to utilise the existing site and simply went with the flow. Was this impious man really convinced that it was divine intervention, or had he found himself a face-saving formula? We cannot now be sure.

The new church had not only survived the dubious patronage of Flambard, a very unpopular King's Clerk and Bishop of Durham, but it had also been built in the best location for the town.

SIX

Remarkable Mudeford Family

The Derhams are one of the main historic families in this ancient and attractive fishing village. Information in this chapter is provided courtesy of both Vic Derham and the *Bournemouth Daily Echo*.

Around the end of the nineteenth century, there were eight strapping sons living in a boathouse built for them at the bottom of their parents' garden. The main house was Crugmere, occupied by Mr and Mrs James Derham together with daughters Ellen and Priscilla, whilst the boathouse was home to Gilbert, Peter, Jim, George, Harry, Tom, John and Roy. Crugmere, a large detached four-bedroom house with double garage, is still there, as is the boathouse with its splendid harbour views to the rear and approached from Fisherman's Bank.

Apart from being able to sit down at the table with their parents and sisters, the eight lads had all they could wish for, including their mother visiting to cook for them every day. Since they all had one or two dogs each, a separate house was a good solution. As James had been a landlord for many years, he knew a large number of local people and kept 'open house' at Crugmere. With the sons also looking in, it must have been a very happy period in the life of the family.

However, as reported in the *Echo* in 1974, a sadder moment was shared by sons, daughters and grandchildren of the 'Boathouse Boys'. Tom had died just before his ninety-third birthday – the last of a notable generation. After a life spent fishing local waters, Tom had retired to his shuttered house at Fisherman's Bank, where he had lived since getting married. When his wife died in 1955, his only daughter, Kathleen, had moved in with her husband and family. There it was that Kathleen, and her cousin Norah, talked with the reporter about some old family memories.

The Derhams were originally of farming stock and, despite being a fisherman, Tom was always keen on horticulture and spent many hours in his greenhouse. When he was born in 1881 as the seventh son, the family were running the Stag Inn at the corner of Purewell and Livingston Road. Due to the deep snow, the doctor had to climb in through the window to attend his birth! James, his father, later became the landlord of the Nelson – which is still there on Mudeford Road – but at that time it was a thatched cottage with a coal business run from a rear store. James used his own barge to bring coal from Poole to Christchurch Quay. When he had the Nelson rebuilt, the coal store was converted into a bar and, naturally, customers were called upon to guess how much coal it would take. On one occasion, the landlord was taken aback to be given the right answer – 200 tons.

The next family move was to Crugmere on Stanpit. As the brothers gradually married, the boathouse at the rear of Crugmere was used more for storing fishing gear. Before the Second World War, it must have been a hard life rowing (without motor power) the three miles out to the lobster pots on Christchurch Ledge. This is the shelf of ironstones now forming an underwater continuation of Long Groyne at Hengistbury Head. In addition, the Derham brothers fished for mullet, flounders and bass in the harbour, under rights granted by the Mills family, who ran the Royalty Fishery on the river Avon at that time. Out of Tom's many fishing experiences, perhaps the one to take the biscuit was the landing of a royal sturgeon in 1912. Reportedly the only one ever to come from the Run, it was 6ft 9in long. At a threepenny charge

Margaret houseboat moored on the south side of Christchurch Harbour
The Derhams provided teas to ramblers and a motorboat service to Convent Walk near to the tram terminus in Church Street. _(Courtesy of Vic Derham)_

to view the 'monster', a good sum was raised for local charity. Thereafter, it was apparently sent to Sir George Meyrick as Lord of the Manor and he forwarded it to King George V as a royal fish.

And so the boathouse eight moved on to other things in life. Roy became an electrician; Peter had a large yacht before settling down to run a hotel near Southampton Docks; Harry became a fishmonger; and George ran the Avon Beach business. Today, Avon Beach has been greatly developed by Vic Derham (George's grandson) and before him by George's son Ken Derham (1908–1994). In 1974, Ken had been involved with the beach business for more than fifty years. It was Ken who received a formal presentation by Queen Elizabeth, the Queen Mother, in 1984 for his fund-raising efforts and greatly helped establish the life-saving facility at Mudeford, now run by the RNLI.

Vic tells me that his grandfather George (1876–1960) went to the grammar school operating from St Michael's Loft in the Priory Church. George met his future wife when selling fish to the Avonmouth Hotel (now the Christchurch Harbour Hotel) Mudeford, where she was cook and housekeeper, and they were married in the Priory Church. Many years beforehand, however, when he was a choirboy, he had an argument with the vicar of the church opposite that hotel. Having gone about four weeks without the agreed rate of pay of one penny a week, he asked for the money, only to be told: 'You should sing in the House of God for nothing.' His response was to suggest to the vicar that the same surely applied to him – for his trouble, he was immediately dismissed from the choir on grounds of misbehaviour! However, this was not the end of the story. At a much later date, the same vicar unfortunately slipped by the steps when trying to board 'Razza's' ferry and fell into the dangerous waters of the Run. Razza was the nickname for another family member. George, who was watching, felt that this was hilarious and opined that the vicar's rescuer should 'push the b★★★★★★ under with the oar'! George, like everyone else, was of course pleased when the rescue proved successful.

In 1911, a houseboat was built in Christchurch for George at a cost of £150. He and his wife, Annie, named it after their daughter Margaret, who died tragically in childhood. It was taken over by the Royal Navy from 2 July 1917 until 26 May 1918 for a total consideration of £44 10s, fair wear and tear excepted. Notably, the rent paid to the family was described as an Act of Grace by the Admiralty.

Around 1918, Ken and his sister Norah needed to get to school in Pauntley Road from the south side of the harbour. He was ten years old and Norah was six, and so they rowed themselves from the sandbank, past the Run to Mudeford Quay! After school, they rowed back again – no wonder Ken's boat-handling skills were so good in later life. Perhaps fortunately, the journey was not needed in the period October to March because the *Margaret* was then quartered on the other side, on land now used as a dinghy park.

The photograph of the *Margaret* is from before the Second World War, and shows that two businesses were then operated – motor ferry and teaboat. The ferry ran a summer service every half hour or so to Convent Walk, 6d single and 9d return as late as 9 p.m. on some days in August. The teaboat became famed for fresh lobster teas served to walkers over Hengistbury Head. In addition, George and Ken still worked as fishermen.

SEVEN

High Price of Leather and Hobble-de-hoys!

Nineteenth-century Christchurch produced a number of anonymous and perhaps eccentric-sounding letter writers to the *Christchurch Times*. In this first typical example of the genre, we have a genuine concern about the tax-induced price of leather expressed with wit, charm and imagination. Mention of 'Paterfamilias' implies that the writer is the male head of a household who has concluded that the foot is both under-rated and badly treated. He also sounds well-read, knowing about the essay published in 1833 by Sir Charles Bell, a most eminent doctor, extolling the merits of the human hand in a document running to more than 200 pages.

There is a probable double-meaning at the end of the letter. A corn-cutter was the Victorian term for what we would now call a chiropodist, whilst a corncutter is also a special blade for cutting corn stalks. Why should the government get extra taxes from leather goods without any prior contribution (sowing) and/or why should foot doctors benefit from the inherent defects of leather boots when a soft substitute might be better? Readers may interpret the letter differently.

SIR, – You remarked last week upon the high price of leather. The frightful price which it is assuming under the dynasty of a sixteen penny income tax sets Paterfamilias on the look-out for a substitute. The wonder is John Bull never thought of that before. What a bundle of habits we are, what slaves of the tyrant fashion. Why an eminent man (Sir Charles Bell I think) wrote a book, a big one too – a *Bridgwater Treatise* – to teach us the use of our hands; can it be, then, that nature designed the foot as in reality a part of what anatomists term, I believe, conventionally, the *inferior* extremity. To shoe the cat with walnut-shells was, in our schooldays, 'fun'; yet what a philosophic lesson if read aright. Look at the ballet dancer – the tight-rope dancer – the sailor – the professional pedestrian who walks for wagers – how little they encumber the foot. Nor are instances wanting of the foot being educated to supply the place of hands, in the use of knife, scissors, and other instruments. Man may be superior to monkey in head, certainly not in heel. Oh, but thin shoes have always been held fruitful of colds, coughs, consumptions – *query* are the shoes or stockings most at fault? who now-a-days confesses to aught so plebeian, as 'stout knitted hose', such as our grandmothers delighted to work. The stoutest boot (of leather) soon ceases to be waterproof, and once soaked retains moisture in proportion to its thickness, to be given out again *insidiously*. Why not wear something of the slipper kind, of some worked materials; surely some soft substitute for leather could be found. Why wear the high wellington boot? What is the use of such; is it for protection? If so, why in the name of wonder wear it *inside* the trowser [*sic*]. The days of the hat are numbered, then let us kick the old boots after for luck. Head and feet both cry aloud for reform. Why should the corn-cutters reap what they didn't sow?

Yours obediently,
SPRING-HEELED JACK
Christchurch, January 28, 1857.

Turning to the second writer, still in the late 1850s, it may be a mistake to consider anti-social behaviour to be a modern malaise with a variety of modern causes. As this letter shows, the young men of the town were not universally of 'morally upright character' as the Victorians might have said.

SIR, – I have been so constantly and seriously annoyed Sir lately that I cannot refrain from writing you upon the cause of my annoyance. I saw in your paper not long ago that a poor old woman, on passing near the corner at Purewell, was stoned by a lot of worthless hobble-de-hoys, who towards evening congregate there and pass their idle time in using filthy language, and in making remarks on, and otherwise annoying, the passers by. I am constantly compelled to pass along the streets in the evening, and the abuse I have received, the disgusting language I have heard, and the disgraceful conduct generally of the young men at various corners in the town, often causing an *actual obstruction* to the passenger, have convinced me that the morals of the labouring poor are low here, and that *something* is required to make them know better.

Yours, &c.,
A MARRIED WOMAN
Christchurch, May 18, 1858

EIGHT

Henry VIII's Last-Minute Reprieve

Having been part of the relentless national expansion of the Roman Catholic monasteries, Christchurch Priory and the Priory Church became vulnerable to King Henry VIII's plans in the sixteenth century. He needed the money at the time to defend the country against the French and/or Spanish, could do without the services of educated monks (as a result of the rise of grammar schools) and had a good understanding of the level of popular resentment. People were very aware of the riches of those supposedly dedicated to poverty by their vows. For instance, despite some medical help, provision of shelter and the giving of alms to the poor, many felt that the charity offered was much less than could be afforded. Although there had been huge expansion since the Norman foundation under Flambard, there was now the probability of total loss by complete demolition. A local debate began about how to carry out a 'rescue from the king', for the benefit of the town. Was such a thing possible?

Around that time, an alternative to Dissolution was being considered – a return to strict monastic values. Unfortunately, it had previously been tried and failed. From the late fifteenth century, bishops had been working to transfer monastic estates to educational foundations and to promote proper observance of the divine office of prayer and monastic rules. This meant a smaller number of larger houses, but there was great opposition from monks and nuns – particularly to the requirement that they remain in their cloisters. Hence, although Oxford and Cambridge Universities had benefited from such suppression, there was little enthusiasm in the monasteries for strict observance.

If the priories and abbeys were to make another attempt at reverting to a severe regime, together with its privations, there was evidence to suggest it would generally lead to apostasy, rebellion and the emptying of the monasteries. It was therefore most conveniently concluded that no such effort would succeed, because the monks were never going to stay on the straight and narrow; too much drinking and corruption would continue.

Consistent with the element of 'monastic dishonesty', or pragmatism, was the evidently phoney nature of some relics. Top of this list might be the story of one church claiming to have some clay left over from the time God made Adam and Eve. Another motivation for the Dissolution was the rift with the Church of Rome. Combining this discord with his acute awareness of the sheer wealth of the monasteries, the king clearly felt that the money was getting into the wrong hands. A successful pilot project in 1536, to dissolve some smaller religious houses, convinced the king that he could expand the scheme nationally with the consent of the people, and so it proved – there was little opposition. Accordingly, his commissioners travelled the country recommending wholesale Dissolution. The valuables, lands and income were to be transferred to the Crown, whilst most priory buildings were set for demolition.

Since Christchurch Priory was rich, there was no sufficient reason for the commissioners' plan to be any different here, despite a favourable report in May 1536 about it to the king. They recommended demolition of most of it, including the Church of the Holy Trinity, which was used both by the Augustinian canons for monastic purposes and by the townspeople as a parish church. The monks' part was beyond the choir screen, and the people of the parish worshipped in the main part from the nave as far as the screen. It is important to note that the 1539 commissioners were pretty hard-line – they had a job to do for a results-minded king who was not renowned for his patience. They reportedly used threats and cajolery as a way of leading up to what was known as the 'surrender'.

However, although it was locally accepted that the monastery had to go, there was a lot of feeling in favour of the church itself. It was probably used for shelter, gatherings, markets, trading and even the supply of legal advice by the monks to the townspeople. Indeed, we know that the north porch of the parish church was a great meeting point between monks and townspeople. It seems that although people could stoically withstand the loss of the canons and all their works, they wanted to keep the church. However, this could be a slightly misleading interpretation locally, in that the Augustinians of Christchurch were much more of an 'open order' than many, and the loss of their work for the town was perhaps missed more than we think. In short, the acceptance by the people of the surrender to the king was almost 'making a virtue of a necessity' and itself leant weight to the effort to save the church. Incidentally, the inside of the building was at that time painted a somewhat garish red. Despite the efforts of the Victorians to scrub away all the paint, traces of it can still be seen today on the bottom of stone columns in the nave.

Following representations from Prior John Draper (and others: Edward Lewyn, Robert Westbury, Thomas Hancock and James Trym), the king was persuaded to let the church itself remain for the town. It has been possible to obtain from the National Archives a copy of the prior's petition, which is now held in the papers for King Henry VIII. The transcription below is made from the sixteenth-century text as supplied to me, although that comes from a 'letter book'. At the time, the petition, or letter, would have been copied by hand into the letter book for the king and the original may or may not have been kept. I am indebted to the historian Ted Baker for the skilled work of exactly transcribing the handwriting with extensions to abbreviations in square brackets.

Spelling, punctuation and sentence construction were then very different. Indeed, because the spelling of a word was written as it sounded in the local dialect, you can get a sense of that dialect by reading it aloud. Another curious aspect is that although the writing is very different from that of today, the meaning still comes across very well. As to detail, 'i', 'j', and 'y' are interchangeable, and there is one unknown letter (shown with a question mark) in a word at the end of a line. A space is left in the transcription after each line of the original document. Although it would have been possible to modernise the whole thing for readability, it has been kept as an accurate historic record of its time:

To the king our Soveraygne Lorde

In the moste humble wise showeth unto your most excellent Highnes your humble obedyent Suppliannt true and faythfull Subiect Chapelyn and daily bedeman John

Draper Prior and commendatory by your moste Royall maiesties high auctoritie of your place of Christchurchwynham nygh unto yo[ur] new Forrest in your countie of S[o]uth[am]t[on]

That where the said place is situate and set in a desolate place of this your Realme and in a very bar[r]en Countrey out and farr from all high wayes in an angle or a corner

having no woodes nor commodiouse countrey about it, nor nygh no good towne, but oonly the said poore towne of Christchurch, whiche is a very poore towne and solenderly

inhabited, nor hath no commodyouse demaynes, neyther temporall townes nor Lordships royall of temporal lands, but oonly certeyn poore villages and grannges, and

the moste parte with farmes of personages and spirituall tythes The churche of whiche place is notoonly a churche and a place for poore religiouse men, but also is the p[ar]ishe churche unto the said towne of Christchurch, and of other hamlotes theraboute p[ar]ishners to the same in whiche p[ar]ishe is the nombre of xv or xvj hundred houselyng people and

above and neyther churche towne nor p[ar]ishe of any substannce where any honorable or honest man may have any succour or refuge on horsback or on foote nygh therunto by

the space of viij or ix myles, and somwayes by the space of xvj or xviij myles, but oonly that poor place of Christchurch, to the whiche both rich and poor doth repayre and repose

So it is moste gratiouse soveraygne that the said place of late yeres was a place of secular Chanous, and by right noble high and puissannt Princes of famouse

memory your Autecessors, was made a place of Chanons regular And although that the said place is so barenly satuate and set yet notonly the poore folkes

Inhabitanntes of the towne and parishe there but also of the countrey therabout are daily there releved and susteyned with breade and ale purposely baked and

brued for them wekely, to no litle quantities according to their fundation, and a howse ordyned purposely for them, and officers accordyng duly geving attendannce to s?ve

them, to there great comfort and releves. Whiche charitable almes appereth in your Maiesties bookes, where it is of yo[ur] maiesties benigne goodness gratiously allowed. And

your said Oratones and their predecessours have used contynually hetherto to kepe a Maister to teache gram[m]er to children and Schollers there, And certeyn of them havyng meate

drynke and clothe. And now accordyng to your godly ordynannce in your graces visitacion is also kept contynually a lecture of Dyvynytie. And if the said place shulde there

be suppressed and lacke, then shulde notonly the said Towne and parrishe, but also the Countrey theraboutes decay, and be right bare and desolate, to the great ruyne and desolation

of that parte of a lytle corner of this yo[ur] Realme, (to great pittie). It may therfore please your moste excellent highness of your benynge goodness and grace especiall[y] amonges

other your manyfolde good dedes of mercy, the premysses tenderly to consider, And therupon to be so good and graciouse liege Lorde unto your said suppliannt Chapeleyn and

bedeman, and to his poore Brothern, as to grannte furder your high awtoritie, that the said place and churche may styll contynew stande and be under suche order and

rule as shall stande with your Maiesties high pleasure, and your moste honorable right wise and discrete Counisayle to appoint them. And this at the reverence

of god and in the way of charitie. And not only your said Suppliannt and Chapeleyn, and his poor Brothern during their poor lyves accordyng to their

bounden duties, but also the poore towne and Countrey for ever shall daily pray to god for the pressivation of yo[ur] moste noble and royall estate and your high

Supremytie in moche honour ioye and felicitie long to prosper and endure

It would be understandable if pondering this use of language dating from a time before the birth of Shakespeare is not to everyone's taste. However, for those who are intrigued by it, there is an expert's tip – read it through three times to gain the full benefit. The prior painted a picture of Christchurch as being a most isolated, poor and desolate place, relieved only by the good works of the church and priory. The implication was that a kindly reprieve by the king would permit continuity and be a lifesaver for not only the town but also its hinterland. Moreover, John Draper did not presume to suggest how matters should be arranged in the future – that was for the king to determine. If he had simply pushed for the removal of the priory support buildings (as indeed the king eventually decided) his argument about providing bread and ale to the poor could have failed. It was a most respectful, skilful and successful appeal.

No doubt the king was influenced by the fact that the prior had been his chaplain in the past. In addition, Draper was, according to his commissioners' report, 'a very honest and conformeable person'. His severance terms were certainly very good, having the use for life of the Somerford Grange mansion and an annual pension of £133 6s 8d. In the event, a total reprieve would not have been considered, but a compromise did prove possible. Part of this involved the appropriation of various valuables. To quote the commissioners –

> thinges of sylver right honest and of gudde valew as well for the churche use as for the table reserved and kept to the kinges use.

Under the Dissolution, a detailed inventory was provided for the king. Some things were sold off, but not all – the king apparently kept twenty-six ounces of gold plate. The lead was even measured and reported at thirty-eight fodders. A fodder is around nineteen hundredweight (cwt), or six sacks of lead where each sack is five fotmal and each fotmal weighs about 70lbs, providing some 12 sq ft of lead sheeting of thickness one tenth of an inch. Carrying the calculation to extremes, we find 0.314 acres of lead at such a thickness, although, in the event, much less would have been sold for the king as the church was reprieved.

One somewhat speculative theory, mentioned by a notice in St Michael's Loft Museum, has it that Draper married the king to Anne Boleyn knowing the marriage to be bigamous, thereby enabling him to blackmail the monarch later – a course of sheer recklessness!

The surrender to the king's commissioners (Southwell, Carne, London, Poulet and Berners) took place on 28 November 1539 and the grant, by Letters Patent to the Churchwardens and Inhabitants of Christchurch, occurred on 23 October 1540. It meant that the Church of the Monastery, the seven bells and the graveyard on its north side became for evermore their responsibility as the Parish Church of Christchurch. The grant was made to the churchwardens and inhabitants as a single legal body with deemed perpetual succession. Stones, timber, iron, glass, lead and roof gutters were specifically included.

Fig. 5, an artistic depiction in the glass of the Cloister Way window, shows nearly all the buildings existing before the Dissolution. Those set for demolition on the south side of the church included the greater and lesser cloisters, prior's lodging, guest house, barn and stables. The other part of the glasswork shows John Draper surrendering the priory's riches to the king's commissioners.

According to Ferrey's *Antiquities*, on 14 September 1540 the king granted the immediate site of the priory and precinct, reserving the church and churchyard, to Stephen Kirton and his wife Margaret, to hold 'by the service of the fortieth part of a knight's fee and the annual rent of 31s 6¼d'. The grant was *in capite*, meaning the tenancy was held immediately of the king. According to the Victoria County History (*see* British History Online in Bibliography), in 1540, the king granted a twenty-one-year lease of the priory to Wriothesley and Avery. In the same year, he granted a twenty-one-year lease to Wriothesley of the Royalty Fishery. In 1545, the priory site and other lands were granted to Wriothesley for life by the king, who granted the reversion to the Kirtons two months later. After several changes of ownership, this priory estate was bought by Gustavus Brander, who was Lord of the Manor and a governor of the Bank of England. The gardens and Priory House, which he erected at the end of the eighteenth century, have replaced most of the old buildings.

The main sequence of events from 1539 to 1540 is clear. It must have been most unsettling for the petitioners and townspeople who were trying to avoid the eventual fate of Beaulieu, i.e. of their church becoming a cleared site. After all, the entirety was surrendered and, much later, there was a royal grant of part of that entirety excluding the church and then, later still, a grant was thankfully made to the town of the church. Hence for some eleven months from the initial 1539 surrender up to the final Grant by Letters Patent, survival was uncertain.

There is a sad footnote to the loss of the town's monastery. Despite helping to save the wonderful church building for the town, Draper was far from universally admired. Perhaps because the prior's compensation for eviction was so generous, and there was some popular resentment against him in the town, he seems to have arranged for his burial to be anonymous, in the church nave. If the people did not know where his body lay, they would not be able to vent their feelings about him or the Church of Rome by desecrating the tomb. Nearly 300 years later, a blank stone in the nave (Purbeck marble, 9ft 3in by 4ft 6½in) was lifted by workmen to reveal for the first time that it was the prior's tombstone, as so inscribed on its downward-facing side. On 28 October 1819, a vestry meeting agreed to sell the space for a pew adjoining the pulpit on certain conditions, including the removal of Prior Draper's headstone. It is reported that, in 1822, the gravestone was relocated to its present position, in front of the Draper Chantry by the south aisle to the quire, the stone being too large to go in the chantry itself.

In the old position, some remains of the prior were found together with a part of his vestments and crozier. In addition, a pewter chalice, a paten (communion plate), parts of leather shoe straps, and a piece of candle, were discovered. It is reported that the candle and parts of the straps were kept by a Catholic antiquary, Francis Bernard Argyle. The sixteenth-century gravestone is still there, this time the right way up for all to see and no longer at risk of desecration. A translation of the Latin inscription engraved around the four sides of the burial stone would read:

The tomb of John Draper: twenty-sixth prior of this church: who died on the 29th day of the month of September in the year of our Lord 1552, to whose soul may God be propitious. Amen.

NINE

Unique River that 'Freezes the Wrong Way Round'

In a science class at Bournemouth School, during my brother's schooldays, a pupil asked the master why it was that the river Avon freezes from the bottom up, instead of in the normal way from the top down. The master duly regained the initiative by saying to the boy that it was an excellent subject for him to research and to bring the answer to the next class! Sadly, that is all I can recall and only now, about fifty years later, have I got round to the matter.

An entry in the journal of the Christchurch Local History Society also drew attention to the strange phenomenon. No other river in the country is believed to freeze in this fashion. Whilst it may be understandable that it can occur in arctic conditions and in North America, where it is called 'anchor ice', what is so special or peculiar about the Christchurch Avon that it can happen here? This is a key question, but first it is best to explore some background.

Since our local winters have been mild for a long time, there is no recent experience of rivers freezing – so masses of ground ice floating down the river would be something of a shock! But for now, let us just consider the significance for the river Avon of some really cold weather; should we have another winter like 1963, we shall indeed see a return of ground ice. Based on 1963, we know that although the Avon will start to freeze from the bottom, when conditions get very extreme, it will also begin to freeze across the top. On the other hand, if temperatures are less severe, then the ground ice will just float to the surface and be carried down by the current.

In the much colder nineteenth century, there would certainly have been ground ice in the Avon, but it did not affect the water supply because water was still obtained from wells. (Indeed, there was then quite strong opposition to the whole idea of piped water, despite its benefits in reducing the risk of cholera and typhoid.) In 1841, a certain Edward Daw rode his horse across the ice of the Stour from Wick to Christchurch. In 1855, it was so thick that people skated all the way from the barracks (a site with frontage to the river Stour in Barrack Road) to Mudeford, the only obstruction being where the Wick ferryman had broken through to ply his trade. It is even reported that shops closed for an hour and everybody got on the ice! An 1881 blizzard made the roads impassable and froze the rivers again. The Mill Stream was frozen in 1890 and, five years later, snow and ice brought back the river skaters.

Eventually, the health benefits of a safe water supply were accepted and arrangements were made to extract water from the river Avon. The West Hampshire Water Company was founded by an Act of Parliament – Royal Assent was given on 24 August 1893 and Knapp Mill waterworks was opened on 13 August 1895.

The *Gentleman's Magazine*, of 8 January 1786, published a 'Query in Natural History' addressed to Mr Urban from An Humble Enquirer:

Persons, I perceive of the first rank in literature, do not think it beneath them to become correspondents in your valuable Magazine. Doubts, whether respecting any part of natural or revealed religion, may modestly be proposed, and depend upon a rational solution. Different appearances of things in nature are accounted for; difficulties are satisfactorily cleared up; and questions, of any kind, answered with polite attention. I hope, therefore, that I shall be excused if I beg a place in your next month's Miscellany, if you think the matter deserving the attention of any of your correspondents.

I have been in Hants some time, and frequently heard the people talk of what they call *ground ice*, or ice that begins to freeze at the bottom of the river Avon, in that county. I imagined this to be a mistake; but have had an opportunity, this season, of ascertaining the reality of the fact, and should take it as a favour if one of your ingenious correspondents would account for it upon rational and philosophical principles. I observe that it generally begins to freeze at the bottom, where the water is shallow, and the current pretty strong. However, I have found the ground ice, in other parts of the river, upwards of six or seven feet deep, where the stream has been so gentle, that one can scarcely perceive the motion of the water. At first, I imagined that this ground ice might possibly have sunk from the surface; but on a minuter examination, am convinced that this is not the case, but that it really begins to freeze at the bottom. Whether this is peculiar to the river Avon in Hants, or not, others may determine. A solution of the above phenomenon would much oblige.

Unfortunately, it has not been possible to trace a solution from a later correspondent. The matter was still deemed worthy of investigation, amongst others, at an 1861 meeting held in the very recently rebuilt Town Hall. The ground ice in the river Avon was described as a 'peculiarity' for enquiry by members of a new archaeological association to be formed in the town. Perhaps, therefore, it is high time to describe the nature of this unusual ice. Normal river and pond ice freezes from the top down as a smooth plate of increasing thickness, depending on the severity of conditions. So much is common knowledge. Ground ice, however, is composed of rough clumps often with debris attached (such as gravel and river weed), once they have floated to the surface. It has been described as 'numerous small crystals adhering to each other in small flocculent masses'. With a certain increase in temperature, the ice will break free from the river bed, rise up and form floating rafts that naturally proceed downstream. It has been described as very like snowballs that have been frozen together, or 'frozen snow masses', and quite different from the usual floating ice slabs, which result from a normal smooth plate. Another turn of phrase from the Water Company is 'cauliflower-like masses', in respect of ice still at the river bottom.

An eyewitness account, given to me by a lady born in 1938, refers to a very cold winter when she was about eight years old and the Avon froze over – almost certainly the severe winter of 1947. It seems that there were bumps of ice within the surface of the frozen top water – in other words, after the initial formation of the ground ice, it seems to have floated to the top, only to be fixed in place by the freezing of that top layer of water. The freeze-up was sufficient for the river to be used for skating that year, except of course for those parts with ice lumps sticking through the surface.

The *Christchurch Times* of 5 February 1954 reports a successful emergency attempt to maintain the water supply by way of an 'ice battle'. Working round the clock at the pumping station, men rigged up steam pipes to keep the water intake to the electric pumps free from ice. A water-driven turbine, which pumped the supply through the town's mains, had to be stopped at 4 a.m. when its intake was at risk of ice blocking. Coke braziers, a steam tractor, and a crane with drag attachment, were all pressed into service. The 'ice battle' photograph gives some idea of the ice dredger that moved blocks around 6ft square and 18in thick. The emergency appears to have involved both ground ice and surface ice, during a freeze-up when the temperature range over six days varied between just 17°F and 33°F.

Ground ice is called 'anchor ice' in North America because it can encircle an anchor, causing it to rise to the surface when sufficient ice has been formed. The Edmonton Fire Service in Canada has pronounced that when cold water cools a river bottom to freezing point, the ice will form on rocks or other solid objects, but be released when the sun warms the bottom. Such released anchor ice will rise to the surface, causing log jams and other navigational hazards.

Ice battle of 1954
Men worked all hours at the
waterworks to keep the intake free,
using this 'ice dredger' amongst other
equipment. (Christchurch Times)

Ground ice at Knapp Mill in 1963
Emergency conditions required the
use of steam-raising plant to maintain
the water supply. (Courtesy of the
Bournemouth & West Hampshire
Water Company)

Thus we have these uneven chunks, sometimes separate and sometimes gathered together, relentlessly floating down to the intake grills of the water extraction plant on the river Avon. The Water Company installed steam generation equipment for just such a contingency. The principle was simple: create steam, pipe it to the intake grills and inject the floating ground ice, thus melting it and preventing the town's water supply from being obstructed. There was, however, one very bad spell in January 1963 when ground temperatures were below 20°F for sixteen days. After the ground ice had formed, the ongoing extreme cold made the river surface freeze right across, with just a narrow channel remaining under the surface. This very restricted water fed the town's supply at 33°F. Fortunately, the steam heating system worked successfully at the water intake point. Although this was certainly the worst winter, the experience of ground ice disrupting the water supply system had been a problem in 1938, 1954 and 1961. On the last two occasions, a mobile steam-raising plant, towed to the water works, had been effective, but the company decided that a permanent installation would be wise after 1961. Descriptions from that time refer to pipes and screens being choked and clogged. Interestingly, the 'permanent' plant was removed as part of a refurbishment around 1998, but the intake point has moved upstream. We may yet see some emergency measures if there is a big freeze.

So what are the conditions needed for ground ice to form and thereby explain its presence in the river Avon, as established in January 1939 by the Water Company? The answer is a combination of things. The cold spell must be very severe, resulting in water temperature at freezing point (32°F) and air temperature even lower. In particular, it is known that night temperature must be at or below 20°F for the water to reach 32°F. Beyond this, water turbulence must be enough to ensure that all the water is no more than freezing point. The absence of cloud is also required as it permits outward-bound radiation and penetrating frost. Another factor is that a gravel river bed, like that of the Avon, will promote radiation, unlike a muddy bed. Since it is relatively muddy and thereby hinders radiation, the Stour for example is not at risk of ground ice. Even the absence of trees overhanging the river bank has a part to play – trees can inhibit the radiation needed for ice formation. The Water Company discovered one more condition essential to the formation of ground ice – clear water. This is easily met by the river Avon, which does run clear, being a chalk stream.

The Christchurch Avon has been subject to ground ice historically, because when the weather is cold enough it meets the ice-forming conditions, thereby posing a real threat to the local water supply. Avoiding any risk of interruption during future severe winters will depend upon the ready availability of mobile steam-raising plant.

Figure 1: Bow House, High Street
Originally part of an eighteenth-century brewery, this property (within living memory) once provided access to enormous cellars under the road.

Figure 2: Alpine Accentor mounted in a glass display cabinet
A typical, lifelike and high-quality presentation by Edward Hart. *(Courtesy of Hampshire County Council Museums and Archives, Red House Museum, Christchurch)*

Figure 3: Priory Church
Although the centuries have seen many alterations, today's congregations still use Flambard's nave.

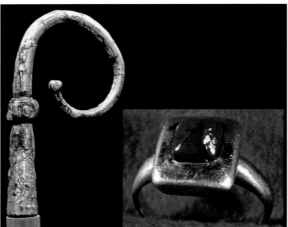

Figure 4: Crozier head and ring of Bishop Flambard
These surviving artefacts belonged to the man who started building the priory in 1094. *(Courtesy of Durham Cathedral)*

Figure 5: Cloister Way window commemorates the Dissolution
Most of the buildings on the south side of the priory and church were demolished, and Prior Draper surrendered the valuables to the king's commissioners.

Figure 6: Extract from the 1539 defence map for King Henry VIII

This extraordinary map shows the extreme vulnerability of the Christchurch area to invasion. *(Courtesy of the British Library Board. All rights reserved. Cotton Augustus 1.i.31,33)*

Figure 8: St George depicted on an arch brace of the nave roof
One of the religious images no longer visible to churchgoers after the nineteenth-century addition of a vaulted ceiling.

Figure 7: Studland Bay Wreck
Scale model by Ron Burt of a contemporary Spanish ship which sank around 1520. *(Courtesy of Poole Museums Service)*

Figure 9: Miraculous Beam that changed the name of the town
Christ placing a miraculously lengthened beam during the twelfth-century building works.

Figure 10: Jim with a supervisory swan. Inset: A thin-head eel image
A wide, flat-bottomed rowing boat is ideal to haul on board a net and place the silver eels in a perforated barrel, later used for storing them in the river. The thin-head, which starts life as an egg and then a tiny plankton-eating fry, drifts 3,000 miles on the Gulf Stream to Europe from the Sargasso Sea.

Figure 11: Roger Castle, Jim Davis, an eel, a storage barrel and a double fyke net
Roger is holding a silver eel with some difficulty in this otherwise tranquil scene.

Figure 12: Salmon weather vane atop the west tower. Inset: The salmon misericord
The golden fish symbol recalls the days when the prior received annual gifts of salmon in return for saying masses for Lords of the Manor. The oak misericord, dated around 1515, provided some support to a monk at the lengthy prayers.

Figure 13: Priory Church's weather vane, until it collapsed in 1969
A lovely traditional copper vane that was rescued by the priory architect in the nick of time – it was nearly disposed of as rubbish.

Figure 14: First known street map of central Christchurch, *c.* 1715
A simple diagrammatic map, which easily allows features like the river Avon, the Mill Stream and the Constable's House to be identified. *(Courtesy of Hampshire Record Office. IM53/1175/1)*

Figure 15: Double salmon catch from 1951
These enormous fish were the same weight at 41¾lbs and taken from the Royalty within a week of each other by the same angler in nearby pools.

Figure 16: Edwards and Hayters Pools as seen from the top weir compound
The double salmon catch from these two pools has ensured their popularity with salmon fishermen. The salmon ladder can be seen in the foreground.

Figure 17: Almonry remains, now bisected by road to Christchurch Quay
A large priory outbuilding, once providing alms to the poor, has been cut through to improve traffic access to the quay.

Figure 18: Stocks and whipping post on the track to Christchurch Castle
To the best of the author's knowledge, these tourist attractions have yet to be used.

Figure 19: 1986 replica contraption at the end of Ducking Stool Lane at Mill Stream
Kelly was happy to pose for this shot in the chair, perhaps because it was not quite extended over the water!

Figure 20: The Run, taken from the Dutch Cottages at Mudeford Quay
The quay will allow the water to flow over it, but the cottages should generally stay protected by the concrete wall.

Figure 21: Mudeford Sandbank is heavily defended to the south-east
Rock groynes and armouring, together with wide beaches, now give the harbour much better protection against a sea breakthrough.

Figure 22: Car 85 is back in town and displayed at the Museum of Electricity
A well-travelled tram like this one is fortunate to survive so long after the Bournemouth system was replaced by trolleybuses in 1936.

Figure 23: Christchurch New Zealand 'wedding tram'
Were we right to abolish our trams in 1936? After all, the New Zealand approach has been a great tourist success.

Figure 24: Sunbeam MF2B being turned in 1966 with Norman castle remains in background
However much we look back with affection, times change and, eventually, the trolleys may be as outdated as the castle. *(Courtesy of Carl Isgar)*

Figure 25: Souvenir tickets for trams and trolleys
A comparison is instructive between the elegant gold-lettered 1936 ticket on the change from trams to trolleys, and the utilitarian 1969 ticket on the sad loss of the trolleys. *(Courtesy of Bournemouth Borough Council)*

No. BCT.......... **235**

Bournemouth Corporation Transport Services.

SOUVENIR TICKET
issued on the last journey
by TRAM
from
BOURNEMOUTH SQUARE
to CHRISTCHURCH
WEDNESDAY,
8th APRIL, 1936

Electric Trams replaced by Electric Trolley Buses on this date.

No **273**
BOURNEMOUTH CORPORATION TRANSPORT

SOUVENIR TICKET
issued on the last journey by
TROLLEYBUS
from Bournemouth Pier to Christchurch
and Mallard Road Depot

SUNDAY, 20th APRIL, 1969

36 YEARS OF TROLLEYBUSES
———
13th MAY, 1933
to
20th APRIL, 1969
———

Issued Subject to the Published
Regulations and Conditions

Figure 26: Turntable today, behind the shops and accessed from Wick Lane
The unique, forlorn and disused heritage feature is now merely part of a yard – no more the excitement of turning double-deckers every few minutes. Yet it remains of national importance.

Figure 27: Trolleybus turning into Church Street
This idealised image from the 1960s contains a telling mixture of modernity and quaint old-world charm. *(Courtesy of David Bowler)*

Figure 28: Law report of a Christchurch poaching case heard by Oliver Cromwell
This is the top left-hand corner of the parchment, dated 7 November 1657 and including 'Oliver' as its very first word.
(Courtesy of the Bournemouth & West Hampshire Water Company)

Figure 29: Hengistbury Head from the Priory Church
The 'ironstone-strengthened headland' of Hengistbury (the low mound on the horizon) has meant two bays instead of just one, so restricting sea erosion and allowing Christchurch to be built in its present location.

Figure 30: Artificial headland of Long Groyne, Hengistbury Head at the eastern extremity of Poole Bay
Poole Bay and Christchurch Bay will be protected from catastrophic future erosion by plans to sustain this 1938 structure.

Figure 31: Ian Jessopp, retired priory architect, marks the position of the presumed tower
The vertical steel rule is at the north side of the old tower – the wall behind Ian simply continued upwards.

Figure 32: Massive Norman arches above the transept of the Priory Church
All four heavily-built arches could have been originally designed to bear the weight of a tower and spire.

Figure 33: Plaque of the Priory Church before the loss of tower and spire
Above the door to Draper's Chapel, named after the last prior before the Dissolution, is this icon from the time of the Catholic Augustinian canons.

TEN

Pipe, Boot and River Keeper

This is quite a detective story. It all began when an angler came across the bowl of a clay pipe. In the middle of the afternoon on 9 January 2008, he had been carefully watching whilst a mole proceeded to dig a hole in the east bank of the river Avon at Trammels, which is a little way downstream from the Great Weir at the top of the fishery. The mound gradually grew until, unexpectedly, a clay pipe bowl popped out at the summit! Of interest were the initials carved upon it: RAOB, standing for the Royal Antediluvian Order of Buffaloes. This is a charitable organisation that operates in the form of a brotherhood with a network of lodges. Details are readily available to anyone interested and can be found by using the initials RAOB for an internet search.

The Royalty Fishery Museum duly looked into the provenance of the find – apparently, it was from the period 1870 to 1925. It was a common custom for smokers of these white clay pipes to treat them as expendable. They would break the bowl off from the stem and discard them after use. Quite apart from this custom, such a breakage was also part of a particular ritual of the brotherhood of the RAOB. Thus far, it is reasonable to conclude that a member of the local lodge had been smoking one of the brotherhood's specially-made and initialled clay pipes on the river bank.

I am indebted to officers of the RAOB and also to West Country pipe expert Heather Coleman for further information. It appears that clay pipes became popular from the early 1800s and were often smoked by women. When used in one of the RAOB ceremonies, a pipe might be broken over the head of the initiate, wrapped in a tobacco leaf and then kept. At least twenty-five pipe designs have been identified, including two particular versions mentioned later – the Cutty having a thick stem and length of some 4.5in and the Straw having a thinner stem, a length of 7in and a more elegant bowl.

Quite separately from the above, on 29 February 2008, angler Rob Stack was coarse fishing at Dick's Hole, which is a swim located on the west bank between the Royalty Fishery building and the railway line bridge just to the north. It was a very good day because he caught a barbel weighing 15lbs 4oz! It seems, however, that the very next cast brought out something entirely different – an old boot. He took his find to Curator Tony Timms, who is well known for wanting any artefacts that might add to the collection. The first job was to remove the mud, weed and smell – after all, it had lain undisturbed for about 100 years. The boot was found to be a 'wading boot' with a studded sole. Although it is so termed, such a boot does not extend much above the ankle

Clay pipe bowl unearthed by a mole on the river bank
The RAOB pipe could have belonged to Keeper Preston.

any more than does its modern equivalent. The angler is kept dry by having a waterproof connection between waders and a kind of proofed socks, currently fashioned from Neoprene. Today's boots are essentially the same as the artefact found and have the same studs to help clamber over a river bank.

Research was duly carried out by a specialist in antique tackle and clothing, resulting in an estimated manufacturing date of around 1900. At this stage, the realisation set in that around the time the pipe had been discarded, the same had happened to this good quality boot. Yet there was still no good reason to make any connection.

A third distinct event brought things together. As part of the ongoing research into the heritage of the Royalty, all the river keepers, or water bailiffs, were being identified. In doing so, on 19 June 2008, a photograph was obtained of a certain Henry Joseph Preston, dated to approximately 1900. He was the keeper from 1873 to 1913. His job at the time was similar to the work still done by the current keeper, involving river maintenance, cutting weeds to improve flow, shoring up banks, repairing habitats to help ducks, bats etc. Clearly, in the photograph, he is dressed for carrying out such duties in rainy weather. However, of particular interest is the fact that he is smoking a RAOB pipe and wearing a boot – at first glance identical to both of the items found at the river.

A close look at the picture of Preston reveals that he was probably smoking a Cutty pipe, whilst the find is likely to be a Straw. Nonetheless, it was normal at the time for a smoker to have a number of pipes. Indeed, another picture of this keeper shows him smoking a third type of pipe, known as a Thorn and closely matched to the Thorn number 130 made by John Pollock & Co. of Manchester. Wilsons of Sharrow in Sheffield, who took over from Pollocks in 1990, advise that although this clay pipe is definitely a Thorn from Pollocks, it is unknown now whether the mould still exists for it. Incidentally, these Thorn pipes had various designs on them, including one which had a witch on a broomstick on the base with thorns on the bowl. It cannot be conclusively proved on this evidence alone that the pipe and boot found at the river Avon were indeed once the possessions of this keeper. As for Preston's very probable membership of a local lodge, RAOB records are not sufficient to confirm this. Yet it is certainly a possibility – the dates and the photographs are persuasive.

There are three unexpected footnotes. Firstly, it transpires that Henry Joseph Preston was the great grandfather of the 2010 editor of the journal of Christchurch Local History Society, Mike Andrews. Secondly, a photograph exists, yet again from around 1900, showing

Boot hooked out from the river Avon in 2008 Made around 1900, this boot is virtually identical to one worn by Keeper Preston in a photograph from that era.

Keeper Henry Joseph Preston, *c.* 1900
Water bailiff of the Royalty Fishery from 1873 to 1913. (*Courtesy of Michael Andrews*)

that cabinet maker Lewis Preston (another member of the large local Preston family) did at one time occupy a building, which still stands next to Waterloo Bridge in Bridge Street. The Preston name and business title was painted on the house's flank wall facing the river. Although that bridge was built in 1816 and named after the Battle of Waterloo, it replaced a timber one named after the family living next to it, the Richmans. Even earlier, the timber bridge had been known after another family living next to it – the Prestons. The third item concerns what might be deemed a health and safety risk these days – Preston was in the habit of clearing the soot from his chimney on an annual basis by firing a double-barrelled shotgun up it! No doubt the neighbours became acclimatised over time.

ELEVEN

Why is the Town Called 'Christchurch' Today?

t is generally believed that the church, and therefore the town, was founded in the seventh century as a result of the pope's plan to reintroduce Christianity to the country, through the work of St Birinus. According to the Anglo-Saxon Chronicles, in AD 635, the year following his arrival, he both baptised the King of Wessex and was also instrumental in founding a church or priory in what is now Christchurch. The town of Thuinam (to use an early Saxon name) was built or subsequently developed by the Saxons as a fortified settlement on land just north of the meeting of the river Avon and the river Stour. This was particularly wise, allowing the founding church to be erected on a sound gravel foundation, whilst the location was also a very good military choice against the marauding Danes. It must have provided a deterrent to such raiders planning to invade by using the rivers.

By the time of the Burghal Hidage, around the start of the tenth century, the name had become Twynam, alternatively spelt Tweoxneam. The town name related to its position between the waters or, alternatively put, 'where two rivers meet'. If St Birinus was indeed responsible for the foundation of a Saxon priory, either personally or through priests sent out by him, there was no hint of the present name of Christchurch in those early days.

Within a short time of winning the Battle of Hastings in 1066, William the Conqueror placed French lords throughout the country. In the same fashion as the castle-building programme, it was a way of showing the Saxons who was boss. The de Redvers family was granted Christchurch as confirmed by charter, amongst many other estates. Although the available eighteenth-century copy of the charter is not dated, the original is known to be from the twelfth century. Strangely, the Latin document includes three words for the town: Twinham, Cristescherche, and Cristesch. In addition, the Christchurch Priory Cartulary translation refers to two deeds from around the middle of the same century, giving differing names. Deed 206 refers to *Twynhm et Canonicus* (meaning Twynham and its canons) and Deed 214 refers to *Prioris de Cristeschurche* (meaning the Priory of Christchurch).

Reports of the decisions of the king's justices in the thirteenth century provide some more names: Cristewewerth, Cristchierche and Cristeschyrch. Bishop Sandale's Register of 1319 refers to the Church of Christ of Twynham. However, there is an ordination document of 18 December 1305 referring to *Willelmus de Christi ecclesia*, i.e. William of Christchurch. Cartulary Deed 216, believed to date from 1351, has another variation: Cristeschurchia.

Spelling was not so consistent many years ago as it is today and various errors were made by Domesday Book scribes, not to mention Shakespeare, who is reputed to have written his own name with different spellings.

The Miraculous Beam of the twelfth century was the reason for the basic change of name from Twynham to Christchurch. Many will simply dismiss the whole business as a far-fetched legend, whilst others might try to imagine how the story might be adjusted to make it more credible, and stoutly maintain that there is no smoke without fire. After all, it cannot be disputed that the name of the church underwent a change, one that was faithfully copied by the name of the town. Flambard began building the new Norman church in 1094, but left to be Bishop to Durham just five years later. According to the website of Christchurch Priory, work was continued in his absence by the Dean of Thuinam Priory. Hence, at 1100, we may say that the building work was at an early stage and there was only one name for both church and town – the one based on the location between two rivers, the Avon and Stour.

The evidence is that, during roughly the next century, the name (with all its variants) of both town and priory did indeed change from Twynham to Christchurch whilst the new Norman church was being built. It is estimated that by AD 1150 the works had reached triforium level, i.e. the gallery of arches above the side-aisle vaulting in the nave. That would leave just one more storey before constructing the roof. It is probable that work began on roof timbers during that century, which is completely consistent with both the story of the Miraculous Beam and the timing of the name change. The builders were said to have become aware of a new carpenter, who did not eat with the others or receive any pay. One day, there was great embarrassment because a structural timber was found to be cut too short and of no use for its planned position within the roof. If true, this would have been a big issue due to the amount of time, cost and effort involved in making such a big component with the very basic tools then available. However, on arriving at work the next day, they found that not only had it been miraculously lengthened but it had been hauled into place. Moreover, no more was the mysterious carpenter seen on site.

The photograph in Fig. 9 is of a stained-glass window from the Cloister Way, one of forty-nine depicting scenes from the history of the church. It is an artist's impression of Christ lifting the beam during the hours of darkness. The legend must have had a tremendous force at the time for the people to change the name of their town in recognition – who else but Christ could have been the carpenter, and was this not truly Christ's Church?

Having dwelt on the town's name at some length, it may be appropriate to express a final thought concerning the name of the church. Surprisingly, the current common usage of Christchurch Priory is not strictly correct – it should really be known as the Church of the Holy Trinity, Christchurch. Indeed, the Domesday Book of 1086 mentions the dedication of the Priory Church to the Holy Trinity, implying continuity of such dedication from Saxon times to the present day. The high altar is specifically dedicated to Christ the Saviour.

In the twelfth century, the evolution of the town's name thus went from Twynham to the Christchurch of today – it was named initially after its location between the two rivers and, following the story of the Miraculous Beam, after 'Christ's Church'.

TWELVE

Invasion Scare of 1539

Christchurch had its part to play in what was a year of great importance for King Henry VIII. His concerns included ensuring the royal succession, dissolving the monasteries and, not least, the very real risk of invasion. The complete break with the Roman Catholic Church had taken place with his excommunication by the pope in 1538, whilst the balance of power had greatly shifted due to a peace treaty the same year between Francis I of France and Charles V of Spain. As those countries, the main Catholic powers of Europe, were no longer at war, he knew that one or both of them would begin to see England as the natural enemy. The Emperor of Spain was indeed still offended by Henry's annulment in 1533 of his marriage to the emperor's aunt, Catherine of Aragon.

It was certainly a deteriorating political climate with the probability of invasion – Henry's response was to plan to stop any invasion fleet before it was able to land an army. There must have been great nervousness in the countryside – at the same time that the king was dissolving the monasteries and removing their medical, food and accommodation assistance to the poor, an invasion was expected. On the orders of Thomas Cromwell, an extraordinary south-coast mapping operation was carried out in great haste for the king. Once the various locally-produced maps and sketches had been sent to London and edited in Greenwich, they were compiled and displayed by the king at his enormous Whitehall Palace. Although the final maps were pictorial, showing ships and fortifications in some detail, they were also usefully factual, with sea and coast measurements. A key idea was to identify landing points with the mind of an invasion commander. Having highlighted such beaches by exaggerating their size, sites for possible forts were added in appropriate locations. Although the work is diagrammatic and inaccurate, it still shows the high local level of shoreline vulnerability and the urgent need for defence measures.

The king duly began building forts and castles to protect all the major ports and harbours along the threatened coastline. Whilst the able-bodied were assembled and the fleet made ready, weapons and mercenary fighters were obtained from abroad. Warning beacons were put in working order and manned. The original mapping, held now by the British Library, is in various sections – the portion covering part of Dorset and Hampshire has a north/south length of 1ft 9in and a width of 4ft 11in. If that seems large, the section from Land's End to Exeter is nearly 10ft wide! As such, they were never meant to be taken on board ship – rather they were an aid to national defence policy in London. The map was intentionally orientated in the opposite direction from normal. With the north point at the bottom, you are looking defensively to the south and out to sea.

Christchurch is a named town (spelt Crechurche) in the 1539 Dorset and Hampshire defence map – extract in Fig. 6. The picture of the church building was purposely portrayed as a small fraction of the size of the nearby beacon structure at Hengistbury Head, so drawing attention to the defence needs. The headland, which at the time was known as Hednes Buria or Hensbury Ende, then lay within the estate of the canons of Christchurch. In the same fashion as the invasion scare of the Second World War, no one would have worried about getting owners' consent for military installations such as beacons or forts. After all, if the country was under threat, it made no sense to suffer delays in arranging the defences. The important thing was to have an effective early-warning system in place and all the beacons would have been prepared without let or hindrance.

The essence of the document was therefore to advise on possible invasion points and what defences were needed. Colour was used to provide a violent depiction of the scene, with galleons sailing, beacons blazing and guns guarding key areas. A beacon comprised a strong vertical pole or poles with a fire basket on top, side struts to aid stability and a ladder giving access to light it and maintain the flames; a hazardous task indeed. Since they are shown in some profusion locally, the threat of invasion here was seen as very real. Certainly, Poole and Christchurch bays were then, and remain now, ideal for ships to make landings.

The map's annotation reads in translation from the old English: 'From Christchurch to Bournemouth is seven miles and fair landings within a quarter of a mile of the land and draws four fathoms of water.' From a discussion with the National Maritime Museum, it appears that this has two possible meanings. It could be saying that within a quarter of a mile of the coast, ships could find good ground for anchoring. Alternatively, it might just mean that ships could approach within a quarter of a mile of the shoreline, without running aground, and be close enough to land parties in boats or barges. Either way, the king was being told that these places were attractively located in the eyes of an invasion force. The 'four fathoms' relates well to the depths shown on the current Admiralty Chart, No. 2615, if due allowance is made for coastal erosion since the sixteenth century. Indeed, the annotation even ties in with the council's tourism claim of seven miles of beaches! The sense of these remarks, about the viability of invasion, was repeated in a 1574 assessment. At that time, the country's fear of the Spanish proved well-founded when the Armada set out in 1588. To quote that report – 'We find at Bourne Mouth, within the west bay at Christchurch, a place very easy for the enemy to land, being void of all inhabiting.'

According to the Anthony Roll of 1546, the king had fifty-eight ships as there described, including the famous *Mary Rose*, although this had sunk by that date. Whilst this resource is of some assistance, it is less than definitive in identifying those depicted on the map by the Greenwich draughtsman. Moreover, it would be beyond the scope of this book to do more than make a brief comment. The galleon nearest to Christchurch, flying the flag of St George, is likely to be over 200 tons but is one of the smaller ships in the navy, although there is provision for six guns in the stern. The larger fighting ships would have had an additional mast and two fighting tops on the main mast. The map also includes a galley with its forward, stepped main mast and no sign of armament – that is likely to be a trading vessel only. Other than that, there appears to be a sprit-rigged local working boat, a merchant vessel and a fishing boat. A subsidiary intention of the draughtsman seems to have been to demonstrate England's south coast as defended, yet engaged in trade and fishing – an altogether attractive pictorial scene.

It is strange to reflect that only about twenty years before this superbly effective map was created, a Spanish galleon had come to grief in Studland Bay. That wreck, now recognised as one of the most important in the country, has been dated to about 1520, when relations with Spain were so much better. Fig. 7 shows a model reconstruction of the Studland Bay wreck. It was 75ft long, 15ft wide and about 175 tons. Despite the scattered nature of the seabed wreckage, there have been 750 finds. As a merchantman, it was an ocean-going, cargo-carrying, gun-defended ship that had foundered near Poole, most probably due either to bad weather or to human error.

So what did the map mean for Christchurch? Perhaps the first thing to note is the placing of the beacons. The most effective local beacon is the one shown at Hengistbury Head, due to its 360° view from the top and its proximity to the town. Here was an ideal position from which to summon local defenders. Other things can be gleaned from this astonishing map. For example, by the Bourne Stream is noted 'Bowurnemothe wer ys feyer landing' and a beacon is placed (bottom edge of the extract) on what is now the town's East Cliff. At the top left are the words 'of Wight' and below are the words 'Chulke Roke', which must be the chalk rock of the Needles. Some place names (off-map) are simple to recognise, such as 'Pooll', 'Northe havyn poynt', 'Corffe castell' and 'Wymbourne'. Others are perhaps less obvious, e.g. 'Brumkesey yle' (Brownsea Island). Starting from the top of the extract, other places are: 'Dorlande' (Durlston), 'Peverell poynt wer ys feyer landyng', 'Swandewyche' (Swanage), 'Hanfaste point', 'Studlande baye' and 'Studlande'.

Defence at this part of the coast included circular blockhouses, i.e. the simple type of fort referred to earlier. One was shown by the Bourne Stream, a likely landing place for an invading force, with its gradual slope inland. Poole is given two gun emplacements, each with two-wheeled guns. Although the landing grounds near Christchurch were clearly to be defended with the aid of a beacon warning, this seems to have been a policy to defend the nation rather than the town itself. No fort was ever planned or built here. Henry's new forts were generally placed to confer a benefit on a major habitation or to protect a military town like Portsmouth, which was therefore extremely well-defended. The line had to be drawn somewhere in such matters, and one might think that Christchurch was relatively expendable. Indeed, Prior Draper described it to the king in most unflattering terms in his efforts to keep the Priory Church for the townspeople, rather than see it demolished as part of the Dissolution. (*See* pages 25, 26.)

As a small, poor place, why incur the cost of a fort? An added force to this expendability argument might be that it did already have its own inland castle. Bearing in mind that the Parliamentarians captured it in 1644, and ordered its destruction in 1652, it might have been regarded as a good defence structure in Henry's time. Then again, it was described in 1540 as being 'far gone in decay', an impression probably not mitigated by its reported use at the time as a pig enclosure. One is forced to the conclusion that the town did not matter enough to justify the expense of a shoreline fort, but was wanted to supply defenders when summoned by beacon.

Hence, Christchurch played its part in combating the invasion scare in two main ways. Firstly, the prior surrendered a lot of property and goods to the king's commissioners, so contributing to defence funds. Secondly, the beacon, overlooking the town, would have drawn many defenders to a battle on or near a local beach, had it been needed and lit. Yet Christchurch was probably not deemed important enough to defend. Be that as it may, at a national level, the threat was very real and the defences which followed the mapping were an effective deterrent. The king had succeeded in his primary duty of preserving the whole country from attack.

THIRTEEN

Some Ancient Decisions of Christchurch Corporation

I n times gone by, Christchurch had to consider and decide very different issues from those arising today. Here are some examples, mainly from the minutes of the mayor and burgesses.

19 December 1586: Agreement by James Coper to take Christian Carpenter a child to foster, bring up and keep for 8 years, receiving 6s 8d a year from the parish. A like agreement by Thomas Galliet to take Elyn Carpenter a child to foster for 3 years to be paid 6d a week for the first year, 4d a week for the second, and 2d a week for the third year by the parish.

1616: The Mace was new made at a cost of £4 15s 6d.

13 February 1643: No man was to be elected Burgess for Parliament unless he be first sworn a Burgess of the Borough according to ancient custom.

27 June 1665: Constant watch and ward was ordered day and night for the better preservation of the Town against plague and pestilence. No man coming from London was to be admitted to Town for 20 days.

7 January 1668: It was agreed that gowns shall be worn by the Burgesses on penalty of being incapacitated from becoming Mayor – to revive the ancient custom before the late unhappy wars.

22 September 1680: The Mayor and Burgesses finding how obnoxious and prejudicial it is to the well governing of the Borough the excess of beer given to the Commonalty upon the Election Day by reason whereof many of them are drunk and very abusive. It was ordered that the Mayor shall entertain his Brethren at his own cost chargeable on his account and not bestow above 20 shillings upon the Commonalty upon Election Day upon penalty of £5.

24 January 1695: Acknowledgement by James Kitch of Preston, parish of Christchurch, yeoman, that he unlawfully ploughed up a common called Woore and so deprived the inhabitants of the Borough of Christchurch of their common of herbage from Lammas to Candlemas (2 February). Kitch pays 12 shillings to the inhabitants as compensation and promises not to plough up the land between Lammas and Candlemas without the consent of the inhabitants. Memorandum dated November 1695 that the fine of 12 shillings paid by Kitch was augmented to 14 shillings and used to buy bread for the poor. [Lammas was a former English festival held on 1 August in which bread made from the first harvest of corn was blessed. Herbage was the right to pasture one's cattle.]

6 September 1718: It was ordered that no Mayor shall swear anyone to be a Burgess without the consent of the major part of the 'In-Burgesses' then residing in the Borough – under a penalty of £100.

26 October 1832: The thanks of the Burgesses were given to John Spicer for his temperate and judicious conduct as Mayor during a period of great popular excitement and unprovoked aggression arising from the protracted discussion and at the subsequent enactment of the Reform Bill.

FOURTEEN

D-Day from Hengistbury Head

A longstanding member of Christchurch Local History Society, Mrs Barbara Jones won a society competition with this short entry entitled 'My D-Day Memories' and has kindly agreed for it to be reproduced here, bearing in mind that Hengistbury Head used to be part of Christchurch:

My father Reginald R. Hayball, having served in the First Great War, was too old to be a fighting soldier again – so he became a member of the Christchurch Home Guard.

I remember him going off to be on night duty in various strategic parts of the town, like the Water Works, Railway Bridge or parts of the harbour. At weekends they went up to the old rifle range at the bottom of St Catherine's Hill to practice their shooting skills. For a while that spring, we had artillery guns manned by Canadians practising every day firing out to sea at the bottom of our garden which ended at that time in Wickfield Avenue. The noise was tremendous and all the houses around suffered cracked ceilings as a result! This was never really cured until the advent of 'Artex'. One summer evening my father went off to do a Home Guard duty over the other side of the River Stour to Hengistbury Head. This turned out to be different to all the other previous duties.

On his return he was so excited and amazed at what he had seen. It appeared they had been on top of the Head. He told us that you could hardly see the sea, for as far as the eye could see there were boats – anchored all the way up the coast to Hurst Castle and beyond, the Solent was choc-a-block with boats of all types.

My sister Margery and I went off to bed that night of the 5th June 1944 not thinking very much about it, but on getting up the next morning the radio was switched on to hear the latest news of how the war was progressing. The newsreader announced that the Allied Forces had landed in Europe. D-Day had dawned – we realised the significance of what my father had seen the night before.

FIFTEEN

Can the Priory Church Endure?

The town's fine and ancient church appears today to be in good fettle, with large congregations and many religious and social functions supplying funds, quite apart from legacies and suchlike. Does this mean that all threats to the existence of this Grade I listed building have disappeared? It has required, perhaps, a charmed life to survive the unsteady founder Flambard, the need for relocation from its designated building site of St Catherine's Hill to where it now stands, and the Dissolution plans of Henry VIII. Sadly, there is a fourth threat to be overcome – the sheer costs of conservation and maintenance.

It is common enough for churches to raise funds for essential roof maintenance. However, the Priory Church has had a lot of different expenses to meet over the years. For instance, the top of the nave used to extend all the way up to the roof timbers, i.e. without the ornamental vaulting now forming a ceiling below them. When that vaulting was installed in 1819 (the date being recorded on one of the nave bosses), the trusses with their decorative images were lost to view. Fig. 8 shows St George, the Patron Saint of England, getting ready to slay the dragon, which is shown on a rafter of the opposite roof slope. Whilst it is not believed that he ever came to this country, the legend of this Roman Christian soldier has been a powerful force for good in that the dragon represents our darker side that has to be slain on a regular basis. No doubt there was some concern about losing sight of these images at the time of the new ceiling.

If this task was a cosmetic upgrade, rather than an essential repair, that probably made it the exception to the rule. For instance, the strengthening of the main roof, overseen in the nineteenth century by Benjamin Ferrey, was needed for reasons of structural integrity. An even more obvious case concerns building works consequential to the believed collapse of the church's central tower in the early part of the fifteenth century. However, the west tower was built around 1470 and houses the bells that ring out over the town today, including two fine ones from the fourteenth century. It was almost certainly designed as a replacement of that central tower, at a time of the priory's considerable wealth.

A very brief summary of recent building works is set out below:

    1928 Lead roofing, buttress and window repairs.
    1930s Bell, transept, roof and gargoyle repairs.
    1950s Repairs to lead roofing, stonework and Lady Chapel screen.
    1970s Stonework and window repairs and major work on bells.
    1981 North Porch roof and works to quire.
    1990s Flying buttresses work and organ restoration.

From this point onwards, the rolling conservation programme using outside contractors was begun, with a view to putting the priory into good condition for at least the next 100 years.

2000 Phase I: Conservation of south and west faces of the tower, including the clock face and repairs to the west window at a cost of £200,000.

2002 Phase II: The North Elevation Project from the north side of the tower to the west side of the north transept at a cost of £525,000.

2003 Phase III: The north transept – a very testing section as it is architecturally one of the great features of the Priory Church. While carrying out this work, a section of wall at a high level was found to be at risk of collapse. Work had to stop and English Heritage had to be consulted about the way forward. After difficult technical negotiations, it was eventually agreed that, instead of 350 stainless steel bolts being used to tie the masonry in place, it would be better to dismantle the wall and rebuild it stone by stone as it was, but with fresh mortar and hidden stainless steel ties to the inner wall. The cost was £285,000.

2010 Phase IV: The north quire from the north transept to the Lady Chapel. This phase is estimated at £418,000 and in the present climate it has become much more difficult to raise the funds and set against increasing costs. Although English Heritage has to be consulted over any proposed work, so far the Priory Church has received no funding from them for any of the projects listed here.

The conservation of the exterior will take another five phases and will probably require upward of £2 million to complete – then there is the interior!

Although it may not be very obvious, the great majority of building jobs are indeed essential to the fabric and have to be done in order to keep the church waterproof and secure. The Repairs Committee, currently (2010) chaired by Barry Beesley, has the philosophy of keeping a living church rather than a museum. Worn historic stonework is replaced only when essential, using matching material and preserving the outlines of changes that have taken place over the centuries. Stone cleaning is needed not just to reinstate the attraction of an old wall, but to be able to identify necessary work. As in Phase III, there is sometimes a temporary disagreement with English Heritage, who are closely involved due to the listing of the building and its classification as an ancient monument.

The Phase IV works projected for the north quire give an idea of the difficulties which can arise. During preliminary surveys, it was found that two buttresses at ground level were leaning outwards. When holes were dug to investigate the adequacy of foundations, it was discovered that there were none! Deep below one of them, a sarcophagus, possibly Saxon, was revealed. So, although they needed support, the work would have to be done by the least obtrusive method. As the buttresses were effectively tied to the wall, they were exerting an undesirable outward pull, rather than pushing inward to prevent the wall leaning away from the building. It is unsurprising, therefore, that the wall is bowed outwards. The solution was to pile onto the good gravel beneath each side of the buttresses and support their undersides with reinforced concrete beams, cast *in situ*. Wall settlement cannot be reversed but at least further movement can be arrested. Interestingly, the Church discovered the same problem with a flying buttress

Buttress without foundations at Priory Church
Instead of supporting the wall this buttress has been exerting an undesirable outward pull. *(Courtesy of Barry Beesley)*

on the north wall in the nineteenth century and removed it. That usefully got rid of the 'pull factor', but the buttress was never renewed. At present, a costly task such as replacement is assessed in exactly the same way as it was then, i.e. as more desirable than essential.

In addition to the carefully planned programme of works, there are always other expenses to be met. For instance, with the increasing risk of lead being stolen from church roofs, security has had to be enhanced by electronic means and the lead itself 'marked' to allow its future identification as coming from the Priory Church, even after it has been melted down several times. Another example is a plaster fall at the Lady Chapel, which, on investigation, revealed a need to replace a disintegrating stone mullion and badly rusted iron bars, i.e. urgent work within Phase V, ahead of the laid-down timescale. Some will see this whole issue of raising the required money as a matter of prayer and faith, others as a question of arranging the right cash flow, and others as a bit of both. Ways to increase income over the long term are constantly under consideration.

Let us hope that essential costs never outrun available income, thereby allowing this magnificent centrepiece of the town's life to survive even when the economic climate is harsh.

SIXTEEN

Humour and Hardship at the Petty Sessions

Christchurch Town Hall – 1 August 1849 (Courtesy of the Christchurch Local History Society)

Elizabeth Sawday and Joseph Sawday appeared before Henry Hopkins and William Popham at the Town Hall. The sentence of the first defendant on a charge of vagrancy was a month's hard labour. The second was also convicted, this time of assault, and suffered a penalty of £2 and costs of 7s to be paid forthwith, or, failing this, to be committed for two months. In this one example (amongst many similar cases) of the administration of justice, the law was indeed fast and simple, with a common expectation of the punishment fitting the crime. That said, the opinion of suitable punishment was much harsher in those days than within our current judicial system. The hearing and sentencing took place the day after the law was broken. The following report, which speaks for itself, is verbatim from the record:

Charles Allen sw:
Last evening about a ½ past 5 o clock I came from my work to Lodge's house where I lodge. I saw Elizabeth Sawday throwing stones at Lodge and Joseph Sawday was standing before Mr. Lodge with a stick in his hand as if he intended to strike him. They were in the Road near the House. I went to them. I am lame I can't walk without a stick. I said to the woman who had stones in her hands 'Put down the stones or I'll strike them out of your hand'. She directly flung a stone at me. I had out my hand and caught the stone with my hand and in so doing knocked my hat off. I then struck her hands to knock a stone out of it – the stone fell – Sawday turned round and struck me when my hat was off with the stick I now produce. I turned and struck him across the arm with my stick. The blow he struck me cut my head open.

X – I didn't strike your arm first. I did not strike the woman over the back.

Harriet Lodge sw:
Elizabeth Sawday came yesterday afternoon to my House and begged for something to eat. I told her that I had nothing to give her. She followed me into the House and said she would not leave till I had given her something. I said I had nothing to give her. She said she would have some victuals. She abused me. She went out and I followed her to the door. My husband came up – in a cart. She took stones and went to him in a threatening manner. He shook the whip at her. I don't know whether he struck her – Joseph then came up with the stick produced. Allen came by and I begged him to assist my Husband. He went to the woman who had a stone in her hand and attempted to strike it down. She attempted to throw it at him. The man then turned round and struck him on the head with his stick. I both saw and heard the blow. I went and led Allen away. I expected him to fall he bled so much. I sent for the Police. I did not see Allen strike the woman.

James Lodge sw:

I went to my House in Christchurch yesterday in my cart. Elizabeth Sawday was giving abuse to my wife and gathering stones. My wife was in the porch and the woman was in the Road 3 or 4 yards distant. 'Halloa' I said 'What's the row here, you had better be off.' She took up some stones and threw them at me before I could get out of the cart. She followed me to the door with stones – I shoved back and she scratched my face – I had a small whip handle about the size of my finger with which I struck her two or three times. Joseph Sawday came and made a blow at me with his stick but missed me. I looked round just after and saw Allen bleeding but I didn't know how he came to be so. I saw the woman throw a stone at him.

X – I did not throw out any beer from my cart as soon as I came up. I took him custody for the Police after he assaulted Allen.

Joseph Sawday:

I was never put to gaol in my life nor in prison. He struck me first.

Christchurch Town Hall – 11 August 1856

On a rather different note, Farr, Popham, Castleman and Dean had to deliberate about a 'chicken situation' as fully reported in the *Christchurch Times*. The real question here is, were those present in court able to keep straight faces?

John Hargrave, painter, was brought up in custody of the police, charged with stealing two Chicken the property of Mr. W. Tizard, Iford. Mr. Tizard said he missed the chicken on 28th July just after the prisoner had been in his alehouse, and did not see them again until a few days ago, when they were at the half-way house in Barrack Road. Another witness said he was in the Alehouse, when prisoner endeavoured to catch the chicken which was running about the house but failed, because he was drunk, and that he said he would have them before he went. Albert Tizard, prosecutor's son met prisoner between his father's house and the barracks, with something in his hand which made a noise like a chick. George Troke was called to prove he saw *a* chicken at the half-way house, but did not know to whom it belonged, and, never saw prisoner in his life! Mr. Eldridge, the tenant of the half-way house, said the prisoner lodged with him, and brought two chicken home that day fortnight, saying a man gave him three but he had lost one. Ives P.C. produced chicken found at the lodgings, which Tizard identified. The prisoner elected to be tried under the new Summary Act, and said the Chicken were given to him by a man, who asked him first to buy them. The Bench considered the case proved, and sentenced the prisoner to 21 days imprisonment with hard labour.

The *Christchurch Times* of 1 August 1857 used the heading 'Not Cooled Down' to report a vexatious court case brought by Mrs Mary Butler against Sarah Edwards for assault and beating. The report indicates that the court felt it was at risk of being used in an ongoing bad neighbour squabble – it was simply not known who was the most at fault.

It appeared that both parties lived at Bargates not far from each other. Mrs. Butler stated that Sarah Edwards met her on Thursday night the 25th June, and without any preliminary, struck her in the face several blows with her fist, at the same time expressing in words strong and pungent, her intense satisfaction now she had got her. In cross-examination, she became a little warm and excited; acknowledged that there had been squabbles before; had a son that she thought *rather* too intimate with the defendant, and that it was a connection likely to lower the respectability of the family, confessed she, as a mother should, had sometimes felt angry; didn't come there to be insulted; had a good character; would not answer any more questions. She brought a witness who said that she on the night in question heard a squabble in the road, and heard Edwards inform Mrs. Butler that her intention was to change her organs of vision by striking both eyes into one. It was urged on behalf of the defendant that this was a series of Bargates squabbles; that the complainant more frequently began it than the defendant, imagining she had good reason to be angry; that the summons was not taken out until nearly a month after the alleged assault, showing that no real injury had been inflicted, but that something must have since happened which had caused the complaint to be made either out of revenge, or other feeling and not from a desire for honest justice. The Bench appeared to take a similar view of the case, and dismissed the charge.

SEVENTEEN

Second Miraculous Beam

*I*t has to be admitted that the astounding story of the Second Miraculous Beam may not be as powerful as the story of the first beam told in Chapter Eleven. Nonetheless, it happened within very recent living memory, is verified rather than legendary and should not be overlooked. The miraculous aspect refers to the lucky escape of people in the church nave, who were sheltering from an extreme storm after a morning service. As a result of the beam, no one was crushed by a falling stone weighing 380 kg or 7.48 cwt. It also serves as a salutary reminder that a church is not merely a building – it really comprises the people who go there.

A structure like this has endless maintenance needs. Here, the instability of some high-level stonework was brought to light in a dramatic fashion in Force 12 winds. In the winter of 1989/1990, during a hurricane-force storm, a pinnacle stone on the west tower was dislodged and came crashing down with a huge bang through the northern roof slope of the nave. Being the north-east pinnacle, and the wind direction being from the prevailing south-west, the stone naturally fell a vertical distance of some 40-50ft, through the roof covering and onto the second main roof truss from the west tower. It is a triangular section truss design, installed around 1840 by the famous Victorian church architect Benjamin Ferrey in order to strengthen the existing medieval roof. The stone came to rest on the lowest horizontal part of the truss and fell no further. Ian Jessopp, the priory architect and Len Newman, the priory stonemason were present at the time and immediately investigated what repairs might be necessary.

The photograph from early 1990, of the stone, the truss and the hole in the roof, shows that one rafter has clearly been severed; the outline of the pinnacle can just be made out. It is also possible to see a previous roof line through the hole. The current church roof is roughly the third one to be built and the line proves that a previous roof was somewhat higher. Fig. 29 shows the nature of these heavy stone pinnacles in full sunlight.

Hole in the nave roof of Priory Church caused by the pinnacle from the west tower
Severe damage from the 1990 storm which dislodged this heavy stone missile. *(Courtesy of Barry Beesley)*

A commemorative plaque explains that the fallen pinnacle overhung the Second Miraculous Beam by about 14in in the position of a large nail. To see the plaque requires walking along scaffold planks, having simple scaffold poles as rails, and taking some care to avoid stepping off to one side onto wire mesh and the lath and plaster of the nave ceiling below.

The weakest point of such a stone feature is at its base. If, as apparently happened here, there are extreme winds with ferocious eddies causing 'side loading', then the break point will probably be where the pinnacle meets the main structure beneath. In the great storm of 1987, the same sort of winds and eddies had been enough to remove heavy stone tiles from the nave roof. Having left the top of the tower, the pinnacle appears to have fallen like a bomb, i.e. without turning over in flight. Those below heard a loud crash from above their heads. Part of the luck, or the miracle, is that it did not drop straight through the lath and plaster ceiling. If you look up, there are two small sections of ceiling damage to be seen from ground level, where fragments did penetrate but caused no injury to those below. The repair was carried out with the aid of some replacement stonework and, crucially, using stainless steel pins as reinforcement. Last but not least of the story's charm is the sheer luck that both architect and stonemason were there at the time in order to investigate and reassure.

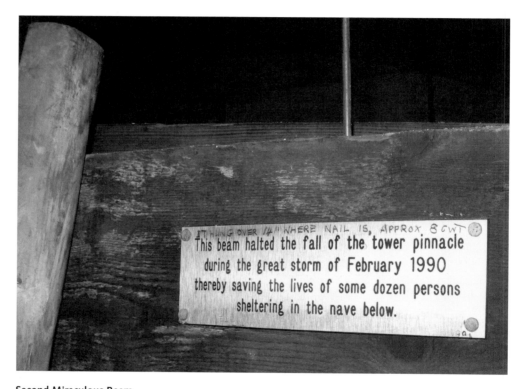

Second Miraculous Beam
The horizontal member of the roof truss that saved the people below from being hit.

EIGHTEEN

Eels of Christchurch

*L*et us begin this somewhat unusual chapter with the incredibly long journey, undertaken as a matter of course by millions of eels. All these extraordinary creatures in the Avon and Stour have travelled about 3,000 miles to get here. Not content with that, many of our rivers' mature eels, that are ready to reproduce, will swim the same distance back to their place of origin! They are indeed unique fish, which are perhaps disliked more than liked. However, even those who say they could never eat the flesh of snake-like animals must admire their amazing ability to metamorphose and to endure a long migration without food. But, first of all, let us look at their life cycle and the story of how they manage, and are managed, in the rivers around the town.

The Christchurch-bound European or common eel, known as *Anguilla Anguilla*, starts off in the Sargasso Sea, an immense and strange part of the Atlantic including most of the notorious Bermuda Triangle. The sea has no shores or currents but a depth of at least two miles; the colour is a deep blue yet the water astonishingly clear; it is extremely clean but with hardly any plant life, except for the masses of Sargassum weed. Upper levels are very salty and warm. Here it is that the eels from our rivers choose to mate (mainly from March to May) at a depth of some 600ft. Then they die. As the exhausted parents fall to their death, the newly fertilised eggs rise to the surface, each on a speck of oil. Within two days they have become larvae and begin drifting across the Atlantic on a journey lasting some two years.

So it is that while the prospective parents swim south-west to mate and die, their predecessors' offspring travel north-east to new lives and through the very same water. The tiny plankton-eating fry is transparent, shaped like a willow leaf and called *leptocephalus* or a 'thin-head', shown inset in Fig. 10. It has no homing instinct for a particular river. Even so, the automatic distribution, by ocean currents of the many billions of youngsters to the European coasts, means that a number will enter the Run at Mudeford and find their way up the town's rivers. Sadly, that number, as generally elsewhere in the world, is only a fraction of what it was in times past.

Once the Gulf Stream has taken them towards the estuaries of Western Europe, the thin-heads undergo their first metamorphosis from the leaf shape into 'glass eels', so-called due to their transparent eel-like appearance. In changing to glass eels, they become shorter, cylindrical in shape and about nine tenths lighter! After reaching the estuaries and becoming pigmented they are known as 'elvers', a major traditional livelihood for fishermen the world over. Hence, although both glass eels and elvers have the same shape of baby eels, there is a metamorphosis from the first to the second – the pigmented elvers then migrate to fresh water. However, numbers in Christchurch are so low that there is no question of harvesting the elvers here. They press on with enormous determination, making full use of incoming tides and waiting out the ebb tides near river banks in slow water. Typically about 2in long, they progress upstream to become 'yellow eels' (also known as 'brown eels') to live and grow over several years, males for typically nine years and the larger, less numerous females for some fifteen years.

Only now do they become sexually mature, turning into 'silver eels' in a last metamorphosis and ready to migrate. Observation shows that the business of becoming a silver eel takes perhaps six months from spring to autumn, resulting in some 'half-silvers' during this time. Some do not return to the Sargasso Sea, remaining instead in fresh water and living – it is believed – to a grand old age of up to eighty-five years! It is believed that the 'decision' to go can depend on factors such as stress or food. However, the general rule is that an eel which lives will eventually migrate to create the next generation. To do so in the tough sea conditions entails this final change into a more muscular fish.

Like it or loathe it, the eel certainly is amazing. It hunts at night, generally lays up during daylight and can live in wet grass for about twenty-four hours. It can travel considerable distances over land if it wants to migrate and does not have the benefit of a continuous river, e.g. because it is living in watercress beds or a pond. The common expression 'as slippery as an eel' is well coined, because its considerable body slime and muscular wriggling can make this fish impossible to hold. Not only that, but they are notorious for continuing to squirm round in a rather revolting fashion after they are supposed to have been killed. The body fluids, including blood, are toxic and only made harmless by cooking. Anyone getting such fluid in a wound should be very careful. Unlike other fish, the eel can be transferred from sea to freshwater and back again at any time without adverse effects, whilst, as a predator, it has been known to catch and eat birds and be a cannibal to its own kind. Like the crocodile, the eel will spin itself round in order to tackle a large prey. In the case of the eel, this is a method of taking a bite out of a large fish.

Yet much is still to be discovered about the humble eel. It is not known why the elvers are sexually neutral and then become hermaphrodite, finally plumping for male or female years later. In addition, despite many attempts, man has so far proved unable to breed and raise them in captivity, presumably due to problems replicating the conditions of the Sargasso Sea. Although fertilisation has happened in artificial conditions, the essential objective has not yet been achieved because the larvae always die within about a day – eel farms are simply stocked by transported glass eels. The raising to full-size eels can be done in about eighteen months only, compared to more like ten years for the wild variety.

At the Royalty, these fish are regularly taken through a system of licensed netting. As the Water Company own the fishery, they are able to grant permission – for a suitable consideration – to Roger Castle, a skilled nets-man, to cull the eel population as appropriate over the year. Although there is a minor commercial element, much of the actual operation is to do with conservation and good river management. For example, otter guards are used on nets; numbers of nets are strictly limited and anything other than eels is thrown back. Roger, like all eel men, is happy to work the variable and sometimes unsocial hours, enduring the hardships along the way. In our relatively prosperous times, however, there may not be local continuity on his retirement. Nowadays, not many younger people are going to commit to a life of tending the nets, dragging the eel barrels up the steep river banks and marketing the fish.

Catches on the Avon were high during the 1950s, have greatly reduced over time since then, but have seen a revival to a minor extent from 2005 with more elvers entering Christchurch Harbour. For hundreds of years, this river has proved very attractive to the eel (certainly more so than the river Stour). As a large chalk stream, it is so rich in food that it is ideal for the fish to grow, whilst the harbour, a wide gently-flowing estuary, is easy for the elvers to navigate. On maturity, larger specimens of 3lbs and 4lbs are not uncommon. Some indeed persevere many miles up the Avon, past Salisbury to the river Wylye. Staying longer in these more remote reaches, they tend to be larger fish.

The prime netting time for the fat silver eels is at the end of October, when they are getting ready to go back to the Sargasso Sea. By way of preparation, their backs turn from green to almost black and their bellies from yellow to silver as a camouflage for the ocean crossing. There is a great increase in feeding, making them much fatter by the autumn migration time – an essential if they are to make the sea voyage back to the Sargasso without eating again. With fat newly-stored in muscles they become firmer, whilst with no more expectation of eating for the rest of their lives, the jaw changes somewhat and the digestive tracts shrink. Nostrils, sex organs and eyes get bigger. The evidence suggests that eels like to start off on their long and ultimately fatal journey on a dark and stormy night. For reasons unknown, they prefer to avoid a full moon, even if it is obscured by cloud.

The 'fyke nets' are ready and waiting on the bottom of the river. Although used throughout the season (26 June to 31 December), this is their prime time. They comprise tubes of nylon mesh kept open with steel rings and having three compartments of reducing size, the smallest being known as the 'cod end' (Fig. 11). The otter guard is fixed at the first and largest funnel-like opening. Since eels do not normally eat carrion, bait would make little difference; so why do they enter? The answer is that the nets are joined together by a section of vertical mesh, a 'leader net', that tends to guide them in (as bottom feeders) automatically. There are some 40 fyke nets at the Royalty, strung together in groups of ten.

To be clear, two fyke nets are joined by the vertical mesh and have the large rings facing each other – that constitutes a 'double'. It follows that, strangely, the eels enter them when moving upstream as well as downstream. Hence, they swim in rather than simply drift in with the current. Five doubles are strung together for each river buoy. Fig. 10 demonstrates how they are raised so that any trapped fish can be tipped into a barrel in the wide flat-bottomed rowing boat. The swan flying above the boatman is purely incidental to this operation! The barrels, having many holes in the sides to allow water to keep passing through, are then sealed with screwed lids and stored in the river until ready for live transport to a buyer or market.

The other local catching method is the eel rack, a staging of steel mesh which traps eels thrown up onto it after opening the adjoining weir sluices to a greater amount than normal. When the fish are heading downstream to start their migration, they are unexpectedly met by a grill set into the river bed at 45°. A fast flow of water will sweep them up onto the horizontal rack. In 1955, according to the *Angling Times*, a ton was caught in just twelve hours on the Christchurch Avon, an amount beyond the wildest dreams of the present day. Although that rack is no longer there, the method is still used on the Stour and with some success. Again, the fish are stored in perforated barrels below the water surface until ready to transport for sale.

Since the Christchurch silver eel has a high fat content, it is most suitable for sending to, amongst other outlets, a specialist shop and restaurant in Somerset for freezing and later, smoking. As some indication of its attraction to the enthusiasts, the price of smoked eel is

Ken Keynes tending the Knapp Mill eel rack in the 1960s
This night photograph shows silver eels ready to be brushed into a tub with a broom at Knapp Mill. The shallow sides and front of the rack prevent their escape in three out of four directions. Large catches were then possible, simply by placing a grill in the river bed at an angle so that the eels were swept up to the rack by the current.
(Courtesy of Mrs Pat Fagan)

comparable to, or sometimes even greater than, that for smoked salmon. This is, however, only a tiny part of the big international eel industry, which has been established for many centuries and involves a whole range of catching and eating methods. Apart from smoking, there is roasting, stewing, frying, grilling, boiling, steaming and probably a few others.

Before saying that commercial eel fishing should be prohibited for reasons of conservation, it should be realised that the total Christchurch eel catch is probably a minority of those that are trying to reach the sea. In addition, the spawn there can be twenty million eggs for a single female! There is no doubt that numbers have greatly dropped, a fall variously attributed to gross over-fishing of glass eels, global warming, increased pollution, loss of wetlands with more building, and to alterations in the Gulf Stream. It may be that the eventual outcome in Christchurch of this particular controversy will be a compromise – to keep commercial fishing but on a restricted basis.

At the time of writing, some 'emergency measures' have been introduced, including an earlier start to the close season, i.e. 30 September instead of 31 December. No new netting licences are being granted and catch limits are being placed on glass eels, silver eels and elvers. It is all part of the EU's conservation policy under the new Eel Management Plans (EMP). One objective is to ensure that more than half of any glass eels caught can be used for restocking. In the UK, a very high-level Sustainable Eel Group (SEG) has been formed from the Environment Agency, fisheries, scientists, senior officials, conservation groups and commercial interests to deliver the EMP – no easy task in light of the problems of monitoring and policing. Both the Stour and the Avon will become centres for eel research projects.

It is also hoped that total eel numbers can be raised in this country by using techniques such as passes to prevent any hindrance on migration of silver eels. Although it must be very hard to measure, another target is to ensure that at least 40 per cent of eels escape to the sea by 2010 in order to migrate. Due to the size of the industry in Europe and the high prices obtainable for elvers, there is bound to be concern on whether all countries keep to the rules.

The least attractive assessment of this issue of declining stocks goes something like this: the almost universal decline in the European elver population has been so drastic over the last fifty years that the wisest course is a full international ban on commercial eel fishing. At this point in the argument, however, a certain difference needs to be stressed – the small-scale operation of the fyke nets in the Avon is probably benign to fish stocks, whereas the large tonnage taken from the enormous continental shelf operation is not. Indeed, research shows that this is the main problem and should be tackled first. An estimated 99 per cent of this lucrative operation is carried out by France, Spain and Portugal, but, sadly, these countries are apparently defying EU legislation.

On the other hand, if there were to be an indiscriminate ban, it would be another sad case of a lost rural industry and folklore, probably never to be replaced. One other possibility is that the eel numbers will (for reasons unknown, despite all the ongoing research) decline to unviable levels. It may be that over the next five years a policy for sustainability will be established. My own guess is that increasing restrictions will be implemented and stocks may recover, either due to this or for other reasons, and we shall still have the tranquil sight of fyke nets being tended on the river Avon for many years to come.

NINETEEN

Mudeford in 1900 with Florence Hamilton

Here are extracts from an article written for the September 1978 journal of the Friars Cliff Residents Association, based on experiences around 1900. They are reproduced courtesy of the association, and paint a graphic picture of a lost age:

A little quiet country lane, where the only traffic one met was an occasional farm cart and the carriages belonging to the houses in the place. In the winter, there would be Broughams drawn by one, or a pair of sleek well kept horses and in the summer the open Victoria would take their place. Various people drove dog carts or pony governess carts, and there was a smart four-in-hand driven by a Colonel with his dainty little wife sitting beside him on the box …

The public transport was provided by a large two-horse omnibus driven by a man called Huss, which ran several times a day between the Railway Station and the beach. One could also hire a four wheeler cab (with its own imperishable odour of horse and straw) or a quaint little pony chaise; otherwise one walked and distance was no object …

The post came three times a day, brought for many years by Postman Troke who walked to and from Christchurch. The road was very muddy in the Winter time and equally dusty in the Summer, when the water-cart drawn by a large horse sprinkled it. There were no footpaths, no street lighting and the forerunner of the corporation road sweepers was an old bent man who mended the roads, filling in holes with stones and a stone-hammer before the advent of tarmac. The roads were seldom, if ever, swept but numbers of little boys with soap-boxes on wheels collected the horse droppings …

There were of course no shops, the nearest being at Purewell Cross, a little sunny baker's shop famous for its Chelsea buns and where Mr. Shirwell made what must have been the forerunner of the present-day rusk then called 'Tops and Bottoms' which was soaked in milk and given to babies. At Purewell Cross too there were the pork butcher, fish and fruit shops, all run by the Clarke family who were renowned for their homemade brawn and faggots … The oil man called weekly with oil for the lamps. In the winter, came the Muffin man carrying his basket of hot muffins on his head and ringing his hand bell …

Entertainments were few. The occasional organ grinder with his monkey and two concerts a year, the Cricket Concert and the Football Concert, held in the village room with complete disregard of the bylaws for safety … The amusements of the young came at regular seasons of the year, hoops, tops and marbles all taking their turn on the then peaceful roads … Cars were seldom seen until the Kaiser came to Highcliffe and drove about the district with his staff in a convoy of five cars …

The path from Mudeford to the Haven had a picturesque little wooden bridge over the Bure Brook which flowed into the harbour there. The Sandbanks now covered with chalets and huts were great sand dunes with a large expanse of beach and only three privately-owned bathing huts … Tea at the Black House, with its famous homemade cake and freshly cooked lobsters or winkles eaten with a pin, was always a treat. There were only a few sailing boats and punts on the harbour then apart from the fishermen's boats … The Coastguards were a fine lot of men and the Coastguard station at Stanpit with its ten neat cottages, white-washed and spotless and with well kept gardens, was a pleasure to see … At the end of the beach was the old Steamer wedged into the cliff between two ilex trees, with beautiful tamarisk trees growing nearby …

On Hengistbury Head the Royal Engineers held their Camp each year and made bridges which were much appreciated by Mudeford residents for many years … Bure Lane was one of the prettiest lanes possible, with its little brook, the watercress growing therein, the countless robins' nests and wild violets in its banks … What was greatly enjoyed was the 'Derham Choir' consisting of the 10 brothers and sisters with their respective families, who came round on Christmas Eve, visiting every house and singing the well known Christmas Carols far into the night …

The uneventful years went by, season by season, and although there was then time to 'stand and stare' there was never a dull moment.

TWENTY

Normans, Weather Vanes and Salmon

*A*mazingly, there is definite historic information available from the charters of the early Norman period about salmon being given to the canons of the priory. Let us begin, however, with the present salmon weather vane atop Priory Church that resembles a fish of pure gold when it reflects the sunlight. In October 1969, a salmon feature (5ft 4in long, weighing 30lbs and at a height of 120ft) was installed as a vane above the west tower of the Priory Church (Fig. 12). The plaque refers to the flagstaff and salmon weather vane being designed by the priory architect Ian Jessopp, donated by three people in memory of assistant verger Theo Brown (1891–1968) and erected by his son and grandson, with the assistance of three others. Altogether, nine were involved in the task. Clearly, the son (together with others) wanted to arrange a unique tribute to his father that could be seen from far and wide. Nonetheless, a vane like this also commemorates a more historic event – one which harks back to the de Redvers dynasty, a Norman family made very rich by Henry I in reward for loyalty in the feud against his brother Robert.

Amongst the family's extensive landed estates was Twynham. As Lords of the Manor, the succeeding generations of this family automatically enjoyed full fishing rights on the river Avon. As Catholics, they were most concerned about the Hereafter and wanted masses said for their souls by the canons, who were Augustinians from around 1150. Out of the three following instances of the de Redvers making a grant or gift of salmon, in the second and third cases, we know that it was in return for commemoration and masses being celebrated.

King Henry I made Richard de Redvers Lord of the Manor around 1100. It was a long time after his death in 1107, that his son, Baldwin, was made First Earl of Devon in 1141. It was this Baldwin who stated in a confirmatory charter (Christchurch Priory Cartulary Foundation Charter Two of about 1140) that the first salmon caught each year, and indeed a tithe of salmon and all other fish, would be given to the canons. It may be that the traditional meaning of 'tithe' is applicable here, i.e. one tenth of the catch. Being confirmatory, it means that the gift had first been made at some earlier date. We cannot, however, in this instance state the reason for the gift.

The second reference to a salmon gift comes in Charter Five of 1161 made by Baldwin's son Richard, the Second Earl of Devon, in return for masses being said by the prior and canons. It was for another salmon to be given every year to the prior and canons on the anniversary of his father's death, which was in June 1155. Hopefully, masses were said anyway during this six-year delay.

We now come to the third and separate salmon gift, made again in Charter Five of 1161 – made indeed in the same sentence of the charter. Richard was here looking forward to masses being said for himself on the anniversary of his own death. Since he died in April 1162, the first salmon would have been given and the masses would have been said in April 1163. After that, it would be annually on each succeeding anniversary.

Although the facts and sense of the charters quoted here are believed to be fully correct, perhaps it should be mentioned that the Latin translation version used is that in the recent publication about the Cartulary edited by Katherine Hanna.

In summary, it was important to the dynasty of this Norman family that masses be said for their departed, and one way to ensure this service from the canons was by giving salmon. To give the translation from the original Latin, an extract of Charter Five reads: '... given them [the canons] salmon ... as a pittance for the celebration of those anniversaries.' In other words, the canons were expected to celebrate each year the deaths of these Norman lords as a way of easing them into Heaven. Salmon, the 'pittance', were the prescribed form of payment or consideration for such masses.

Looking at the salmon from a totally different angle, it might well have been regarded as an ideal icon for the Catholics of the town, because a very early symbol of the Christian faith was a fish. And what better fish is there than the salmon, so plentiful in the river Avon from time immemorial? The Greek word for fish is *ICHTHUS*, the letters of which each stand for a separate word and, put together, they read: Jesus Christ Son of God Saviour. At the time of the Roman persecution of the early believers, the symbol was apparently used as a kind of secret code or password between strangers, where one person would make a curve in the dust with a foot and the other would make an opposite curve, thereby forming the simple image of a fish. Both would then be able to talk safely.

There is a further strong indication of the town's connection to the salmon in the form of one of the priory's misericords, as shown inset in Fig. 12. These are wooden carvings acting to support the monks' hindquarters, as it were – to make the lengthy prayer sessions more bearable! The seat carvings are grotesque and bizarre in general, giving rise to adverse comment from some Victorians. But in this particular case, a good representation is provided of a salmon lying on rocks, accessorised by nearby eels and various carved letters. It is formed in oak and has been dated as around 1515, just six years into the reign of Henry VIII.

Strangely, there is another facet to the whole story of the salmon vane's Norman origins – it was only erected because the corroded supporting pole of the old one collapsed. Naturally, the vane fell, damaging the lead-work of the sloping roof within the tower parapets. Rather than retain it and undertake significant repairs, it was replaced. The previous one was in traditional copper, about one eighth of an inch thick, having decorative scrolls and surmounted by the later addition of a simple cross. It was 4ft 6in long and 1ft 6in high, with the cross adding another 1ft 6in to the height. The design featured a normal pointer, back paddle and fishtail – not remotely like a salmon anyway. Fortunately, this unique piece of heritage was rescued from disposal in the nick of time by Ian Jessopp – it is now displayed to great effect on a white painted brick wall, as seen in Fig. 13.

Although discoloured with air pollution and tinged with green copper carbonate in places, remains of the original gilding in gold leaf is still evident. In its early years, it would have reflected the sunlight just as much as its replacement does now. The copper vane appears on a drawing from 1840 by priory architect Benjamin Ferrey, and also on an engraving from 1857. However, another engraving from 1783 shows only what appears to be a small flag at the top of the staff. Taking the best view we can, and bearing in mind some artistic licence with the engravings, it is probably about 200 years old. When the replacement was done, the opportunity was taken to improve access to the new vane by designing the supporting pole so that it can easily be lowered for maintenance. It has also been supported by stays, thus greatly reducing the stress from wind-loading.

Intriguingly, the architect's drawing of May 1968, in respect of the previous and proposed vane structures, does not show the points of the compass, although they can be seen today just below the golden salmon. They are indeed an additional and later fixture. It would appear that only recently, after hundreds of years, has it been felt necessary, in the face of some controversy, to show north, south, east and west. It is because so many people are no longer aware that as a general rule, churches are aligned approximately east-west.

The old vane has a legend of its own – holes were reputedly made in it by a Luftwaffe machine gun in the Second World War! In 1943, the Germans used machine gun raids in many parts of the country as part of their terror offensive against the civilian population. If you look closely at the photograph, two grey patches can be seen. Having seen the vane, I can say that these are definitely lead repairs of holes. The third hole is again seemingly made by a bullet and has not been patched – the white wall is visible through it. Perhaps a rather more likely explanation is that suggested by Ian Jessopp, who designed and supervised the whole removal and replacement task. Someone could have been taking pot-shots at the vane for the satisfaction of hitting it and seeing it spin round and, having repaired two bullet holes, the church left the third one alone. It would certainly have been hazardous to repair due to the sheer height above the walkway by the parapet, some 35ft. Being placed so far above the centre of the lead-covered pyramid forming the roof of the west tower, it was most inaccessible and dangerous to approach. Another pointer in favour of this explanation is that any holes made by a German fighter plane would all have been lead-filled at the same time, and to imagine a second attack on the vane by a Messerschmitt pilot is probably stretching the imagination too far.

Vying with – and perhaps exceeding – the Luftwaffe-based tale for implausibility, is the story about the vane being turned as a signal in order to assist smuggling at Hengistbury Head. Imagine being the smuggler designated to climb the 35ft in order to wiggle the weather vane, especially on the kind of dark and stormy night preferred by the free traders! How visible would it have been to the party waiting at Double Dykes? If standing behind the parapet of the tower anyway, why not signal in an easier and more effective fashion with a light? Was there even a vane in place at that time? (bearing in mind the absence of one on the 1783 engraving). One suspects that this smuggling story is a myth.

TWENTY-ONE

Astonishing Catches and the Royalty Fishery

During her five-year reign beginning in July 1553, Queen Mary I (1516–1558) made a Royal Grant of fishing rights under the title of the Royalty Fishery. The Grant was renewed by Queen Elizabeth I (1533–1603) and the Royalty became one of the best salmon fisheries in the country. However, even before Queen Mary, the fishery was recognised in state papers, as in the following extract from 1540:

> … by the presents do grant convey and let to farm to our dear servant Thomas Wryothesley Esquire all that our fishery of Stowre and Avon from the river called Stoure Were and Wildewere upon the aforesaid waters to the sea coasts next adjacent. As well as le leyre of le Lampro formerly at the bridge of the late Priory of Christchurch in the County of Southampton with all nets and other engines to the said fishery appertaining or in any way belonging parcel of the possessions of Margaret Countess of Salisbury attainted of high treason.

(Patent Roll 31 Henry VIII Part 6. Translation extract
Hampshire County Council Museums and Archives, Red House Museum, Christchurch)

Many centuries earlier, there is every reason to believe that salmon had been taken by the town's monks, right back to Saxon times. Understandably, there is limited information on this subject before the Norman Conquest of AD 1066.

Long after the fishery was established, the River Avon Navigation Act of 1664 sought to enable commercial vessels to reach Salisbury by improving the channel. In Elizabethan times, we can imagine a fairly slow, meandering river in quite a wide and shallow flood plain, but navigable for small boats. With some disruption caused by floods and the need for repairs, the commercial navigation under the Act continued from 1684 up to final abandonment in 1730. The other big man-made change around that time was the new cut through Mudeford Sandbank in 1695, so diverting the Run to a different course. One wonders whether the salmon, returning to the Avon to spawn, were surprised or disorientated to find the Run diverted in this way! After some years, the harbour entrance naturally re-established in its old position, but even now, the 1695 breakwater remnant, known as Clarendon's Rocks, remains to be seen and to be avoided by boats.

Around 1715, the lands around the Avon at Christchurch were parcelled out into different ownerships and used as indicated on the map extract from that time in Fig. 14. Unfortunately, there is not enough space to reproduce the full document, which is believed to be the earliest street map of the town. It should be said that the accuracy of maps pre-dating the Ordnance Survey is limited. Nonetheless, we can see the general shape of the river, the Mill Stream and the rights of a number of people, in particular Sir Dewey Bulkeley. A salmon house can be seen on the river bank, perhaps for the smoking of salmon or storage with the aid of ice blocks. Certainly, much of the map is broadly correct and many of the place names are valid. However, one inaccuracy is that there is no indication of the eastern branch of the river Avon, implying that the section now running under Waterloo Bridge did not then exist.

Considering the weir at Eldridge's Corner (off-map to the right), Wild Ware is first mentioned in the 1540 document extract and appears again on the map. It was a simple affair of stone blocks set across the river, with spaces in between for timbers that could be raised or lowered. Although the blocks are shown on the map as only going part way across the water, at one time the whole width of upstream water (and therefore water feeding the Mill Stream) would have been height-controlled. It must have been necessary to have sufficient height of water in the Mill Stream to work the mill properly. At the Constable's House remains, the stream can be about 2ft above the river Avon and that difference could be further controlled by the gate on the connecting weir running under Convent Walk. It is highly relevant that the Mill Stream, which formed the boundary of the burgh in Saxon times, took its water from the Avon and discharged it below Place Mill into the Stour. As a result of this rare system of running a mill stream between two rivers, it was particularly important to have weirs to ensure the right level of water at the mill – they could be adjusted to reflect changes in the relative water heights of the two rivers. Since the mill no longer uses water power, there is now no need for what was once known as Wild Ware. More recently, the river has seen the Knapp Mill water extraction works and, downstream of these, an outfall from the Burton sewage works. Although the water was extracted until recent years at Knapp Mill, it is now taken from the Avon upstream at Matchams and piped to Knapp Mill for treatment.

During the 1880s, the fishery slowly started to give more opportunity to angling with rod and line. Until then, it was purely commercial fishing, which included the practice of netting – as still used in a very restricted way at the Run. However, all commercial fishing, excluding the Run, ceased in 1929 when the owner, Miss Mary Francis Mills, sold it to the West Hampshire Water Company (now the Bournemouth & West Hampshire Water Company). The latter has appointed Southern Fisheries to look after the Royalty under a fishery manager.

In 2006, a permanent exhibition room was dedicated and has since been built up enormously by museum curator and salmon angler Tony Timms. The Royalty Fishery Museum displays a wealth of historical information in an ideal setting next to the river Avon. The collection continues to be extended in various ways, throwing light, for example, on the background of many local families over the generations. Research has also revealed details for all keepers since 1794, together with a wide variety of exhibits, such as that referring to the (then) British record barbel of 13lbs 12oz caught in the Railway Pool on 18 October 1962 by Joe Day. Indeed, the Avon reputedly has as large a variety of fish as any other English river.

The present syndicated membership of twenty-one salmon anglers is subject to a waiting list of several years, although it sanctions fishing only once a week per member from 15 March for three months. Allowing for guests, the largest number of rods permitted on any one day is just six, spread over three beats, and all fish have to be returned to the water for conservation reasons. On 16 June, the coarse fishing season begins and day tickets can be bought for both coarse and game fishing throughout the summer. With the absence of competitions, the rules about acceptable baits and the limitations on tickets, both types of angler happily co-exist at the Royalty. Although the netting season at the Run is limited and all salmon netted have to be returned to the water, sea trout can be retained. Records of rod-caught salmon indicate that the most prolific years were the 1950s. Now, the Environment Agency has automatic monitoring equipment to check fish movements and numbers at Knapp Mill throughout the year.

ASTONISHING SALMON DOUBLE

We now move to the territory of 'stranger than fiction'. It concerns the landing of the two salmon shown in Fig. 15, a photograph taken in the Fishery Museum. On 11 April 1951, the first was taken in Hayters Pool by the incredible angler G.M. Howard and a week later, on 18 April 1951, the second was caught by the same angler in Edwards Pool, both using silver sprat.

The second catch was far from easy, taking forty-five minutes to gaff the fish and needing Howard to recover from falling over in flood water during the process! These two pools are shown by the photograph in Fig. 16, an idyllic location for the serious angler if ever there was one, and still considered the best two pools. The extraordinary thing is that each enormous salmon had precisely the same weight of 41¾lbs, and the second one was caught within a week of the first. For this to happen, and through the efforts of the same angler, is believed to be unique. At that time, these were the largest fish taken at the Royalty since 1929. A careful look at Fig. 15 demonstrates why Mr Howard described the first fish caught as 'very deep-bodied' and the second one as 'like a torpedo'. Clearly not content with this achievement, he proceeded on 27 February 1952 to catch what is even now the record salmon for the Hampshire Avon from Greenbanks Pool, at a weight of 49lbs. To add some perspective, the all-time national record is held by Georgina Ballantyne for a 64lb monster caught on 7 October 1922, taken after a major battle from the river Tay. There is also the salmon caught in the nets at the Run (and so not qualifying as a rod and line river catch) of 53lbs on 13 April 1880, and presented by his supporters to the loser in that day's election, J.E. Moss.

But this is far from the end of the story. In those days, the catches would have been eaten without too much delay. Fortunately, before that happened, a careful plaster cast was often made. Although it was known that Mr Howard's family had casts of the two 41¾lb fish, nobody knew that they also had a cast of the record 49lb fish. Indeed, as it was fifty-five years before all three casts were made available to the fishery by the family, it meant that Tony Timms was the first angler of the modern era to see the 49lb salmon. Now that the fishery had access to the casts, plans were laid with a Bolton specialist to produce fresh ones for display purposes. It is a very skilled operation, creating most durable and lifelike replicas from fibreglass-based composite material. The reason for using such a distant taxidermist was that he, and he only, would guarantee to return the casts to their original condition if damaged when in his care.

The first cast to travel to Bolton was the record 49lb fish. Although a somewhat heart-stopping journey was needed to transport the original brittle cast by car, it was successful. No doubt that was due – at least in part – to the gigantic amount of bubblewrap used. Lloyds of London underwrote the insurance of the expedition at a premium of £256, based on a value of £8,500. The charges of the taxidermist and artist, including mounting the new cast on polished oak with gold-leaf lettering, came to £2,800. After the record salmon was put up on display, it then became the turn of the 41¾lb specimens – Bolton and Lloyds were re-contacted and the operation was done all over again. These three fish have since caused many times the work involved in simply being caught by Granville Martin Howard in the first place! In all, over 2,000 miles were travelled in order to produce such a magnificent display for the museum.

TWENTY-TWO

From Helping the Poor in 1372 to Helping the Traffic Now

lthough King Henry VIII had good reasons for closing down the priories in the Dissolution, there were major losses to the country. Whilst evidence had been found of the Catholic monks becoming corrupt, fat and rich at the expense of the people, many religious houses did provide a lifeline to the poor – there was medical help and the destitute, in need of a bed for the night, were not turned away. Christchurch Priory seems to have had a better record than most in terms of helping the poor with food and drink. There was an almonry and gatehouse building at the entrance to the priory complex, where the needy would have gathered on the appointed days and times. Since the remains of it are still there, and the long side is about 50ft, it is clear that this was a substantial facility for the poor.

Occasions for the distribution of alms were anniversaries, including the following: Richard de Redvers the Elder, Adeliza, Hadwise, another Richard, two Baldwins, William, Earls of Devon, Lady Joan of Briwere, Bishop Henry de Blois, Martel, Adeline, Prior Reginald, Prior Nicholas, Isobella de Fortibus, etc. The actual amounts given depended on just who the anniversary commemorated. Every day, two masses were said for benefactors, bringing total daily masses to around six. It was all part of the life of the priory. The records from 1372 show the distribution for that year – 1,354 loaves, 467 gallons of beer and 934 dishes from the kitchen. It is hard to know how far that went to alleviate local poverty, but we can say that its loss with the closure of the priory must have been felt by many. There must also have been many cases of extra help given to individuals on a one-to-one basis by kindly monks. Even as late as the 1930s, there was some residual giving of alms from the church, when bread was given to the needy from the kitchen adjoining the west tower.

Now, the needs of road traffic seem to be paramount. Fig. 17 shows what is left of the almonry, with a tarmac road going through the middle of it leading to the car park and Christchurch Quay. It has been commented that the structure might have been a late medieval development, or even erected by Gustavus Brander as an eighteenth-century imitation. However, that idea does not seem to be supported by any evidence. The better theory may be that which is outlined in this chapter, and consistent with the eminent work, *Monasteries of Dorset*.

If you examine the masonry, it can be seen that a modern match has been made where the front wall was cut through. The match is most evident perhaps when facing the car park (from outside the original site) and looking at the wall to the left of the road. The false impression, that this was the entrance to the original monastery site, is enhanced by the concrete spheres above the wall on each side of the road, as if these were indeed ornamental gate posts. In fact, the position of the entrance has shifted since the Dissolution. The old gateway, between the almonry and what is now Priory Lodge, has been walled up in favour of the idea of driving the road through the almonry itself. The roof and rear wall of the almonry have long since been removed and now there are two large trees growing within the area of its original walls on either side of the present road.

It is rather startling to realise that on driving to the quay, one is passing through a building, once largely dedicated by the Catholic monks of Christchurch to providing bread and beer to the destitute.

TWENTY-THREE

Stocks and Ducking Stool – For Visitors

The first thing to make clear is that the title of this chapter is not meant to imply wholesale corporal punishment of tourists. Rather, it means that the replica 'equipment' now in Christchurch has been installed only recently and has never been used for its intended purpose. Since such punishment is no longer meted out, the town's replica stocks and ducking stool exist largely for visitors to marvel at the barbarity of our past – on the other hand, some may rue their loss!

STOCKS

Many towns have a set of stocks to remind us about days of yore. They always seem to be of heavily-used gnarled oak construction with ancient iron clasps. One can well imagine the satisfying feeling of throwing old fruit and rotten eggs at the hapless and helpless criminal. Justice is generally supposed to manage three functions – punishment of the offender, protection of society through deterrence and reform of the offender by rehabilitation. In those times, the stocks were certainly deemed to play their part.

When in the stocks, the victim would sit facing the apparatus and two boards were placed above and below the ankles, locking the feet in place. The more drastic pillory imprisoned head and wrists, whilst the miscreant remained standing. Some devices did both at once, having the wrongdoer's head, wrists and ankles all poking through holes. Stocks were meant for the humiliation of minor offenders and deserters, who had to endure all weathers and were often given only bread and water. The range of offences was very wide – in one Christchurch instance, an offender was sentenced to four hours in the stocks in 1665 (by order of the mayor, Henry Rogers) for failing to keep a watch to maintain quarantine during the plague. Apart from being bombarded by refuse, the person under restraint could be beaten or even tickled. Although the stocks had been generally discontinued in this country by the middle of the nineteenth century, they have been used elsewhere, including Panama, as recently as 1995.

One glaring omission, therefore, from the heritage credentials of Christchurch, was the recent absence of any stocks. It seems that an ex-mayor of the town, Michael Hodges, decided something should be done, because he secured some Japanese oak and personally made a replica. But, where should they be put? That was the question. The task demanded a prominent position where they would be seen, but all such spots were either taken already or would never get the requisite consent from the authorities. Here indeed was some potential use for the new stocks – they could be erected and used without delay for any public official who objected to the plan. Or perhaps to punish the wrongdoing of the person responsible for the illegal installation!

It was time to take a calculated risk. They were fixed in position one dark night in 1973 on the access-way to Christchurch Castle from Castle Street. The expected official reaction never came. Maybe everyone assumed that someone else had given the necessary consent, or turned the proverbial 'blind eye'. Eventually, due to the original wood being not quite right for the job, the stocks needed repair or replacement. By then, they had no doubt fooled thousands of residents and visitors regarding authenticity – a job well done! The council proceeded to replace them, as shown in Fig. 18. A main difference was the lettering provided – 'Ye Olde Stocks'. Thus it would appear that things have been regularised with the passage of time. The height of the tourist contraption may not be quite correct, because the holes for the protruding feet need to be set lower or, alternatively, the seat behind should be raised.

The town's most recent genuine stocks were located in front of the eighteenth-century jail at the Pit Site, Barrack Road. The whole area has long since been demolished as part of the road improvements connected with the bypass. It has not proved possible to discover what happened to those old stocks – most probably, like the ancient Town Chest, they were disposed of as rubbish. Sentences were reportedly handed down by the Court Leet, which also had the option of punishing by use of the town's ducking stool.

DUCKING STOOL

There stands, my friend, in yonder pool
An engine called the ducking-stool;
By legal power commanded down
The joy and terror of the town.
If jarring females kindle strife,
Give language foul, or lug the coif,
If noisy dames should once begin
To drive the house with horrid din,
Away, you cry, you'll grace the stool;
We'll teach you how your tongue to rule.
The fair offender fills the seat
In sullen pomp profoundly great;
Down in the deep the stool descends,
But here, at first, we miss our ends;
She mounts again and rages more
Than ever vixen did before.
So, throwing water on the fire
Will make it but burn up the higher.
If so, my friend, pray let her take
A second turn into the lake,
And, rather than your patience lose,
Thrice and again repeat the dose.
No brawling wives, no furious wenches,
No fire so hot but water quenches.

Benjamin West, 1780

Ducking stool from the good or bad old days – let the reader decide!
Perhaps the victim looks resigned, whilst the onlookers are happy to be present at a normal social event of the day.

Fig. 19 illustrates how the punishment would appear, except the wrongdoer might be less cheerful – I would like to place on record my thanks to sporting volunteer, Kelly Williams.

If there was to be a change in the law that would encourage a rebirth of medieval punishments, at least the stocks would serve well without alteration except for the seat height mentioned above. The same cannot be said of the ducking stool placed by the Mill Stream at the end of Ducking Stool Lane. The shallow depth of water means that it is a tourist attraction only, rather than a working apparatus. Perhaps this is just as well, or the temptation for some might be too great. Nonetheless, it would be easy to make it fully serviceable by making a pit in the Mill Stream with adequately shored-up sides. The padlocks could be undone and the main beam slid forward to allow the chair to be centrally placed above the water, whilst the weight of the miscreant would be balanced via the fulcrum by whoever was administering the retribution at the other end of the beam. It would be important not to overlook the need for an iron band to be placed around the sufferer to prevent him or her from falling out during immersion.

There is perhaps some ingrained nostalgia connected with the installation of the Christchurch replica, placed as it was on the site historically used for ducking. It was all part of the town's centennial celebrations of the 1886 Borough Charter. A notice on the stool reads: 'This ducking stool was made and erected near its original position for the re-establishment of the ancient Court Leet at the time of the Christchurch Centennial festival in June 1986.' The court exists to beat the bounds and may still have the power to punish wrongdoers. The impact on the visitor is further consolidated by another notice carved on the chair itself: 'Of members ye tonge is worst or best – an yu tonge oft doeth breed unrest.'

The particular Christchurch design is unknown, but the idea was always the same – place the victim in a strongly-made chair and fully duck him, or her – both to provide punishment and for the appreciation of the townsfolk. The illustration shows one type of stool, but there were other variations, e.g. the Leominster one, which had the benefits of a waist-high fulcrum, a four-wheeled base and a hinged main beam for compactness. Some had a kind of see-saw over the axle of two large wheels in order to make for an easy trip to the river side. Since the town's ducking stool was reportedly kept in the north porch of the Priory Church, it was most likely to have been a mobile design. However, a reproduction of that type would perhaps have been a little too shocking to reinstall in the north porch in 1986 – much better to put one without wheels in Ducking Stool Lane. That said, the original Leominster stool has resided in their Priory Church since 1895, albeit with a current notice including a prayer asking for God's pardon!

Probably the most important purpose was to duck 'scolds' as a corrective of nagging behaviour. Other offenders were witches, slanderers, unruly paupers, common brawlers, prostitutes, dishonest brewers, apothecaries, butchers and bakers. Sometimes, a quarrelsome couple were tied back-to-back and ducked at the same time. It is a measure of the importance of these devices that local authorities could be fined for lack of maintenance. The fact is that they were well used by magistrates throughout the country as a practical form of rough justice. When somebody was ducked, it is safe to say there would have been much discussion in the crowd about the severity or lenience of the sentence – should he or she have been immersed more times or fewer?

Ducking stools were popular in the seventeenth and eighteenth centuries, with Leominster distinguished by its last recorded use in 1817. However, that occasion was poorly planned because the pond level was too low and the offender, one Sarah Leeke, was merely wheeled round the streets in the chair. Reputedly, this was the Saxon practice, which made use of a somewhat different piece of equipment called the cucking stool and involved no water. It simply comprised a chair for parading the woman through the town to the accompaniment of a jeering crowd.

By 1824, a Pennsylvanian appeal court had to review the judgement of quarter sessions that the 'defendant be placed in a ducking or cucking stool, and be plunged three times in the water'. Duncan J. considered the judgement of the lower court to be cruel and ludicrous, expressing the hope that 'we shall hereafter hear nothing of the ducking stool, or other remains of the customs of barbarous ages'. Part of his reasoning was that this unsatisfactory element of British law had not crossed over to his country – not only that, but it was a sentence no longer used in Britain anyway. Although this sounds like fair comment, our own parliament could not bring itself to consider whether being a 'common scold' was against the law until 1967. That year, the Criminal Law Act abolished the offence of being a common scold, amongst others: '… any distinct offence under the common law in England and Wales of maintenance (including champerty, but not embracery), challenging to fight, eavesdropping or being a common barrator, a common scold or a common night walker.'

PHYSICAL PUNISHMENT CULTURE

From the Middle Ages to the nineteenth century, there was a simple common creed of retribution:

> The day being fine, the streets were dry and free from mud, but the defect was speedily and amply supplied by the butchers of St. James's market. Numerous escorts of whom constantly supplied the party of attack, chiefly consisting of women, with tubs of blood, garbage, and ordure from their slaughter-houses, and with this ammunition, plentifully diversified with dead cats, turnips, potatoes, addled eggs, and other missiles, the criminals were incessantly pelted to the last moment. They walked perpetually round during their hour [the pillory swivelled on a fixed axis]; and although from the four wings of the machine they had some shelter, they were completely encrusted with filth.

> From a report about the punishment of the Vere Street Coterie in London, 1810

Although everything was on a big scale in London, the thinking was no different from that in Christchurch. For example, it was reportedly a family trip out at the time of the workhouse (now the Red House Museum) for the children to look through the windows at the suffering inmates. Apart from being a strict lesson to ensure that they knew to avoid finishing up in the workhouse, the parents could satisfy themselves that the Poor Rate they were paying was being properly applied, i.e. conditions were so harsh, they would discourage the idle and feckless from becoming inmates. Given that life was tough for them as ratepayers, they reasoned that the workhouse was to be used only for those in utter need.

Quite separate from the general poverty was the violence of the past. For instance, the Shire Reeve (the old name for sheriff) of the town was apparently stoned in 1663, and it has been known for the mayor's life to be threatened. Presumably, a time traveller from those days would see today's society as appallingly soft. Idlers and vagabonds were considered suitable for whipping by the Elizabethans – an even more severe punishment than the pillory, involving being tied by the wrists to the back of a cart and drawn around town whilst being beaten. It seems that this kind of mobile public flogging continued to an extent even after slightly less painful static whipping posts were brought into use. The town's replica whipping post (Fig. 18) is made of stout timber, with a chain at the top so that the victim could be tied before getting the lash. A record exists from the Southern Circuit of 1788 that William Gould was in court for stealing three bushels of barley, the goods of Joseph Aldridge. He was to be publicly whipped at Christchurch for the space of 100 yards on Monday 7 July and then discharged.

It is easy to forget that corporal punishment has generally only fallen out of favour fairly recently and in some countries is still in full use today. Certain other forms of punishment or 'restraint' might be mentioned, although even this is not a complete list. To prevent a prisoner escaping, Christchurch had two pairs of shackles and an iron collar attached to a post. To make a miscreant sick and giddy, the town also had a whirlygig to spin him or her round a pivot set in a frame or rotating cage. Like the ducking stool, the whirlygig was reportedly kept in the very prominent location of the north porch, a constant reminder and deterrent to all. The most serious offences were met with hanging and leaving the corpse to rot at the gibbet at Parley on the old county boundary.

Suffice it to say that Christchurch, like the rest of the country, once vigorously operated a system of physical punishment, as shown by the replica equipment installed – but now, it is merely for the 'benefit' of the tourist!

TWENTY-FOUR

King Canute, Climate Change and Christchurch

The existing town of Christchurch stands in an area which was open sea in pre-history and it will return to open sea in the future. The story behind the sea/land/sea progression is as curious as anything else in the book, but certainly requires travelling beyond normal matters of purely local interest. How concerned should we be about rising sea level and extra storminess in a low-lying town like this one?

King Canute was rather tired of being told that he was all-powerful by a somewhat sycophantic bunch of courtiers. Some 1,000 years ago, this powerful monarch set his throne by the sea at an incoming tide which refused to obey him. He said:

> Let all men know how empty and worthless is the power of kings, for there is none worthy of the name, but He whom heaven, earth, and sea obey by eternal laws.

Thus was the flattery of his courtiers rebuked – it is a common myth that it was he alone who thought he could command the waves. One report even has it that he insisted on his court staying there, at risk of them all drowning, until they finally admitted he could not stop the tide! However true or otherwise the legend may be, there has to be much sense within that quote.

Will mankind now succeed in controlling climate although Canute failed to stop the tide? If not, what does it mean for Christchurch? Looking firstly at the global picture, the omens for control by mankind are poor. For most of the Earth's life there has been no ice at all, and consequently much higher sea level than today. During the development of human civilisation, we have been going through the warm part of a warm/cold cycle within the current Ice Age. The cycle results from orbit changes, axis tilt and a wobble in the planet's axis of rotation, and repeats on average every 100,000 years. Our climate is also greatly affected by solar flares. Assuming that the planet will perform as it always has in the past, we can expect that, one day, the Ice Age will end. There will then be a very warm phase without any ice. Coastal lands will again become open sea. Since these things have happened throughout prehistory without mankind's activities, they are almost certain to continue whatever we do. In the meantime, no doubt debate will continue about how much – if any – of global warming is man-made and whether we are coming to the end of the current Ice Age.

Assuming, therefore, that mankind cannot control climate, where does that leave Christchurch? If there is indeed relentless long-term global warming, there will be higher sea levels and more severe and frequent storms. An eminent coastal engineer has even told me (half-jokingly) that he considers it best for us all to live on high ground at least ten miles inland. Bearing in mind the current rise in sea level is about 3mm per year, a big average increase in this figure to 5mm would mean a rise of 5m over 1,000 years and render most of Christchurch uninhabitable. But frankly, such predictions are unreliable.

As for severe snow falls in Christchurch, they have been so few in recent years that our recollections may be based more on the Dickens-inspired Christmas card. Because he had great nostalgia for the snow-ridden winters of his childhood in the second decade of the nineteenth century, his writing reflected that – the groundwork had truly been laid for today's attractive snow-based Christmas feeling! But the Little Ice Age (with varying opinions of a start date, and more consensus as to the end date, roughly 1300–1850) was indeed coming to an end. However, just recently predictions have been made for ten years (and other predictions suggest thirty years) of very cold winters.

Having decided that the future is uncertain, what can be done to safeguard the town? The past suggests that we should simply continue with defence works. There have rightly been plenty of public sector actions to deal with flood risks over the years. Willow Drive is raised above the playing fields of Twynham School; many properties fronting the river Stour are designed with ground-floor levels of utility rooms and garages only; and then there are the flood walls. For instance, the Dutch Cottages at Mudeford Quay, once inundated by water overtopping the quay, are now surrounded by a gated protective concrete wall (Fig. 20). A stream to the river Avon used to run along Bridge Street (Rotten Row) from Stoney Lane to Waterloo Bridge. As recently as the 1954 storms, the road water was 3ft deep. Since it has been culverted, and no doubt other works carried out to improve local water management, the notorious flooding of property there has mainly stopped.

But it is an old problem. After the notorious floods on 5 November 1916, the ward councillor for Purewell, J. W. Vickery, pressed the matter in a way we would recognise today: 'What were the people of Christchurch who lived in the "Highlands" going to do to help the people in the "Lowlands"?' Mudeford Sandbank has seen an enormous scheme for sediment retention with groynes and rock armour, thereby protecting the harbour from all but extreme events (Fig. 21). And so the list goes on. Whilst it is good that these forms of protection have been put in place, we should be aware that they will not last forever. Christchurch does suffer from particular vulnerability – low ground levels, flood risk from the two main rivers, and the experts' agreement that one day there will be a sea breakthrough to the harbour near to Double Dykes.

The answer, regarding safeguarding, has to be that a major public budget should be provided for cost-effective climate defence works over the long term. Sometimes, improved defences will be needed to keep pace with the increase in risks and sadly, on occasion, there will be times when the costs will be deemed too great for the benefit to be gained and no protection will be provided. But it all depends on what transpires – if global warming does take place aggressively for 200 years, it could then be time to start thinking about the higher ground, because coastal defence may not be practical. Alternatively, if it is much slower, then there might be a delay in reaching this stage and, yet again, if instead we get another 500-year Little Ice Age, we will need a different set of building works.

As recognised by King Canute, in the very end the sea will have its way. Perhaps the best attitude is to place faith in our ability to adapt over time. Intriguingly, if the forecasts of very cold winters for the next thirty years do prove correct, snow falls and freeze-ups might yet become a matter of personal experience rather than Dickensian nostalgia at Christmas!

Flooding in Bridge Street, looking towards Waterloo Bridge from the town centre
This engaging 1950s photograph tells its own story of fun in the water.
(Courtesy of Hampshire County Council Museums and Archives, Red House Museum, Christchurch)

TWENTY-FIVE

Now We Have Trams!

Compared to the horse-bus operations in the latter part of the nineteenth century, trams must have seemed the very latest thing. How much more civilised it was to take a tram over a brand new, stronger Tuckton Bridge than go to Poole, dragged by horses – so much so, that, in location after location, as soon as a tram route came along, the horse-bus service ceased. Yet if we go back even further, it has to be admitted that the horse-buses themselves were an improvement for many travellers. Before that time, one was restricted to walking, riding or being hauled by one or more horses in anything from a trap to a carriage. The inconvenience and cost of using horses would have often restricted the poor to walking. In such a world, the horse-buses must have been most welcome.

The picture of Church Street, dated about 1875, captures all the atmosphere of the era. The man pushing the handcart was headed towards Church Lane and the white, probably timber-framed, building on his left was rebuilt and is now the location of the Copper Skillet restaurant. Behind the white building is the Eight Bells, so-called since the Priory Church had seven bells and it was like going to the 'nineteenth hole' after a round of golf. Like many old, small pubs, it appears to be a normal house with the front room for customers – hence the derivation of the term 'public house'. Although it is not evident from the picture, lives were then starting to change with the gradual advent of public transport.

Much earlier, in December 1856, Mr Newlyn of the Kings Arms was advertising his return Sunday omnibus service from Mudeford to Christchurch to allow passengers to attend a church service. Three years later, he provided a daily service from Christchurch to give passengers five hours in Bournemouth. By that time he was also running his omnibus service both for private hire and regularly to Christchurch Road station, which is where the A35 crosses the former Ringwood line at Holmsley. However, such horse-buses were hardly frequent by today's standards.

Another early horse-bus route was run by a Harry Beamish from Southbourne to Bournemouth in 1872. A main regular service from Boscombe to Westbourne has been dated from 1889. Services were known as the Penny Bus and had a large front sign of '1D', three horses and a driver wearing a bowler hat. Local press reports in the 1890s mention that the buses weighed 25 cwt (1¼ tons) and carried thirty passengers. From the same decade, a newspaper correspondent talks about the hot summers and that 'it was most painful to see the drivers whacking their horses to race their buses against each other. The steam rose from their backs in great clouds. On my way to school I saw horses collapse.' In 1944, the *Bournemouth Times* reported that the horse-buses had been illuminated by smoky oil lamps and had straw put down in the winter, presumably for warmth. When two-horse buses were brought in by a so-called 'pirate company', the older-established three-horse firm took great exception, thereby perhaps increasing the racing to the stops and the passengers.

Yet it must be said that the era of exuberance, or one might say conflict, was not completely over with the arrival of trams. For instance, the trams in the High Street could pass each other only where there were parallel lines and one often had to stop until the approaching tram entered the loop line – these were known as 'passing loops'. There were reportedly many cases of 'tram rage' on the network, where the drivers would race to be the first to their next loop. It meant that the 'losing driver' would have to reverse to the loop behind him.

The present Tuckton Bridge was built in reinforced concrete to accommodate the weight of the new and exciting electric trams. It replaced an inferior timber one that was completely inadequate for the purpose, albeit successful at creating the lowest bridged crossing point of the Stour in order to open up Southbourne for development. That said, we do not have a very heavy duty structure for today's traffic. One hopes that a lorry driver will not be tempted to mount the bridge kerb for any reason, as that action alone could apparently send the vehicle into the river.

The spacing of the tram rails and wheels was the narrow-gauge at 3ft 6in. The reason was that when Bournemouth, after much controversy and a court case which nearly went to the

Church Street, c. 1875
A slow pace of life still dominates this scene, although by now horse-buses and railways were becoming operational. *(Courtesy of www.thepastinpictures.co.uk)*

Old 'penny bus'
Perhaps this early horse omnibus would not have looked out of place in a Western – it certainly looks noisy and uncomfortable! *(Courtesy of the* Bournemouth Daily Echo*)*

House of Lords, finally decided to run electric trams, the Corporation's first job was to take over the existing system in Poole. This had been run by a subsidiary of the independent British Electric Traction Company from 6 April 1901. Since that was a narrow-gauge design, the whole network, which began to operate from the next year, needed to be the same. Hence, the cars were only around 5ft 10½in wide versus 6ft 3in of a typical standard-gauge tram at the base of the body. In addition, the upper levels had no roofs, due to Ministry of Transport concerns about the operation of 'top-covered' cars on 3ft 6in gauge track, particularly at exposed coastal locations – very pleasant in a January snow storm! However, it was necessary to consider the power of side winds on top-covered cars in south coast towns. Certainly, even standard-gauge top-covered trams were blown over on occasion in Blackpool and elsewhere.

The service to Christchurch began on 17 October 1905, with the last tram running there on 8 April 1936. On the first date, a greatly festooned Tram No. 1 travelled in style to Christchurch followed by five decorated double-deckers over the new Tuckton Bridge – so new, in fact, that there was no fencing on its east side! Bournemouth had purchased Car 1 as a luxury single-decker, initially planned for private hire and civic inspection tours, having mahogany internal walls, a ceiling hung with tapestry, and a crimson Wilton carpet. For good measure, it sported twelve upholstered chairs, four mahogany tables and a buffet in one corner. It was the mayor's parlour car but soon became known as the 'picnic car'. Sadly, its last years after the scrapping of trams were spent as a bus shelter at Iford until 1951, followed by its removal and use as a shed at the rear of a hotel near Ringwood.

There is little doubt that the later quiet trolleybuses were cheaper to run and much preferred to the older trams, especially as over time the trolleybuses stayed quiet whereas older trams on old track became noisier. But perhaps we should take a pause before implying that the trams were primitive and poor. In 1905, a time of mainly horse-based transport, they suddenly provided a service from the Priory Church to Poole station every sixteen minutes – indeed, with intermediate cars, it was every four minutes between Fisherman's Walk and County Gates. Poole to Christchurch by tram was typically one hour thirty minutes, compared to today's motor buses at one hour three minutes – unless a late-night service, suffering less traffic congestion, is used, which takes fifty minutes only.

Trams also had an advantage in being 'double-ended'. Since they were able to reverse all their seats whilst the driver went to the cab at the other end, there was no need for any turntable. 'We never needed any new-fangled turntable in the good old days of trams,' someone is bound to have remarked in 1936! Old maps of Christchurch show that the trams retraced their steps in this fashion with the aid of a tramway terminating near to Wick Lane. One would pass along the High Street and come to the terminus in Church Street, so presenting a tram-side view to anyone in Wick Lane, before reloading with passengers and taking exactly the opposite direction. That stop had the benefit of a rail 'siding', so that two trams could be side by side.

The fare from The Square to the Priory Church was 5d (five old pennies or 2p in current money) including the toll at Tuckton Bridge of ½d. On 1 May 1918, a range of new staged fares was introduced – 6d to Tuckton Bridge East including the unchanged toll of ½d, and 1d from there to the church. Bridge tolls were not discontinued until 1943. Although the new total was a major increase, it does compare with current bus fares if you take a broad inflation multiplier of about fifty since 1918. As for pay, who would now be tempted to work a sixty-hour week (six days at ten hours a day) for about two pence an hour as driver or conductor? Although that wage level admittedly applied at the start of the tramways in 1903, an inflation-adjusted figure is still on the low side by the mores of today.

Fig. 22 is of tram No. 85, which served the Corporation from new in 1914 and was sold to the Llandudno & Colwyn Bay Light Railway in 1936, where it operated as Tram No. 6. It was built by the United Electric Car Co. Ltd, Preston. Width over pillars is 6ft 4in, length over car 35ft 6in, and the initial seating of sixty-two increased to sixty-six later. It operated for a further twenty years in Wales when it was sold to a Mr A. Richardson from Rhyll. His courting had been done on the upper deck of a Bournemouth tram! He gave it to the Museum of British Transport, Clapham, which closed in 1974, the tram then falling into the ownership of the

Tram terminus in Church Street, Christchurch
People are clearly fascinated by the 'transport method of the future' in this Edwardian scene. *(Courtesy of Hampshire County Council Museums and Archives, Red House Museum, Christchurch)*

London Science Museum. That year, it was transported to Bournemouth's depot at Mallard Road on permanent loan, where in 1977 it was beautifully restored to the Bournemouth livery under the paint-shop foreman Bob McClumpha, finally coming back to Christchurch in October 1998 to rest at the Museum of Electricity in Bargates. It has been displayed from 1999 in the same building which originally generated its power whilst it was running in the Borough of Christchurch. My thanks are due to Ian Peterson, the driver in this picture. So it was that some eighty-five years after first going into service, Tram No. 85 returned to Christchurch. As an Artefact of National Importance, this tram was reportedly worth nearly £100,000 in 1998.

Redolent of an era long past, it is very easy to get out those rose-tinted spectacles. Yet we might also take care before asking which of us now would swap the convenience of one's own car for using a tram on a daily basis. The answer might be unexpected. Fig. 23 is a photograph taken in the New Zealand sister town of Christchurch, Dorset. Apart from their large and modern town centre being extremely different from ours, a regular tram service operates, including a tram restaurant and a wedding facility!

TWENTY-SIX

England's Last Surviving Bus Turntable

*M*any times as a family in the 1950s, we would take the No. 21 trolleybus from Fisherman's Walk, Southbourne, to central Christchurch and alight at the turntable by the Dolphin in Church Street. When the passengers had left the bus, the driver (in principle always with help from the conductor) would slowly turn it through 180° for its return journey. There was always someone watching such an unusual operation, fascinated that it was possible at all for one man to turn round such a large vehicle.

The task began with the swift lowering of the two trolley booms to stow beneath the retaining hooks at the rear of the upper deck roof. It continued with the hard work of rotating the enormous steel turntable and ended with the replacement of the booms on the running wires once the bus was facing the opposite way. On turning into the yard, the bus stopped to allow passengers to disembark before going onto the turntable itself. Drivers developed the habit of turning the steering wheel just as their trolleybus rolled onto the plate, thereby prompting it to turn somewhat – some reduction at any rate in the manual labour required! In the meantime, the conductor would have taken one of the bamboo poles that hung from a traction pole at the rear of the yard or pulled one out from underneath the trolleybus. It was not unknown for a trolley boom to 'escape', swing round and cause damage to windows. The driver would often lean against the nearside front pillar of the bus, in preference to using the operating handle, to coax the turntable into motion.

As can be seen from Fig. 24, white lines were painted on the moving part as well as the ground to ensure the bus was correctly lined up for its return journey. The particular purpose of the lines was to aid the driver in achieving the best balancing point on the turntable for the return journey. The waiting room was on the south side of the yard at the corner with Church Street. Once the vehicle had turned, the driver usually pulled forward off the turntable to make it easier for passengers to walk around the bus and board. Incidentally, the small figure appearing in the driver's cab is merely a reflection of a woman pushing a pram. This bus, No. 297, was bought for preservation in the care of the Bournemouth Passenger Transport Association and ran at the Trolley 21 event at the Black Country Living Museum in June 2008.

As I recall, we would often proceed to buy a crab from near the quay to take back home for tea. Little did I then realise that these silent electric buses had replaced the slow, rattling trams and were soon in their turn to be followed by the smelly diesel vehicles. One might think that the 1936 local upgrade from trams was sluggish, bearing in mind that the first trolleybuses were run in Bradford in 1911. However, Brighton only did this in 1939, Southampton trams continued until 31 December 1949 before motor buses took over, whilst the last tram to trolleybus conversion in the UK took place in Glasgow in 1958.

The 1936 gold-lettered souvenir ticket (Fig. 25) makes clear that the replacement trolleybus system to Christchurch began running on the very same date that the trams were withdrawn. By contrast, the more utilitarian 1969 souvenir ticket for the last day of the trolleybuses made

Christchurch bus turntable under construction in 1936
The former yard of the Dolphin Inn at Church Street became the site of England's only surviving trolleybus turntable. *(Courtesy of Hampshire County Council Museums and Archives, Red House Museum, Christchurch)*

no mention of motor buses taking over. It is almost as if the arrival of the trolleybuses was welcomed before the war and their passing was mourned in 1969. The last normal service tram from Bournemouth was No. 108, whilst the highly decorated No. 115 displayed a prominent notice on the front of its vestibule: 'Last Service Tram to Bournemouth. Souvenir ticket issued.' In fact, this one carried all the dignitaries. The mayors of both towns alighted from it at Tuckton Bridge, where a trolleybus was waiting. The Mayor of Christchurch inaugurated the trolleybus service to his town and the other mayor did the same for Bournemouth. Tickets were formally handed to the two mayors and later a speech was made stressing the greater viability of the trolleybus. Ministry of Transport consent had been given one hour before the inauguration. Car 115 duly completed its final forlorn journey back to The Square.

England's only original public turntable left is this one in Christchurch, making it both important and unique. It is well worth looking through the covered vehicle access way from Wick Lane to see this piece of history. When you walk towards Church Street, the ground level opening is on the right-hand side of Wick Lane, leading to security gates through which the turntable can clearly be seen. As a listed structure of historic interest, consent is needed before it can be altered or removed. The formal wording is: '1936. Manually operated turntable for trolleybuses, believed to be the only one remaining in England.' Fig. 26 is a photograph of the turntable at the present time, and how incongruous it looks! This picture does more than any words can to demonstrate that there is sadly no going back to the days of light traffic and public transport. In stark contrast, Fig. 27 is a painting of an idyllic scene from the 1960s, as a trolleybus negotiates the turn out of the Dolphin's yard towards Christchurch High Street.

The turntable is now at the back of a small commercial redevelopment. When the old Dolphin Inn was found to be at the end of its economic life, the site was rebuilt, but in such a way as to preserve the feature – by then, the trolleybuses had been withdrawn and it was decided to make Church Street one-way only. The opening date for the shops and offices scheme, known as the Dolphin, was 28 August 1975. Since it has never been destined to come back into use, this example of engineering heritage looks mournful as it continues to reside in the town centre – buses could no longer reach it anyway due to the width and headroom restrictions on the access from Wick Lane.

Going back to the very start of construction, steelwork was provided by Sanderson Brothers Ltd of Gateshead-on-Tyne in the form of a thirteen-plate platform. Below this, and completely out of sight, must be a precision and robust installation to take the weight of the turning operation. Bournemouth's heaviest trolleybuses weighed 10 tons 6 cwts unladen. Although it is noteworthy that the mechanism has never failed throughout its working life, my information from the landowners' advisers is that it has not been maintained since the Dolphin redevelopment scheme.

Very rarely, turntable maintenance was required
In 1963, the raised turntable meant that the buses were very restricted and performed three-point turns back into Church Street. *(Courtesy of the* Bournemouth Daily Echo*)*

Around the clearance gap on the edge are heavy-duty blue engineering bricks surrounded by tarmac. The bricks appear to be the same as when built, which according to the manufacturer's plate was 1936, i.e. the start date of the Christchurch trolleybus service. That company has long since disappeared and their premises in Gateshead have been redeveloped. Established in 1900, by 1939 they were known as a firm of mechanical and electrical engineers, who often designed, manufactured and installed special machinery to meet customers' requirements. Evidently, although a relatively small company, Sandersons won the turntable contract from the Corporation due to their proven expertise, as well, no doubt, as being competitive for price. The Transport Committee of 20 March 1936 notes that this firm provided the lowest of six tenders at £380. There were five tenders for the building work in the coach yard of the Dolphin Hotel, resulting in a win for local firm Bryant & Trowbridge in the sum of £197 10s.

Two occasions when the turntable was affected by maintenance were in May 1958 and November 1963. The first time, Church Street was closed for road repairs and the buses initially did three-point turns using Wick Lane, and later turned at the Pit Site (which is now at the Fountain roundabout) with a motor shuttle from there to Church Street. The second time was due to a need to resurface the tarmac around the turntable in a fashion that required it to be raised some inches above ground level. The illustration also shows a bus completing a three-point turn into the Dolphin yard by using T poles – long poles with cables that connect the overhead wires to the trolley boom contacts, when the booms are secured to the bus roof.

Curiously, it might never have been built at all. In September 1934, Christchurch Council agreed for the trolleybuses to turn round in the High Street at its wide point, opposite the Town Hall. Although they were happy with the idea of such a turning circle, other things were a cause of friction with Bournemouth, e.g. Bournemouth Corporation's wish to run the buses down Barrack Road and their refusal to reduce fares for Christchurch even when the figures justified it. Negotiations continued on the basis that Bournemouth would be amenable to lower fares in Christchurch and buy property for a turntable in Wick Lane, so dispensing with the need to turn round in the High Street, if Christchurch were to drop its objection to the Barrack Road route. In the very end, matters were resolved without buses in Barrack Road and the turntable was built. Even though the mechanism worked effectively, some care had to be taken in the design of the turnaround system. Automated 'traffic lights' were installed in the High Street indicating a bus on the turntable – eastbound drivers then knew to hold back until it had emerged. Otherwise, two buses could not safely pass east of those lights without holding up other traffic. As it was, vehicles parked in Church Street made turning awkward sometimes.

Other turntables, although extremely rare, have existed. Two of them, within the grounds of Sedgley and Bilston depots on the Wolverhampton trolleybus network, were closed in 1931 and 1965 respectively. Another mainly London phenomenon (but without public access) was the 'traverser'. Tram depots sometimes had (at floor level) moving steel platforms. These ran on rails over pits. A tram could thereby be shifted sideways by electric power on the traverser, primarily to avoid expensive tramway points providing access to each siding inside a depot building. When the 'double-ended' trams were abolished in South Lancashire, the traverser was altered to include a turntable for the purpose of traversing the forward-only or 'single-ended' trolleybuses. The same principle applied in the London Transport depots, so equipped. One must imagine a trolleybus entering the depot and coming to rest on the platform of the traverser. The whole platform moved to one side within the depot and also turned through 180°. The bus could then exit forwards in the opposite direction.

One famous public bus turntable was at Longwood, Huddersfield, also built by Sandersons. Indeed, this is the only other one in the country with the same feature of public access as Christchurch. Long since demolished, it had an unusual cantilevered structural support due to being located on a steep hill some 15ft above a field. Moreover, the road used for the twelve-minute trolleybus service was obliged by the geography to follow the hillside contours. The reason for its construction (to allow the buses to turn round in a restricted location) was exactly the same.

However, Longwood had trouble turning buses in wartime conditions, mainly due to conductresses being employed together with elderly drivers, instead of filling such posts with two able-bodied men. These conductresses and wartime drivers often proved not strong enough to turn the bus round. It was also hard to see the wires for the booms to be replaced in the blackout. In view of this, the turntable was locked and thereafter used simply as a reverser, a somewhat less desirable solution. As if to prove the point, on 13 February 1967 a 1959-built Sunbeam S7A trolleybus 634 reversed through the railings at the back and crashed into the field, becoming a complete write-off! Fortunately, the bus was empty of passengers and there were no serious injuries. Nonetheless, the reverser worked from 1942 to 1967. Again, in a replica of the Christchurch situation, the Longwood turntable was no longer needed because motor buses took over the service requirement. Certainly, had there at any time been an unfulfilled requirement for public transport along Bridge Street, Christchurch, trolleybuses could have been used – in practice, the motor buses from the tram era simply carried on providing the service.

The new buses were quicker than the trams, which had had a single line running in both directions on much of the network. However, congestion has meant journey times are little better now by motor bus. A trip from Christchurch to The Square is, at the time of writing, timetabled at thirty-two minutes, compared to thirty minutes by trolleybus in 1963. Can we say this is progress? Using a very broad comparison between the local trams and trolleybuses, the latter had a better safety record, if only because of the 7 May 1908 tram disaster in Avenue Road between The Triangle and The Square. Tragically, there were seven deaths resulting from the runaway and overturned tram, and new regulations were introduced followed by a redesigned braking system. In contrast, on 11 September 1947, an empty trolleybus rolled away unattended in High Street Christchurch, demolishing a Keep Left bollard, no doubt the one at the corner of High Street, Church Street and Castle Street. The driver admitted he had driven off the turntable and not placed a 'scotch' under the offside front wheel. A Mr E. Hiscock had jumped into the cab and applied the handbrake. A scotch is a brick-shaped piece of wood, concave at one end, that was carried in the cab of all these buses to prevent just such an occurrence.

Increases in post-war prosperity worked against the continuing success of the trolleybuses, despite the fact that they were less likely to break down than motor buses. In 1950, there were a record sixty-four million journeys across Bournemouth Transport. However, with petrol no longer rationed, changes in society and the five-day week, the buses came to be used much less over the years, so leading to higher fares and less frequent services. For certain periods both before and just after the war, the turntable was in use every six minutes during the day because both the 21 and 21A services ran at twelve-minute intervals. But heavy passenger use at this sort of frequency was not destined to continue. The roads became so congested that the buses were slower and less able to keep to their timetables, thereby hastening their decline. In their later years of operation, costs of spares increasingly became an issue for the trolleybuses, whilst alterations to overhead wires due to road improvements were again too expensive for the passenger numbers to justify. Spares were difficult to purchase simply because the manufacture of trolleybuses in the UK had virtually ceased whilst, unlike any other country in (today's) Europe, changes to the overhead equipment were not considered an integral part of the cost of the road layout changes.

During the whole period of these attractive, quiet, electric vehicles, motor buses were running. Although they did not compete over the same routes in the same way, both operators and the public were well aware that they were an alternative means of public transport. For example, a motor bus service ran from The Square to Purewell from November 1930. When numbering was instituted from the start of the next year, it was allocated No. 1. Another motor bus route, service No. 2, also ran between the two town centres from the same time – both used new Thornycroft thirty-two-seat single-deckers. Today, Transdev, the operators of Yellow Buses, run three services over mainly the same route, numbered 1a, 1b and 1c. From being very rare when the trams began, motor vehicles (including buses) became very common by the 1960s and well impressed on the public mind. Such 'go-anywhere without needing infrastructure' buses were more suited to less frequent timetabling. There was perhaps some inevitability to the final triumph of the motor bus, the design of which has greatly improved over the years.

Did the final days of the trolleybuses lead to the redundancy of the turntable? In view of the planning situation, the answer is a moot point. The planning consent for the Dolphin scheme was given in two stages: on 21 January 1974 for the main area, including the turntable, and on 1 May 1974 for the units on the corner of Church Street and Church Lane. The planning consent shown here is taken from the second application, as it gives a better idea of the whole redevelopment built with all three road frontages – the Wick Lane frontage can be seen as the new access point for the new rear service area, incorporating the bus turntable. The earlier consent includes planning condition 5: 'The existing vehicular turntable shall be retained for turning purposes in the service area.' The reason for the extraordinary condition was 'to secure a well planned development'. My view is that the council accepted a high density (and therefore more lucrative) commercial design, having regard for the benefit of being able to turn vehicles in the yard. The condition was all about turning vehicles in the future so that the new development worked well, and not about preserving a heritage feature. It follows that the council saw the designed yard as rather too restricted in terms of access and space to manoeuvre cars and delivery vans, but thought the turntable to be an acceptable palliative. After all these years, it is no longer kept operational and the parking spaces allocated in that consent are now only used partially.

The last day of operation for Bournemouth Corporation trolleybuses was 20 April 1969. I wonder whether it was an emotional day for many, or whether most people simply welcomed the new order and did not mind the general scrapping of the trolleys. For me, one great loss, compared to the latest motor buses anyway, has been the inability to race after a bus and jump on it. Although it is possibly less safe, I never came across any accident or injury from this very common technique, then known literally as 'running for and catching the bus!' It is intriguing to note that after the last trolleybus, the replacement motor buses used the turntable for some time – the very last use was reportedly on 11 June 1973.

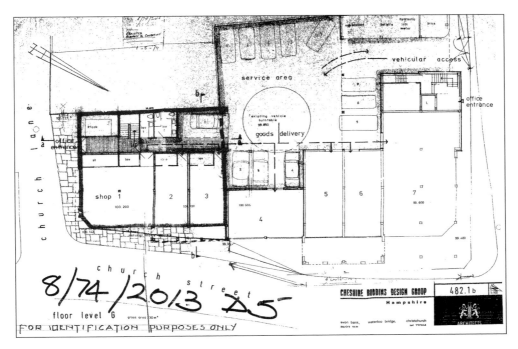

Planning consent preserves the turntable
The high-density Dolphin commercial redevelopment left the turntable as part of the rear yard, but with a planning condition for it still to turn round vehicles. *(Courtesy of Cheshire Robbins Design)*

But what does the future hold for trolleybuses? Abroad, new trolleybus routes are still being opened and new trolleybuses still being built. In Zurich (and many other cities around the world, including Edinburgh), even new trams are still being delivered. In public referenda, citizens generally prefer trolleybuses to motor buses as they are quiet, produce no pollution on the street and are not dependent on imported fuel. The irony is that, like trams, they are now regarded as beneficial for the environment – a factor accorded no importance at the time of their demise. But then diesel was once felt to be much better than petrol until the risks of particulate emissions were realised. Despite nothing ever staying the same, large-scale reinstatement of trolleybuses seems unlikely – re-use of the Christchurch bus turntable is even less so. As if pointing to the endless changes caused by the passage of time, Fig. 24 shows the remains of the Norman castle in the background. Maybe the day will come when the turntable is regarded not only as curious, but quite as outdated as the castle seems now.

TWENTY-SEVEN

Oliver Cromwell and the Salmon Thieves

A major Christchurch law dispute was brought before Cromwell in 1657 at Westminster, or to quote the report: 'Oliver the Lord Protector of the Commonwealth of England, Scotland and Ireland and the Dominions thereto belonging.' Since the report says that the case came before him at the Upper Bench, we know that he personally heard the pleadings. His involvement makes the matter of historical importance.

As the ownership of the Royalty Fishery changed hands over the centuries, many legal documents were regularly passed to new owners with the deeds. The Water Company, who are the present owners, recently decided to have a clearout of old boxes from their archive room, including an enormous old chest about 1.5m long and of unknown contents. Amongst many other documents was a large sheet of handwritten parchment dated 7 November 1657, fortunately preserved in very good condition – it is now at the Dorset History Centre, Dorchester. Fig. 28 is a small extract including the very first word, 'Oliver'. The original has now been properly saved for posterity, with a copy displayed in the Fishery Museum together with a full transcription.

At a time when the Royalty was much larger than it is today, and even then was renowned as one of the best salmon fisheries in the country, its three joint owners found themselves beset by what seems to have been an armed party of twenty-one poachers. They claimed that 110 of the fish had been 'taken, filled and carried away' on 28 March 1657. The word 'filled' could simply refer to filling a cart with these large fish. Since salmon were extremely valuable, the temptation for 'trespas' (a word then meaning theft) would have been very great to many locals for economic reasons, yet the miscreants were certainly not all from the working class. Perhaps the most recognisable name from the list of defendants is John Tregonwell, but there is also Robert Fenn, who was from a wealthy and landed family.

The three plaintiffs (Thomas Catchmayd, Peter Dolbey and John Maynston) claimed that the defendants had taken salmon from many identified sections of water running all the way from the Run at Mudeford to Throop on the Stour and to the Royalty's top boundary of Alderbush on the Avon, just downstream of Winkton. A calculation of the damages sought, at £1 per fish giving £110, gives a present-day value of approaching £8,500! Netting would have been used in places with a good flow of water, where the fish were known to rest and congregate. The identity of the defendants must have been established and noted on the day by the owners of the fishing rights – or their bailiffs, who were probably so outnumbered they could not prevent the theft. It is likely that there were some angry confrontations. The law report specifically refers to 'with force and armes etc.'. Hence the claim was for financial loss arising from a large-scale armed raid on the fishing livelihoods of the plaintiffs.

In the first hearing at Southampton, the claim had also included the statement that the 'trespas' had continued in all of these areas until 16 April 1657, and 'other wrongs to them did against the publiyue peace', thereby justifying a further claim of £240 – by now, we are looking at a £350 total, which at present values, on a different conversion method, would buy about sixty-four cows or fifty-four horses. One can only conclude that salmon was an expensive delicacy of the times. Although it is unclear whether the £240 was to compensate for the continued fishing or for other wrongs, it is evident that the defendants were somewhat outraged and felt they should appeal to the highest legal authority in the land and have the benefit of a jury. Perhaps the reference to disturbance of the public peace means that there were some scuffles on the river bank or some old scores to settle. The Westminster case report indicates that of the twenty-one original defendants, fifteen decided to appeal to the Lord Protector and plead 'not guilty' to everything. It is unclear whether the lower court in Southampton enforced *pro rata* damages against the six who did not appeal.

Twenty-four jurors were called and twelve sworn in for service, every one of them identified as a 'gentleman'. The three plaintiffs had just Christian names and surnames. The fifteen defendants included two esquires and one gentleman; of the six who failed to appeal to Oliver Cromwell, there was one esquire and one gentleman. It would probably have been one man's word against another man's word but for one legally unusual aspect – the jurors put their local knowledge into the decision! The case reads in transcription: 'And the jurors ... come who to speake the truth ... as to the trespass aforesaid in fyshing ... places called Gunters ... and Bryants.' In other words, it appears that the jury knew that the poaching took place in only two pools and this meant that the defendants were only partly guilty as charged. In effect, they were acquitted or found not liable for most of the damages claimed. Hence, instead of succeeding in their demand for £350 plus costs, the plaintiffs were awarded just £65 13s 4d plus costs of £3. Indeed, the decision refers to the plaintiffs' 'false clamor' against the fifteen appellants for the 'residue of the trespass', believed to mean that for which £240 was claimed. After the jury had decided the extent of guilt in the usual way, it most probably would have been Oliver Cromwell who determined the level of damages.

Let us digress to how these fish were caught; here I am indebted to the very experienced local fisherman Mike Parker. In those days, fish were caught in nets, as rods were simply not in vogue. In addition, netting is much more effective. A very wide rectangular net of cotton would probably have been used, including a central section called a 'bosom' some 15-20ft wide and of 4in mesh, a suitable size for the salmon. With fifty-five meshes, it means a total net depth of some 18ft. On each side of the bosom were long 'arms' to the same depth, but having a 5in mesh only, and not designed for catching the fish – rather, the arms were there to guide the fish into the bosom. The bosom was made from thicker cotton twine than the arms because it had to carry the heavy weight of the fish. The two arms and the bosom together give a total net width of 125 yards and a depth of 18ft. Ropes of 1¼in diameter with cork floats were run through the top edge and with lead weights through the bottom edge, in order to aid floating and sinking respectively. The bosom had a central buoy so that its position could be judged in relation to the current.

It was most important to hold the top and bottom ropes together during the operation. A man would stand on the bank with one end of each rope, whilst a punt (with the other rope ends) would be taken round in a circle on the water and eventually back to the bank. As the net spread out downstream, the current would make an enclosed loop of 4in meshing that would ensnare the fish. With the ends being firmly held, the ropes would be above each other in the water whilst the 4in mesh 'ballooned' in the water, whether it was fast or slow. Having hauled in the catches for the day, the nets had to be spread out to dry to minimise the cotton rotting, and weeds would need to be removed. Since each netting task would have involved four men, it follows that there may have been about five netting teams if all twenty-one defendants were at work.

A fascinating feature of the story is the surprise about the high-born identity of two members of the 'armed party', and what could be the real motives for the dispute. Richard Fenn (aka Venn) Esquire was one of the appellants and Robert Fenn (aka Venn) Esquire was one of the six who did not go to appeal. An earlier Richard Fenn was a London alderman, who bought the Manor of Christchurch, Twynham in 1630 and conveyed it to his brothers Robert and James, including the church and priory property. A year after the Dissolution, the manor excluded the church which had been separately granted to the town by Henry VIII. However, in 1545 it is reported as containing extensive property including a fishery on the Stour and Avon. In 1664, Robert resettled the manor on himself and his wife Frances, and afterwards his son Richard. Following Robert's death, his widow and son were holding court in 1667. After son Richard's death in 1683, the manor descended to his sister Jane Tregonwell, widow of John Tregonwell who had died in 1680.

At the time of the poaching expedition of 28 March 1657, it seems that one of the many John Tregonwells was a contemporary and brother-in-law of Richard Fenn, prospective owner by inheritance of the Manor of Christchurch, Twynham. These two defendants were likely to have been close. It is perfectly possible that Richard's father, Robert, had previously granted the fishery out of his manor to the three plaintiffs at a rack rent without reserving proper rights for himself and his friends and family, but not anticipating any trouble – after all, he was the Lord of the Manor. The elderly Robert clearly decided that a court appearance in front of Cromwell was not for him.

Perhaps this was because he was an ex-Royalist who had already suffered for his sympathies. As someone on the 'wrong side' of the Civil War, he and his son had paid the heavy fine of £904 6s 8d in 1648. The grant of a pardon and the return of property was an 'Ordinance to clear them of their Delinquency'. However, following the 1660 Restoration, he was officiating for Charles II as a Clerk of the Green Cloth. That year the Clerks were securing House of Lords approval to estimates for 'Necessaries for the King's present Reception' amounting to £14,501 19s. Delinquency indeed!

One might further surmise that political leanings lay behind this intense poaching dispute. Perhaps the fishermen, who were plaintiffs and Parliamentarians, wanted a battle with the wealthy landowners, who were defendants and Royalists. But it could be that the poachers were a combination of the well-off and some local fishermen, working together. The latter would have the equipment and skills, and do most of the hard work. One side – or more likely both sides – seem to have avoided seeking an out-of-court settlement through the agreement process that was specifically available and known as 'imparling'. Yet one thing does seem plain – an exaggerated damages claim was made by the fishery against some poachers, including a most prominent ex-Royalist. It failed to a suitable degree in a court personally directed by Oliver Cromwell, and that looks like justice.

TWENTY-EIGHT

Wartime Evacuation to the Cadburys

At the start of the Second World War, Eric Harris was sent, along with many thousands of other children, away from London. Although the pre-war predictions of deaths from bombing were greatly excessive, the government was still most concerned when many children returned to their parents. However, it appears that that did not happen in the case of the boys and girls at Beacon Lodge, Highcliffe. From the extracts of Eric's evocative account given here (courtesy of Hampshire County Council Museums and Archives, Red House Museum, Christchurch), it seems to have been an excellent evacuation facility. It is now a dental practice.

A short drive in buses took us to Highcliffe where we assembled at the 'Enterprise Hall' which was situated at the East end of the village (now a block of flats). Here we were to be sorted out into 'families'. Brother Gordon and I were chosen but not youngest brother John. We explained that we had promised Mum and Dad to look after him and stay together. This was quickly put right and John was invited to join us ... We followed the chauffeurs out to some large cars – luggage was loaded – then we were off back through the village, past the recreation ground at Wharncliffe Road (only a gravel driveway then) and past the long wooden wicket fence (it is still there) and then turned left into a driveway that said it was Beacon Lodge.

At the front of the house we were greeted by Major Egbert Cadbury and his wife Mary, owners of the Cadbury Chocolate Company, and their two sons Peter and Patrick. We had arrived – our journey was over – we were 'home'. The staff of the house were introduced to us – Mr Biles the butler and his wife who was the housekeeper and daughter Betty, and I recall Nancy who was one of the maids ... and the chauffeur Sid Carpenter who was also the dog handler.

The east wing was to be our war time refuge and we settled in very quickly. Each had their own space in a large room which became a dormitory and we had our own storage spaces for clothes and other belongings. Everything was ready for us and we were soon feeling quite at home ... The first task was to write special cards to our parents to let them know our new address ... During the first few days we learnt about the estate – where we could go and where not to go. I well remember the apple tree that grew one apple every seven years. This was out of bounds ... In the east wing were the squash and badminton courts, also the billiard and snooker tables. It was here that we would spend time watching Peter and Patrick Cadbury play with their friends. We would score for them and at the same time acquire the taste for chocolate which was always in plentiful supply. Another great pastime was to ride pillion behind the Cadbury sons on their motor cycles, and we would ride along the very edge of the cliff, in front of the cannons which stood on the lawn facing out to sea. In those days, the drop was quite considerable as erosion of the cliff was rare. What would our parents have thought?

In a wooded area we found a small concrete building and decided it would make an ideal 'den'. Permission was asked for and given. In no time the undergrowth was cleared, the hut cleaned and within a day or so this became the focal point of our free time. Great fun was had here and many a feast eaten around a smoky fire during the fine weather. The people of the village were very kind and generous in the giving of their time to the evacuees, and did much to ease the difficult time some children experienced ... The ladies played a large part in caring for us ... Life carried on quite happily ... I recall my brother Gordon was taken very ill with Quinsy which is an inflammation of the throat, a fever and suppuration of the tonsils. He was a very sick boy and required round the clock nursing which was given by the ladies of Beacon Lodge, the doctor and local nurses. Our family were very grateful for the wonderful care he received.

Then, as if to remind us of what the war was all about, on the 23rd August 1940 Roberts Adlard (builders and paint merchants) and Station Road New Milton were bombed and suffered a death toll of 24 and many were injured ... We were all given instructions on procedures if the air raid siren sounded when walking to school from New Milton (no school bus all the way for us). When it sounded we were to go to the nearest house and seek shelter ... Our first Christmas at Beacon Lodge in 1939 was a great time with the celebrations which included the Highcliffe Village Band who played carols at the house and we all took part. On Christmas Day presents were many and varied – football kit, winter clothes, toys, probably something for our schoolwork and of course the inevitable Cadbury Selection box, one for each child.

Going home to our families for Christmas, Easter, Whitsun and August Bank Holidays was not encouraged by the authorities ... Things were suddenly changing for the whole country. We at Highcliffe saw barrage balloons for the first time in 1940, and the blackout ... Although some things were kept from us, we would soon see what the war meant for the people of Great Britain. Despite all this, a number of us had become involved in the village activities such as Boy Scouts and Cubs. My two brothers and I became members of St. Mark's church choir when the Rev. Gould was the vicar and Mr. Clayton was the organist and choirmaster ... We were still there during Rev. Brownlow's time. One could only admire him for the courage he had as he worked under great physical difficulties. A truly Christian man and a real friend.

TWENTY-NINE

Childhood Memories of a Victorian Mayor

James Druitt (1816–1904) was one of the main figures in nineteenth-century Christchurch as mayor, burgess, solicitor and property dealer. He played, for example, a key role in the 1859–60 relocation of the Town Hall from Market Place to the High Street, where it now stands as the Mayor's Parlour. He was mayor in 1850, 1859, 1867, 1888 and, at the age of eighty years, in 1896. The present Druitt library in the High Street was once his family's home and occupied (together with other family members) by his son, the prolific and scholarly local historian Herbert Druitt, who died in 1943. It was Herbert's enormous archive which gave such a firm foundation to local studies today. It is perhaps surprising that despite James's major contribution to the town of Christchurch, much of his brief verbal autobiography concerns early experiences in Wimborne. The reason is that, sadly, the autobiography remains incomplete, extending as it does only as far as his start in Christchurch as a solicitor around 1838.

Fifty years later, he dictated the beginning of some rather diffident reminiscences to his daughter Barbara. When these were typed out from handwritten sheets, they were described as 'fragmentary'. However, remarking that after six years it was difficult to call to mind exactly what he intended to have said, by far the greater part of the document appears to have been added in 1894. His outlook and personality shine through the words. Clearly, Druitt had received a privileged upbringing which enabled him to practice the law in Christchurch for the rest of his career. Some extracts are now given (courtesy of Hampshire County Council Museums and Archives, Red House Museum, Christchurch).

My dear Daughter

All the world (as you are aware) knows the ancient town of Christchurch and watches with an anxious gaze the deliberations of its Borough Council. All the world therefore is aware that I have the honour to be the Mayor of that venerable town … It seems to me however to be rather a cheeky and also rather a difficult thing to plunge into autobiography when one has so little to say and when, from inexperience in the art, one can scarce determine on the best means of dwelling on the good qualities which one flatters oneself to be possessed of and avoiding mention of the defects which one hopes to conceal from one's neighbours …

I was born on 10th May 1816 in the West Borough of Wimborne, the second Son of Robert Druitt who practised medicine in that very pleasant little town as had his fathers for several generations, though now, alas! no such representative of the family is to be found there. My mother was Jane, daughter of the Revd. James Mayo, Master of the Wimborne Grammar School. At four years old I was sent to a school kept by Mr. Peter Hawke, a Wesleyan local Preacher, an excellent man whose friendship I retained till his death. When five years old, I was admitted to the Grammar School at which I continued for more than ten years … At that time any boy could receive at it an education comprising Latin and Greek grammar, Mathematics and some instruction in French, at an annual cost besides stationery, of £1-11-6 …

I left school at Christmas 1831 and after an interval of some months, entered the office of Mr. Henry Rowden ... and was articled to him in December 1833. I served my clerkship with him and his London Agent Mr. William Dean, an old friend of my Father's. From both these Gentlemen I received very much kindness.

Of my Father, I do not recollect very much ... My elder Brother and I were sometimes allowed to assist him in making pills and I believe we both learned the alphabet from the letters on the drawers in his surgery. I remember but little of his last illness in March 1822 ... Aunt Mary coming to our bedside and telling us of his death. My brother Robert and I attended his funeral, one on each side of our Uncle James. He was laid under the yew tree in Wimborne Churchyard ... It is altogether out of my power to do justice to the patience and self-denial with which my Mother thenceforward devoted herself to the care of her children.

Sir James was a proud and rather parsimonious man, the latter quality being an unusual one for a Hanham ... One of the School Governors, a respectable but not opulent farmer, living at Hill Butts, had the presumption, when calling on Sir James to knock at the front door. Sir James met him in the hall and said to him: 'How d'ye do Misther Hart, glad to see you Misther Hart – will you go round to the back and wipe your thoes (shoes).'

[Referring to famous smuggler Isaac Gulliver] ... He used to be wheeled in a bath-chair and it is said that his old practice of evading the Revenue gave him a liking for evading small payments. It was reported that he had said to his man: 'John, thee draw me up to the 'Harns' (a small inn about a mile from Wimborne) 'and I'll gi'ee a pint of beer,' but that when he got within 100 yards of the inn, he said: 'I be tired John, thee must turn about and get me whoam.'

I must not omit John Carnegie M.D. an army surgeon who had served in the Peninsula, and who settled to practise at Wimborne as a physician somewhere about the year 1820 or 1821, an eccentric but warm-hearted gentleman, skilful in his profession, very fond of talking politics and of professing radical opinions which were extreme in those days, but would be considered very mild now. He was a great friend of my Aunts Druitt, the eldest of whom, Sarah, he always called the Duchess and their house the Palazzo. Unfortunately for himself he had an enthusiastic belief in the newly born Spanish-American Republics, and he invested, and induced my Aunts to invest, a considerable portion of their small fortunes in Mexican bonds, an operation which straitened the resources of both ... Of my schoolfellows I think that only John Carnegie is now living.

The schoolroom was a long low building with fixed benches and desks on each side and lockers under the desks, with the Master's desk at each end, and a smaller desk at about the middle for a French Master who generally taught writing. When first I went to the school, a place was assigned me on a small form in the middle, where with Henry Place son of the Rector of Hampreston, and a son of Sir James Hanham I sat and puzzled over the Latin Accidence. The time for school was from 6.15 am to 8 am which was Breakfast time, 9 am till noon and 2 pm till 5 ... and then an hour or hour and half an hour was spent in the evening in preparing lessons. This was done in the dining hall by a scanty light from candles.

Each boy that chose had at dinner and supper two draughts of home brewed ale, which was generally very good, served in mugs holding half a pint or more. If a cup was broken, the boy who broke it had to provide another, and boys showed their general liking for the ale by purposely breaking any small cup and buying a larger one. I have known the boys of a morning make a rush to the bread room and make a capture of hunches of bread which they ate dry. On Sundays the dinner was always roast fillet and shoulder of veal, followed by baked plum pudding. The time for rising was fixed by the ringing of one of the bells in the church tower – in summer at 5.45 am and as I grew older I used, when I could, to get to the tower, where the sexton, Dick Gratman, would allow me to ring the bell, and witness, and assist in the operation of winding up the clock.

Mr. Philip Elsdon was appointed Usher or Under Master of the school and continued to be so after I left. He dressed in black, with white cravat, and took large quantities of snuff with which his cravat and waistcoat were generally sprinkled. He was, I believe, a good scholar and was very painstaking with the Boys. He was strict and made some use of the cane, but out of school he was very pleasant and good natured ... Elsdon was attacked by paralysis about 1833 and died very poor ... There were also Boys from Poole and a good many from Christchurch. Goddards, Jeans, Sandersons, Humby, Daw and for a short time Tucker and Benjamin Ferrey afterwards the Architect.

The Easter vacation we generally spent with our Aunt Hill at Howe. Oct 6 1894 [presumably the date of dictation]. In Midsummer 1825, I spent a considerable part of the vacation with my Brother Robert at my Uncle Charles' at Winchester. My Grandmother was of the party and they went in a post chaise to Picket Post, to which place Robert and I were driven in my Uncle James' four wheel. My Grandfather had always driven a high yellow gig, but my Uncle established a one horse four wheel. We were there met by a chaise sent by Purkiss, whose son was at the school by Stoney Cross. We drove by way of Romsey where the horses stopped to bait, and we looked at the old church and then on to Winchester, where Uncle Charles lived in a large house in St. Peter Street formerly called Fleshmonger's Street, where your cousin Mary now resides.

From his remarks at the start of dictation, it seems that James Druitt's heart was not really in the whole idea of doing an autobiography – it was started in 1888 and continued in 1894 in 'fits and starts' over several months. Our loss.

THIRTY

Town That Should Not Be Here

Looking both at the Saxon town before the Norman Conquest of 1066 and that of the present day, why should it not be here? The answer is because, by rights, the land on which it stands should have been washed away by the sea in a process that began about 2,000 years before the Conquest!

Since the highest level of ice about 20,000 years ago, the sea has risen some 125m. A tongue of water steadily encroached to the east from the original shoreline that ran between Cornwall and Brittany, following the line of the English Channel River. After the chalk ridge running from Old Harry to the Needles was breached, the remaining chalk pillars were destroyed by water action and Poole Bay was carved out. Instead of the ancient view over a shallow river valley to a chalk ridge in the distance, today's observer from Bournemouth sees only water.

After the breach of the ridge, we were separated from the continent at Dover about 8,600 years ago. Much later, some 3,000 years ago, what is now the Isle of Wight was cut off from mainland Britain. With the loss of the land connection to the Isle of Wight, the sea began the job of creating and scouring out Christchurch Bay. The existence of what might be termed a relatively strong headland at Hengistbury, is the reason for the shape of Christchurch Bay. That strength arose from the Head's ironstones which fell from the eroding cliffs over time to provide a very large shallow pile around the current position of Long Groyne. By behaving like an enormous rubble groyne, the stones stopped erosion, i.e. of the land which is now Christchurch. In short, without the ironstones, the headland would have been washed away and instead of Poole Bay and Christchurch Bay, we would now have a single set-back bay from Studland to Hurst.

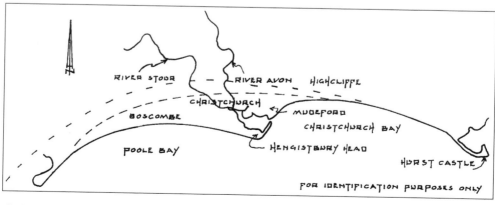

The headland's ironstones enabled today's Christchurch – but what of the future?
The broken lines on the sketch give alternative possible coastlines.

Fig. 29 shows Hengistbury Head with some adjoining low and vulnerable land, as photographed from the top of the tower of the Priory Church. Consistent with this, the sketch shows two possible alternative coastlines. The broken line nearest to the coast is my idea of the minimum expected loss of the land of present-day Christchurch over the last 3,000 years without an ironstone-fortified headland. The broken line further inland is from a 1981 opinion of a future bay shape, assuming no groynes or sea walls over the long term. In the event, we do have existing hard defences that will be improved in the future and delay any such thing happening for a very long time.

St Birinus was reportedly so taken with the natural advantages of the site in the seventh century that he established the Saxon monastery, where the Priory Church now stands. Without the ironstones, there would have been no sheltered harbour and he would have had to go inland. As for the infamous mid-nineteenth century removal of the fallen stones by a mining company, this was controversial even at the time and had a disastrous impact by greatly accelerating coastal erosion. Indeed, a good start was soon made by the sea in creating the single bay. Bournemouth Council finally replaced the lost natural headland of ironstones in 1938 by constructing Long Groyne (Fig. 30). It is a heavy-duty reinforced concrete and rock-armoured 'super-groyne' jutting out from the eastern end of the Hengistbury Head. By causing the longshore drift to build up a wide beach west of the structure, it does the same job as the old headland of fallen ironstones. This key defence is now to be maintained and improved as a top priority in the interests of both Bournemouth and Christchurch.

The present location of Christchurch town centre is therefore a matter of luck, resulting from the ironstones of Hengistbury Head. They were formed in the warm water of a river delta millions of years ago and thousands of miles to the south. Yet they had the future potential to be a natural rubble headland even before they were moved here on a tectonic plate. The protected, drowned estuary of the two rivers – which we now call Christchurch Harbour – and the development of Christchurch itself, was thereby enabled.

To sum up, whilst the precise, alternative line of the coast may be open to some debate, it is clear that, without the ironstones, the town could not have been built where it now stands – that area would be open sea!

THIRTY-ONE

Railway Workers' Rescue Boat on River Avon

Around the start of the twentieth century, the absorbing photograph in this chapter was taken of a railway maintenance gang working on a bridge over the river.

In the years before the postmark date of 1911 on this postcard, there would then, as now, have been some need to publicise safety awareness. It was clearly a staged shot with the photographer's cumbersome equipment on the very edge of the river, if not above it. Nonetheless, that would have been no problem at the time since there was a lifebelt and safety boat available! The initials on the lifebelt, of the London & South Western Railway (LSWR), show that it was company property.

Rather like the story of the railway dog, there is no doubt about the location of the bridge because it remains unchanged – its present structure and rivets are identical to the photograph from around 100 years ago. They are part of the permanent route taking the main line from

Rescue boat on the river Avon
Despite the boat, work was clearly hard and risky for the maintenance workers shown in this early photograph. *(Courtesy of Ian Stevenson)*

London to Christchurch above the Railway Pool of the Royalty Fishery. The fishing potential of that pool was greatly damaged in the 1990s when the railway authorities decided to dump truckloads of stone upstream of its piers. The safety requirement was to prevent undue scouring from storm-water and debris, and the consequent risk of instability. Sadly, there was permanent harm done to the swim because the salmon are no longer to be found just above a gravel bed – they will now be over stones, which can easily snag the angler's line and require him to present the lure with undue difficulty, i.e. in the higher level of the swim.

Returning to the photograph, some points of interest can be seen. The bridge was being painted at the time of the picture, which indicates progress from the left to the right. The metallic sheen could have been an early use of micaceous iron oxide. The painters are the second and third men from the right.

This bridge has longitudinal timbers instead of ballasted track. It appears that the third man from the left at the higher level has a large adjustable spanner in order to maintain those timbers.

The man at the top left, who seems to have been carrying a bundle of rolled-up flags, was likely to have been a lookout. He would also have had a warning device such as a horn or whistle. Again, we find how seriously safety was taken. The boat and lifebelt would have been essential for this type of work, involving as it did a risky and swaying under-slung platform. Indeed, safety boats continue in use today for such reasons.

The hammers, held by the men on the platform, may have been to chip off old paint and rust, in preparation for recoating.

More information could perhaps be gleaned from a present-day trackside inspection and photographs, but the issue of safety has quite rightly raised its head yet again. With some understatement, I was told: 'It would be a bit of a chore to organise because of the risk involved from moving trains and the electrified equipment.'

Possibly the main story of the picture is a common one – from the facial expressions of the workers and their evident hardships, we have (in material terms at any rate) come a long way from the bad old days.

THIRTY-TWO

Did the Priory's Old Tower and Spire Collapse?

he following story is conjectural because of an absence of written historical information about changes to the priory building. For example, the disastrous cotton fire of 23 October 1731 destroyed a lot of documentation, some of which could have confirmed the existence of a former tower. Sir Robert Cotton (1571–1631) had amassed a great collection of Anglo-Saxon charters and medieval cartularies, which were held at the time of the fire in Oxford. Sadly, the Christchurch Cartulary was greatly damaged that day at the Cottonian library in Ashburnham House. One would have expected some building records in the Cartulary or a separate document, but virtually none have survived. They might also have been lost at the Dissolution. Now, we must rely upon theory rather than evidence.

Hence, without definitive records, the drawing shown here is merely Henderson's artistic impression of how the priory may have looked from the north side in around 1400–1450, before the assumed collapse. Although another possibility is that it was demolished on purpose, this is not very likely for a large and expensive structure that was only perhaps 100–200 years old. In addition, there are plenty of other examples of definite collapses of central church towers elsewhere in the country, where (unlike here) there is no lack of evidence that it actually happened. It appears that problems arose due to a shortage of building expertise concerning structural integrity at the time such central towers were erected.

Compared to the present day (see Fig. 3), the drawing depicts certain differences, quite apart from the central tower and spire. For instance, by the time of the Dissolution in 1539, the Lady Chapel and St Michael's Loft had replaced what has been surmised in the drawing, i.e. a single storey and a two-storey building (sanctuary and choir) to the east of the central tower. The west tower, of course, is not shown, as it was probably built in replacement for the collapsed central one. The timing of the construction of the west tower during the fifteenth century is certainly consistent with it being needed as a replacement after the collapse. It now forms an immensely strong buttress to one end of the Priory Church.

It is perhaps possible to digress too much at this point on the subject of the mixed architecture of the building, an enormous subject in its own right. Suffice it to say that it has progressed from the Norman period through Early English (from 1200), Decorated (1200s and 1300s), Perpendicular (1400s) and finally the general stoppage caused by the Dissolution. Since that time, when the large income from the priory estates dried up, maintenance and updating tasks were carried out, but no major original work. No longer would it be financially feasible to change Norman windows for larger ones and install vaulting with such alterations enabled by flying buttresses. And so we are left with that most attractive mixture of styles, which the English do very well.

Retired priory architect, Ian Jessopp, considers that there was most probably a central tower at the priory, but that an additional spire is a little surprising due to the enormous extra weight that would have to be supported. If the tower on the drawing is conjectural, the spire is even

An artistic impression by A.E. Henderson of the priory with a central tower
This conjectural drawing depicts the building before the probable collapse of the tower in the early part of the fifteenth century. *(Courtesy of Hampshire County Council Museums and Archives, Red House Museum, Christchurch)*

more so. On the other hand, a spire could have been a determining factor in any collapse for that very reason of extra weight. Part of any repair works would have included continuing the main roof of the nave above the crossing (where the tower had been) and providing a stone gable wall (which is still there) in the position of the former east wall of the tower. Fig. 31 shows Ian demonstrating, with a vertically-held steel rule, the position of the north wall of the former tower. In the background is the continued nave roof, abutting the aforementioned gable wall. The stone gable can also be seen behind the north transept roof in Fig. 3.

Another difference between the present structure and the drawing is that we now have a shallow-pitch lead-covered roof east of the transept, compared to the steep-pitched roof presumed for around 1400–1450 on the drawing. Certainly the artist, A.E. Henderson, conjectures that the sanctuary and choir were 're-erected in 1295, demolished in 1502 and erected as at present'. This opinion implies a fairly short period to build the present structure (Lady Chapel and St Michael's Loft) before the 1539 Dissolution stopped all work. It also does not quite tally with the believed age of this part on the current architectural drawings – fifteenth and late fifteenth century. Whatever the truth, the north porch and north transept roofs are now easy to walk over, being of a similar shallow-pitch roll and drip lead-work design. Moreover, there are remnants of mortar flashings on the east gabled wall of the former central tower, indicating that the roof of the supposed 1295 building was actually much lower than shown in the drawing, i.e. much less than the height of the main nave roof. The windows and the spiral stairs at the north transept are also rather different, whilst the present main roof of the nave is somewhat lower and less steep than shown by Henderson.

A key argument, for the theory of a collapsed tower, is the structure of the crossing (Fig. 32). On all four sides are extremely substantial rounded Norman arches on massive stone pillars, taking the weight of the superstructure – so substantial that they seem designed for much more weight-bearing than is now required. The structure of the south transept side shows signs of being older and less disturbed, so the presumed fall was likely to have been towards the north-east. For instance, the south side still has some low-level original Norman windows compared to the north side, which has seen rebuilding.

There is yet more support for the central tower and spire theory from a most attractive stone plaque above the door of Draper's Chapel (Fig. 33). The chapel was created within the main (probably fifteenth-century) masonry as that section of the priory was gradually rebuilt from the east to the nave on the west. However, the screen – and therefore the plaque – seem to be sixteenth century, when Draper died – virtually within living memory of the former tower if it did indeed exist and fall in the fifteenth century.

On balance, it is fair to say that although we cannot be certain about the existence and loss of a central tower at the priory, the arguments in favour are indeed persuasive – the plaque alone hints that it is most unlikely to have been a figment of the imagination!

THIRTY-THREE

Billy Combe's Last Fight

To end this book of curiosities is a tale from a manuscript of uncertain provenance dated 16 May 1888 and owned by L.C. Preston of Harbour View, Purewell. According to the Christchurch historian Herbert Druitt, he borrowed the original in 1924 from Nutman the printer and made a handwritten copy which corrected various errors of spelling. Druitt rather doubted that the author was the prolific W.H.G. Kingston (1814–1880) as claimed, and this seems right – certainly, it is not amongst the listing of some 177 titles on a website dedicated to him and my Google search has failed to make any connection. A typed reproduction (of Druitt's copy) is held by the Christchurch Local History Society and the reproduction used for this chapter is courtesy of the society.

The document describes a desperate smuggling run and its outcome (complete with revenge by a woman scorned) in 1778. It is a most romanticised and swashbuckling yarn very much of its time, with the planning and landing of contraband set in the notorious smuggling town of Christchurch. There is some similarity with the famous and real Battle of Mudeford, 1784, the facts of which are mostly verified. That also involved the *Orestes* and a certain George Coombes, a smuggler who was hanged at Wapping and his caged body cut down by friends at Mudeford Quay. Space permits only a small part of the many pages of the manuscript but it is hoped that the additional notes will make the plot clearer and not too disjointed.

> Billy Combe was as bold and dashing a fellow, as gay and handsome, as fearless and as careless as ever, wore a pigtail, chewed tobacco, swore an oath, or kissed a pretty girl without first asking her leave. He figured upon the earth and sea, for on either element he was equally at home, somewhat about 60 years ago more or less … Billy argued that if no laws existed there could be no crime; and that of all laws, strict revenue laws and high duties being most detrimental to the state, he not only did not feel himself called upon to subscribe to them, but to oppose them to the utmost of his power …
>
> If Billy Combe had like other men his faults and failings, he had, which is all that can be said for the best of us, his good qualities also. He was generous in the extreme, he never turned a beggar away with a surly frown and without a groat, and while he had a shot in his locker, it was at the service of a shipmate … The only people he did were the revenue officers, and them he did with a vengeance but at the same time, he considered such doing all fair and above-board.

The narrative then explains how Billy was captured and forced to serve the king for a year in lieu of prison – he did so cheerfully, and successfully fought against his former smuggling friends, before returning to the Free Trade in a new ship, the *Rapid*. This magnificent vessel was partly financed with prize money collected by him when working for the revenue men. In the meantime, he promised to wed Mary Dawson of Hamble after a few more trips.

> Jim Dore was his first mate, and, if unlike him in some respects he resembled him strongly in his attachment to smuggling … 'We'll just heave the cutter to while I go on shore for an hour or so, see Tom Doxon and the other sportsmen, arrange about collecting the people, and settle

the time for running the crop, look in at the Haven House, get a swig of Betsy Seller's ale, and then away to Cherbourg, eh, Jim?

Although the smuggling venture had been arranged at the Haven Inn, Mudeford, the landlady, Widow Sellers, was sorely put out on being told by Billy of his planned wedding. Brandy and silk were then run across from Cherbourg to Hengistbury Head (called by its old name of Christchurch Head in the narrative) but in bad weather, the *Rapid* narrowly missed hitting the *Orestes*, a sloop-of-war.

The cutter's sails were filled, and away she darted through the foaming waves, the main boom almost grazing the sides of a sloop-of-war, which came rolling down past her before the gale … 'Lower away the try-sail, my boys; set the main sail; two reefs in it will do; out with the second jib' … As soon as the King's ship had hauled to the wind, she let fly one of her after guns as a signal for Billy to hove to … At last one past [*sic*] right through her mainsail … 'Well, then, my fine lads, let's train our lee guns aft, and try and knock some of the feathers out of yon fine bird.' … It struck one of the smugglers' crew carrying away his arm, and dreadfully lacerating his breast … His shipmates, laying his body at the front of the mast, covered it up with a sail till they had time to give it a sailor's simple burial … 'Let us get well in with the land, and then goodbye to the Orestes.' … 'I promised to be off Christchurch Head by twelve tonight.' … Having made Cowes Point, the remaining reefs were shaken out of the mainsail … At last the dark outline of Christchurch Head appeared on the larboard bow.

There might have been sixty persons, or more, engaged in the work, besides the crew of the Rapid, every one armed to the teeth with pistols, blunderbusses and swords or pikes … Pistol shots were rapidly exchanged, their flashes lighting up the scene … 'Yield, you rascal, yield,' cried the officer aiming a blow with his cutlass at Combe's head … 'I did shoot him and I scorn to deny it,' answered Combe boldly …

After eluding the *Orestes* and losing one man in the process, Combe finally exchanged signals with his lookout on land, had the contraband taken to shore, and met up with the well-armed landing party. When the goods had been landed and mainly dispersed, the *Rapid*, commanded by Jim Dore, was attacked at sea by the revenue men and returned fire. Soon after, a naval officer landed with his men and demanded that Billy yield, but instead he shot the officer so that his crew had to retreat to their boats. Later, in conference with his smuggling colleagues, Combe scorned to deny that he had fired the shot that killed the master of the *Orestes*. But he did take the advice of his friends to lie low in France. He gave a number of letters to Widow Sellers to post, including one to Mary – poor Mary never got it. Instead, Combe was arrested as he tried to leave the country. And so to the finale …

Combe was placed in the dock, and in the witness box, appeared a female. She turned her head towards the prisoner and he beheld the vindictive features of Widow Sellers … That night was one of storm and rain, and the bodies of the malefactors swayed to and fro in the gale, while the creaking of the gibbets, added their powerful music to the howling of the wind … But when the poor girl beheld the pallid and distorted features of her dead lover, uttering a loud shriek, she fell back fainting into the arms of her friends … It is extraordinary with what care and forethought the smugglers had made arrangements for fulfilling their friend's dying request … Soon afterwards, a simple gravestone was erected on which was inscribed the name of 'William Combe; Died AD 1778 – Aged 30' … Mrs. Sellers was ever afterwards pointed at, as an example of the extremes to which a widow's vengeance might go when she is crossed in love.

Bibliography

Anderson, R.C., *The Tramways of Bournemouth and Poole* (Light Railway Transport League, 1964)

Anderson, R.C., *Bournemouth and Poole Tramways* (Middleton Press, 1995)

Bowler, David R.H., *Bournemouth Trolleybuses* (Trolleybooks, 2001)

Cockain, Eric, *Miraculous Beam* (1999)

Cockain, Eric, *Saxon Face of Christchurch Priory* (Natula Publications, 2004)

Eels, David, *Medieval Fairs and Markets of Christchurch* (Christchurch Antiquarians, 2008)

Ferrey, Benjamin, *The Antiquities of the Priory of Christ-Church, Hampshire* (Henry G. Bohn, 1841)

Goad, J.G., *Hurst Castle, Hampshire* (English Heritage, 2003)

Hanna, Katherine A., ed., *Christchurch Priory Cartulary* (Hampshire Record Series, 2007)

Haslam, J., *Anglo-Saxon Towns in Southern England* (Phillimore, 1984)

Hodges, Michael A., *Christchurch Castle: A Short History* (Natula Publications, 2003)

Hodges, Michael A., *Prepared for Battle* (1982)

Hoodless, W.A., *Hengistbury Head: The Whole Story* (Poole Historical Trust, 2005)

Hunt, H.T., 'Faithful Friends of Woking Homes and Others from 1881, with Railway anecdotes.' (2003)

Jarvis, Keith S., *Excavations in Christchurch 1969-1980* (Dorset Natural History and Archeological Society, 1983)

Knighton, C.S. and D.M. Loades, *Anthony Roll of Henry VIII's Navy* (Ashgate, 2000)

Lavender, Ruth, *Last Days of Christchurch Priory* (Bournemouth Local Studies Publications, 1988)

Miller, Alan, *Monasteries of Dorset* (Albemarle Books, 1999)

Morris, Colin, *Bournemouth Transport* (Ian Allan Publishing, 2002)

Newman, Sue, *Chain Gang* (Electronic book)

Oakley, E. Russell, *Priory Church, Christchurch* (1945)

Page, William, ed., British History Online. Sponsor: Victoria County History. 'A History of the County of Hampshire: Volume 5' (1912)

Samuel, Olive J., *An Edwardian Garden, from the Diaries of Herbert Druitt* (Smada Publications, 2008)

Savage, Anne, *Anglo-Saxon Chronicles* (Salamander Books Ltd, 2002)

Tullett, K.C., *Augustinian Priory in Christchurch, the First 300 Years* (Natula Publications, 1992)

White, Allen, *History of Christchurch High Street* (Revised by Red House Museum, 2008)

Wiltshire, K.F., *Christchurch Priory: The Choir Stalls and Misericords* (Red House Museum)